Growing Up
in Moscow

Growing Up
in Moscow

Memories of a
Soviet Girlhood

Cathy Young

(Ekaterina Jung)

Ticknor & Fields

New York

1989

For information about permission to reproduce selections
from this book, write to Permissions, Ticknor & Fields,
52 Vanderbilt Avenue, New York, New York 10017.

Library of Congress Cataloging-in-Publication Data

Young, Cathy.
Growing up in Moscow : memories of a Soviet girlhood, /
Cathy Young (Ekaterina Jung).
p.   cm.
ISBN 0-89919-511-3
1. Young, Cathy.   2. Soviet Union — Description and travel — 1970–
3. Youth — Soviet Union.   4. Girls — Soviet Union — Biography.
5. Immigrants — United States—Biography.   I. Title.
DK275.Y68   1989   88-36576
947.085'092'4 — dc19   CIP   [B]

Printed in the United States of America

Q 10 9 8 7 6 5 4 3 2 1

Although the events and conversations described in this book
actually took place, the author has changed many names
and other details to protect the privacy of individuals.

To the memory of my grandmother,
LYDIA DUBOVITSKAYA
(1905–1983)

Acknowledgments

It has become a stock phrase to express gratitude to people "without whom this book would not have been possible." In my case, at least, the book indeed would not have been written without the generous help of my friends and mentors. William Tucker was the one who first suggested that I should write a book about my experiences as a teenager in Moscow. William Vesterman, of Rutgers University in New Brunswick, New Jersey, supported this idea and guided me from the start to the end of my work on the manuscript with his valuable criticism and comments as well as his encouragement. Robert Atwan brought my project, then in its embryonic stages, to the attention of my wonderful editor at Ticknor & Fields, Katrina Kenison. Katrina will always have my gratitude for her willingness to take a chance on a first-time author, then an undergraduate who had never written anything over twenty pages in length. Her suggestions and advice steered me through the book and were vital in shaping it as it is today. Liz Duvall did an excellent job as my manuscript editor, and Corlies Smith, Laurie Parsons, and Neil Street were invariably gracious and supportive, helping make the experience of working with Ticknor & Fields a most satisfying one.

Susan Jacoby kindly took the time from her busy schedule to read portions of my work and offer detailed comments, helping me develop a better style and suggesting new angles from which to approach various topics. Andy Kaufman, of John Jay College in New York City, read the entire first draft of the manuscript and made many perceptive remarks, thanks to which (even when we disagreed) I was able to gain a better understanding of the kinds of questions my potential readers would ask and the kinds of things they would want to know. Victor Davidov's comments were most helpful in developing and crystallizing my views, expressed in the epilogue, on the recent changes in the Soviet Union under Mikhail Gorbachev. Jerry Cohen of Brandeis University raised a number of valuable and thought-provoking points.

My parents, Alexander and Marina Young, not only were the source of many excellent ideas but jogged my memory of various episodes in my story. They have been among my toughest critics; to this, I should add that I doubt I would have been able to finish this work without their emotional as well as material support. To my aunt Vega Rosen, I owe some of the best anecdotes in this book.

For their personal support and their confidence in my abilities, I would like to thank John Michael Koroly, Robert Haworth, Eleanor Levine, Mark Popovsky, Steve Bluestone, and Dave Clark.

Contents

Prologue

A FEW WEEKS after my mother was released from the maternity hospital following my birth, she went to the district clinic for a checkup. As she was getting dressed and ready to leave, the obstetrician casually remarked, "So I guess the kid died, eh?"

I was born two months premature at the Moscow Institute of Obstetrics and Gynecology, in a ward reserved mostly for pathological pregnancy cases, where my mother had gotten a space through the intercession of some valuable acquaintance. Covered with bluish skin, I weighed in at one and three quarters kilos, just under four pounds, and Mama was given to understand that I didn't have much of a chance. For the first two or three days, she was not even allowed to see or to hold me, because, they told her, I was too frail to be carried downstairs from the babies' ward. Meanwhile, Mama lay in bed with postpartum fever. Father volunteered to bring an ice pack from home to replace the leaky hospital one, but that was against the regulations. Two days after the fever was gone, the hospital staff got around to moving Mama to the "infection ward," in a different wing of the building. Regulations required a mother and her baby to be in the same wing, so on a very chilly day in February I was wrapped in a blanket and carried across the hospital yard. "But wait a minute," pleaded my mother. "I was just told that she was too frail to be carried *down the stairs!*"

Later moved back to the maternity ward, Mama stayed with

me at the hospital for a month instead of the usual five or six days; they could not discharge her until I weighed at least two kilos. These two kilos became a catch-22: I gained weight very slowly, for the simple reason that the nurses often forgot to wake me up for feeding. Once I finally got home, I started gaining weight rapidly and soon turned into a chubby infant with dimpled cheeks.

Twenty-six years later, I am leading a life that no one, by the wildest stretch of imagination, could have predicted for me when I was born — a life I could not have envisioned for myself even ten years ago: reading the *New York Times* in the morning and going through all my favorite comic strips in the *Daily News;* shopping at the local Shop-Rite for orange juice and bananas and whatever else catches my fancy; writing on a word processor; watching movies — *North by Northwest* and *A Clockwork Orange* and *Tootsie* — on cable TV or the VCR; going out to Pizza Hut or a Chinese restaurant for dinner with my parents in our 1987 Honda Accord; strolling through a shopping mall. On the train to New York City from our small New Jersey town, I am surrounded by commuters in business suits, carrying briefcases. I submit to the indignities of the subway and jostle through the melting pot of the street crowds, window-shop along Fifth Avenue, find a place to eat whenever I feel like it. I dodge Moonies asking for my signature on a petition for a crusade against atheistic communism and for a God-centered society in America; two blocks away, a nice middle-class girl, an earnest look on her face, distributes leaflets calling for solidarity with the revolutionary people of Nicaragua or El Salvador. A weatherbeaten Communist Workers Party poster on a wall proclaims "Death to Capitalist Imperialism"; a nearby shop window displays books on Zen Buddhism, yoga, reincarnation, and karma; an agitated black man paces back and forth with a loudspeaker, warning the hurrying passersby of the horrors that await them in hell unless they accept Jesus Christ as their lord and savior.

It sometimes happens, usually in the middle of something utterly mundane, that I am struck by the sudden thought *Wait a minute — I'm in America! I wasn't supposed to be here!* For a moment, everything I do seems as fantastic as if I had become a colonist in outer space. I am living in a place that once existed only in movies and in books — *Catcher in the Rye, To Kill a Mockingbird,* short stories by John Updike and Joyce Carol Oates and William Saroyan, Lew Archer and Nero Wolfe novels, and my favorite sci-fi novel, Clifford Simak's *They Walked Like Men,* in which a gutsy reporter stumbles onto a plot by aliens to take over the Earth by buying up real estate. (I read all this literature in Russian translations, in English-language Soviet editions, or in foreign paperbacks, which were available in some libraries as well as in a couple of bookstores in Moscow — at discouraging prices.) How strange it is to reread these books now that places, objects, social types, and customs that were nothing but abstractions to me then — a shopping mall, a real estate agent, a motel, Central Park, tabloids, a business card, a press conference, Main Street — have come to mean something very concrete and are a part of the everyday world around me, just as huge posters of Marx and Lenin in the streets, a line in front of a bakery, and the sparkling ice-skating rink in the Sokolniki Park in Moscow once were.

More often, however, it's the thought of having lived in Russia that strikes me as fantastic. America has been a good foster mother to me, the kind who makes it easy for a child to forget she is adopted. She feels so *mine,* with her movies and her music and her holidays and her cities, and even her problems and agonies. I realize with a shock, looking at a 1979 issue of *Time* magazine, that when this issue was on the newsstands I wasn't here, but in a world where *Time* magazine did not exist. Every once in a while over these past nine years, as I have read an article about the Soviet Union or seen the gray streets of Moscow on my TV screen, with the familiar drab crowds bustling through the city and people stopping to read newspapers posted in the streets, I have struggled to understand that I *lived there.* When it has sunk in, so has the knowledge that I could be there still (now there's a creepy thought), indeed *should* be, by all the laws of probability.

Yet most of the time, vivid as my memories are of the people and places from my past, it's all somehow unreal. The Soviet Union of the mid-1980s is something of an abstraction to me; the *real* Moscow I left in February 1980, and the people I left there, are forever frozen in time. It is hard to imagine someone else, with different furniture and different curtains and different wallpaper, living in our old apartment in Moscow — Second Boyevskaya Street, House 6, Apartment 35, on the fourth floor, the apartment where I spent seventeen years of my life.

*Growing Up
in Moscow*

1

Beginnings

IT WASN'T what I would call a typical Soviet childhood. The living standards of my family would have been the envy of at least 80 percent of the Soviet population, for the simple reason that we were lucky enough to be in Moscow. My parents were college-educated professionals, my mother teaching piano at one of the two top music schools in the Soviet Union, my father earning a good salary as a sound engineer for the State Radio Broadcasting and Sound Recording House (an income he supplemented by moonlighting for the state record company, Melodia, and for movie studios, and as a substitute violinist for several orchestras; sometimes he put in a seventy-hour work week).

Of course it never occurred to me as a child that we were so lucky, or that our apartment — two bedrooms, a tiny spare room, and a kitchen — was in any way special. After all, most of the people we knew had apartments that weren't any worse. In fact, they were usually nicer-looking. Our place was quite shabbily furnished until my parents finally scraped up enough money to redecorate, when I was ten or eleven. Most of the furniture of my earliest memories had been bought secondhand by Grandma before her wedding, and was in such bad shape that my parents didn't pay too much attention when I vigorously scraped its wooden surfaces or attacked it with a ballpoint pen. Sometimes when I was taken along to visit relatives or family friends, I would ogle their modern lacquered furniture and their fashionable Oriental rugs, embodiments of luxury. Not that I was troubled by feelings of inferiority; at that innocent age, it never occurred to me that we did not have better furniture because we couldn't have it, because we didn't have as much money as others — because we were worse off. That was just the way we lived. That we were better off than others never crossed my mind either. How was I to know that simply having an apartment of our own, instead of a room or at best two in a communal apartment shared with another family, or other families, was an impossible dream for so many Soviet men and women? (Even today, as recently disclosed statistics show, 28 percent of the inhabitants of Leningrad — a large city, with much higher overall living standards than the provinces — live in communal apartments or in dormitories for workers.)

And we had one luxury that only a few of the people we knew could boast of: a dacha, a summer home, in a country place called Kryukovo, a forty-minute train ride away from Moscow. A rather nondescript little cottage of two tiny rooms and a veranda, with no indoor plumbing (the sanitary facilities consisted of an outhouse in the yard) and no heat except for a wood stove, it was built on a plot of land the state had leased to my late grandfather, a high-ranking engineer at an airplane factory.

Kryukovo happened to be in the vicinity of a town called Zelenograd, a so-called satellite town of Moscow. Slated for expansion, this brainchild of the disgraced Khrushchev was eventually to swallow up all of Kryukovo, including our dacha; when I was a child, the boxlike white and gray modern buildings were already creeping closer and closer to us. One day, when I was about fourteen, appraisers came to calculate the value of our possessions: the house, the apple trees in the garden, and so on. We were to receive a very meager compensation for the house, not nearly enough to buy a new dacha, even if we had, by some fantastic stroke of luck, found one for sale. Then it finally sank in: our little cottage and Grandma's beautiful garden were going to be bulldozed and plowed over. I'm glad we didn't stay in the Soviet Union long enough to see that happen.

The garden had far corners overgrown with tangled, prickly

raspberry and blackberry and gooseberry bushes, and a pond where one could poke a stick at the exquisite green blanket of algae and watch a window of pitch-black water open and then slowly close again, and brown frogs and preciously tiny baby frogs hopping in the damp grass. There were stocky apple trees to climb, and strawberry patches that yielded a modest harvest of berries, most of which I picked before they were fully ripe. There were the woods right across the road, and a stream where the water even then reached only to my waist. My father occasionally took me to splash around there, until one summer we found that the water was covered with a shiny film of rainbow colors.

It was so hard to imagine life without our dacha, without moving there every spring — a ritual that had been part of our life from as early as I could remember: the fuss of packing, the trip in a rented truck or in the car of my mother's brother, Yura. After a long, lonely winter, the cottage was chilly and damp and had a moldy smell about it; Papa and ever-energetic Grandma would chop some firewood and the fire would crackle cozily in the wood stove, and soon the house would be well heated and filled with the delicious aroma of Grandma's raisin puffs baking in the oven.

Such was the good fortune to which I was born: our own apartment; a dacha; parents who went out of their way to keep me supplied with rare delicacies like bananas and bottled Bulgarian tomato juice and apples in midwinter. I was also lucky in that, unlike the vast majority of children, even those from relatively well-off urban professional families like mine, I never spent a day in nursery school or kindergarten.

Conventional wisdom in Soviet society has it that children are better off in day care. A number of well-educated people whom my mother knew prided themselves on their freethinking and would have been mortally insulted by the suggestion that they subscribed to any part of Soviet orthodoxy, and nevertheless they asserted with full confidence that children who did not attend kindergarten were almost certain to grow up selfish, spoiled, egocentric. Maybe this was merely a rationalization to sweeten the pill of the practical necessity of day care. Many, if not most, parents preferred not to send their children to kindergarten if they had an option (usually a grandmother who could stay home with the child), if only because kindergarten conditions left a great deal to be desired. If one child came down with a cold or with scarlet fever, everyone else was sure to catch it.

I was able to stay at home thanks to Grandma, and whatever cravings I had for the company of my peers could be satisfied in the playground in the back yard of our building, which had a swing, a seesaw, a sandbox, and a few other contraptions. Many of the kids in the building all but lived in the back yard when they were not in kindergarten or school, chatting and playing games that are, I suppose, much the same the world over: jump-rope, hopscotch, hide-and-seek. Indeed the yard, *dvor*, is a major part of the typical Soviet urban childhood; a child will say, "There's this one girl in our yard," not "in our building." I ran down to the back yard every once in a while, and had a couple of pals, but most of my pastimes were indoor and solitary; I kept myself busy with toys, books, and whatever else came to hand.

Was I a Jewish Soviet Princess? There's no such term in Russian idiom (although a Russian will instantly understand what a "Jewish mother" is), but every Soviet child of my generation and my milieu, especially one who was spared kindergarten, was something of a prince or a princess, Jewish or whatever. This royal status could last for quite a while — the parents' lifetimes, in some instances. My Uncle Yura's second wife, Tamara, of all things a child psychologist, would say of her brassy daughter from a first marriage, "If Alyona wants our apartment to herself when she gets married, I'll just rent myself a nook somewhere and let her have the place!" (Alyona reciprocated by loudly proclaiming, whenever she had an occasion, that she hated her mother's guts.)

Why Soviet parental love had a tendency to become so hysterically self-sacrificial would be a good topic for a psychosocial study. My guess is that it had to do with all the hardships the older generations — my grandmother's, and to a lesser extent my mother's — had endured. They spent much of their lives surviving quite literally from hand to mouth in cramped apartments, freezing and starving through the war and for years afterward. They were used to denying themselves comforts, and they wanted their children to have the comfortable lives they had never had, to have chocolates and fruits and toys and nice clothes and movies and anything else they desired. The preponderance of only children, especially among urban couples (of the forty-odd kids I knew in school, no more than six or seven had a sibling), might also have had something to do with it. As a teenager, I heard older people remark — sometimes with censure, sometimes with envy — that young couples no longer were all that eager to knock themselves out for their children's sake. Indeed, in the mid-1970s, men and women in their twenties weren't as used to drudgery and self-denial; nor were they as likely to look to their children for vicarious fulfillment of their own dreams of a good, or at least decently comfortable, life.

My parents would not have been content to huddle in a rented "nook" so that I could enjoy an apartment of my own, but the life I led was certainly sheltered, certainly carefree. And there to pamper me as the most precious of princesses was the fifth member of our household, Nanny Olya.

My nanny Olya — Olga Ivanovna Korneyeva — was a small, bony, withered woman in her fifties. She wore cotton flower-print dresses (usually the same one every day for about five years), and her thin gray hair was always plaited into a bun at the nape of her neck. Her round little face had a sallow tint and broad cheekbones, and an air of peasant harshness about it. Once my mother's nanny, she had worked as a domestic in our family for many years, ever since coming to Moscow from her native village at the age of twenty-five. In those years, it wasn't unusual for urban families to employ girls from the countryside as live-in help. The girls were eager to work even for meager wages with room and board, since it was a way to get a Moscow residence permit.

In later years, after the war, the policy of issuing residence permits to live-in domestic workers was revoked, and the complaint "You can't find any good help these days" would have struck a responsive chord in many a relatively well-off Moscow family. The few domestic workers who were available took full advantage of the scarcity, and in addition to charging an arm and a leg were very hard to please. A 1970s skit by the famous Soviet comedian Arkady Raikin showed a hired nanny taking over her employers' king-size bed immediately on her arrival in the household, banishing its owners to the couch and dispatching the mother to take the child for a walk. This wasn't totally unlike the complaints of the one or two of my mother's friends who still had domestics coming in a few times a week; if the *domrabotnitsa* ("domestic worker") was offered an apple from a bowl, she might grumble that it wasn't fresh enough.

By the time I was born, Olya no longer lived with our family but had a room of her own in a basement apartment. She worked every other day as a janitor and then an "elevator woman," a combination of elevator operator and concierge. On her days off she came to our place. Her help wasn't of much value, but she was lonely and had grown used to being with our family. (She had never married and had no children of her own. Grandma recalled that she had had several suitors but had showed little interest in them, saying, "What do I need a man for, anyway — to wash his socks?") No one had the heart to tell her she wasn't needed, so she kept coming over and my parents kept meekly paying her wages. When I grew older, Mama told me not to call her Nanny anymore; the word "nanny," she feared, might arouse antagonism in working-class neighbors. So I began to call her Aunt Olya (children commonly call all adults "Aunt" and "Uncle").

Olya had little to do to fill her spare time, and when there was no housework to keep her busy, she would just perch on a stool in the kitchen and stare up at the ceiling, her hands folded placidly in her lap, and occasionally smack her lips. She did like to talk, mostly about her quarrels with her sisters and nephews, or to tell war stories from her job: "I'm shoveling snow the other day and this fellow comes up, dressed real nice, maybe even an engineer [in fact a laughably low-paying and low-status profession, but the height of prestige in Aunt Olya's eyes], and says in this polite voice [civility infuriated her], 'Excuse me, may I go through?' and I say, 'No, you may not!' and he had to go look for some other way. I could have let him through, you know, but just think about it — me, a janitor, telling this fellow who may be an engineer what he can and what he can't do!" Once, irritated because Grandma was reading a book and wouldn't listen to one of her stories, Olya grumbled, "It's a good thing I don't know how to read — just gives you headaches and screws up your eyes, that's all." It was, however, with an almost superstitious awe that she would say of her college-educated nephew Volodya, "He knows everything there is to know — plain *everything.*"

She had little more interest in radio or television than in books. Back in her young days, Grandma would suggest that she go to the movies, and she would shrug: "What am I gonna go to the movies for? I pay money and then I just sleep. I'd rather sleep at home for nothin'." (Aunt Olya spoke Russian the way Eliza Doolittle spoke English in her pre–Henry Higgins days — and for a long time I talked to her in her own manner, to my parents' consternation.) It took her over thirty years of life in the city to make a discovery she excitedly reported to Grandma: "Lidivenna [her way of pronouncing "Lydia Yevgenyevna"], I figured out when they talk on the radio, it makes some kind of sense! I always thought they were just babbling away!"

The concept of fiction was utterly alien to her. One evening when I was about twelve, I sat in the kitchen reading to Mama, Grandma, and Aunt Olya an excerpt from Anatoly Rybakov's adventure novel *The Dirk;* the passage had to do with a classroom and a pretty young teacher. Aunt Olya astonished us all by asking me when the book had been written.

"Oh, about twenty years ago, I guess. Why?"

"What I mean is, when was all this happening?"

I told her the action took place in the 1920s, and then Aunt Olya said with sudden, vehement bitterness, "Well, here we are reading about this teacher and we're probably wasting our time 'cause she must have died a long time ago!"

With utter conviction, she told stories of witchcraft back in the village. Our favorite was the one in which her uncle went to town to buy a pig, came back without pig or money, and explained that as he was taking the pig home in his buggy, he lit up a cigarette, whereupon the animal suddenly said in a human voice, "Hey mister, can I have a smoke, too?" Horror-stricken by this clear-cut case of demonic possession, the uncle threw the pig out of the buggy, and it scurried away into the woods.

"But Olya," Grandma said, "maybe your uncle just spent all the money on booze or gambled it away, and then made up this story."

"Oh no," Aunt Olya said confidently. "Uncle wouldn't lie." She firmly believed that there had been witches and sorcerers before the Revolution, but the Soviets had done away with them all.

After years of life under the Soviets, Aunt Olya had lost all traces of the religiosity instilled in her by her village upbringing. (If you drank milk during Lent, the parents used to tell the little ones, the priest would cut your ear off.) When she first came to live with my grandparents, she dutifully said her prayers every day before dinner and at nighttime. Then one day she asked, "Lidivenna, how come I pray and you don't?" Well, Grandma explained uncomfortably, trying not to offend the girl, she just didn't observe these customs. Olya considered this reply, then asked, "What about me, then — should I say my prayers or not?" Oh, that's up to you, Grandma said. Olya pressed on: "But if I don't pray, I won't get into any trouble, will I?" Grandma assured her she would not, and she stopped praying. It should have been obvious even to a simple country girl that in the Soviet Union in the 1930s, one was much more likely to get into trouble for saying one's prayers than for not saying them.

Aunt Olya recalled that in the first years of Soviet power, the people in the village used to say among themselves, "They're going to herd everyone into a commune, even if it's just for a day." Notions of what the commune would be like were vague; there was talk of group marriages and the whole village being forced to sleep under one gigantic blanket and to share all household items. That was as far as rustic imagination went. When collectivization finally came to Olya's village, it wasn't just for a day. The family of her uncle, with whom she lived after her parents' death, was roused from sleep one night and deported to Siberia during "dekulakization," the policy of ridding the countryside of its rich peasants. Her uncle died on the way. Olya alone was spared, since she was seen as a poor orphan exploited by her relatives the kulaks — who were counted as such because they owned a cow. (The only people who didn't have cows, Olya insisted scornfully, were bums and do-nothings.)

Olya somehow became engrossed one night in a TV movie about valiant Komsomol members (Young Communists) fighting villainous kulaks. Her sympathies were vocally with the Young Communists, which Grandma found amusing. "But Olya," she prodded, "your people were supposed to be kulaks too, weren't they? And these Komsomol members, aren't they just like the people that sent your family off to Siberia?" Forced to grapple with the complex fact that it wasn't right for her to sympathize with the people who were so clearly the good guys in the movie, Olya floundered and hemmed and hawed, finally exclaiming, "Lordy! I reckon that's true."

My father used to say, half jokingly, that our Olga was a living embodiment of the mysterious Dostoyevskian Slavic soul. On the one hand, she was so slow-witted that she couldn't get the simplest joke, even if you spent a quarter of a hour explaining the punch line to her; yet now and then she made a remark that had the brevity and the quiet humble wisdom of a proverb. For instance, turning down someone's offer of a few rubles for doing an odd job around the house, she would say, "Well, you can't get your hands on all the money in the world." She would quickly bend to pick up a coin or a ruble bill she had just seen someone drop in a store, yet she would give the shirt off her back to her nephews, or offer to take a rain check on her wages so Mama could get herself a new winter coat.

Devoted as she was to our family, she did not hesitate to tell a story about this old woman in her village who used to say, "The Jews, you know — in a way they're human, and in a way they're not." (Or, to convey the flavor of Aunt Olya's speech accurately: "Them Jews, y' know — in a way they're 'uman an' in a way they ain't.") I'm sure no offense was meant, and none was taken. My mother retorted lightheartedly, "But Olya, how can you say that? Don't you know that Jesus Christ was a Jew?" Aunt Olya, who no longer said her prayers but presumably held Jesus in some esteem, asked suspiciously, "Jesus was a Jew? Well, how do *you* know? Did he have a Jewish name or something?"

Aunt Olya gradually faded from my life, as she grew feebler and had to curtail her activities because of various ailments. (She died of stomach cancer when I was fifteen.) In her last few years, she no longer worked for us but only came by to visit once in a while, less and less frequently. But that was yet to come; in my early years, she was always there and she adored me. Fiercely protective, she would get very angry when Mama, Papa, or Grandma scolded me for little things like not saying please or thank you. Whenever I was pretending to be a character from some book or fairy tale and insisted on being called, say, Cinderella, she would dutifully call me by that name. She bought me apples and oranges from her meager income, and when she took me for a walk, I had only to ask for a cake or a bagel.

Even though I took full advantage of Aunt Olya's indulgence, I think I knew, deep down, that it wasn't too good for me in the long run. When I was seven years old, in first grade, I wrote a one-page essay entitled "Raising a Child," in which I assumed the persona of a mother writing about her daughter, Marina (my mother's name). Marina, need I say, was my alter ego, and I had this to say about her: "She is growing up healthy but spoiled. Of course it is not I who spoil her. She is spoiled by Olya, her nanny. 'Oooh, the little one is crying! Oh, you want a piece of candy? Here you are!' And when she misbehaves, then everything is blamed on me, by Olya of course. My only helpers are my mother and my husband."

"On Second Boyevskaya, almost all children have grandmothers." This was a line from an even earlier literary effort of mine, a little autobiographical sketch penned when I was four or five years old. "Almost" was inserted as an afterthought. Not that I knew all that many children on Second Boyevskaya, but my most frequent playmates did in fact have grandmothers living with them.

Mostly this was not by choice but because no separate housing could be found — not even in Moscow, where the problem wasn't as bad as elsewhere. Many young parents would have gladly packed the grandmother off to a place of her own (as most émigrés wind up doing once they find themselves in the United States). Mother-in-law jokes must strike a much more painful chord in the average Russian than they do in Americans, and some are very nasty indeed: *What is the definition of ultimate hypocrisy? A man pushing his mother-in-law out the window and then shouting, "But Mama, dear, where are you going?"*

However, since nearly every couple consisted of two wage earners — one harried housekeeper and one person who hardly lifted a finger around the house — a grandmother could be not just a helper but a lifesaver. When children were still too small to walk to school unescorted, most of the escorts were grandmothers. On exam and recital days in Mama's music school, fidgety grannies would wait outside the performance hall to pick up their darlings and pester the teachers. Indeed, for a pampered middle-class child (the only kind I'm qualified to speak for), there was nothing more natural than a granny in the house. Once, expounding on the importance of not neglecting one's duties to an eight-year-old student who had forgotten to do her homework, Mama illustrated the point by saying, "Just think what would happen, for instance, if I forgot to do the shopping or to make dinner for my family." The child stared at her in surprise: "But you have a granny, don't you?"

For all the benefits of these arrangements, they often ended up creating more problems than they solved. My few brushes with the outside world were enough to impress on me the fact that most households weren't as peaceful and harmonious as ours. One summer, when I was five or six, I suddenly decided to go live with some other family; I even packed some clothes and a copy of *Tom Sawyer*. I considered several options among our

Kryukovo neighbors (it never entered my head that they had any say in the matter) and finally asked a girl I sometimes played with if I could come live with them. She made a face and said, "You wouldn't like it one bit. All I hear day in and day out is Ma and Pa fighting with Grandma."

In spite of a few mean-tempered exceptions, grannies had a reputation for extravagantly spoiling little ones and trying to anticipate their every whim. However, in our home this role was monopolized by Aunt Olya. It's no wonder that I regarded the grandmother as the mother's ally in my "Raising a Child" opus.

My grandmother, Lydia Yevgenyevna Dubovitskaya, was fifty-eight years old when I was born, recently widowed, and working as a piano teacher twice a week at an amateur arts school. As far back as I can remember, she looked older than her years; her face was very wrinkled, perhaps because she smiled so much and her features worked so actively when she spoke. Her haircut looked very out of place with the granny image: an un-selfconsciously liberated woman since her youth, she wore her hair cropped as short as a boy's, insisting that she was simply more comfortable that way.

Her feet and hands were so crippled with arthritis that it was a wonder she could tackle a piano keyboard. But she did that and much more. It was she who single-handedly took care of our garden at the dacha, digging, weeding, carrying buckets of water to the flower beds, her hands blackened with soil. Grandma herself made good-natured fun of her passion for gardening. She once wrote (exclusively for our entertainment) a little play, or rather a series of comedy skits, about our life at the dacha; the "stage remarks" at the beginning of each scene read "*Grandmother is working in the garden.*" Once in a while she would get Papa, or on even rarer occasions Mama or myself, to pitch in, but the garden was really her territory. "What's going to happen to my flowers after I'm gone?" she would often say with a sigh, at least until it became evident that the dacha was likely to go first. She grew peonies, tulips, irises, begonias, and would speak of a new flower or a new variety of apple tree with all the enthusiasm of a scientist sharing a new discovery. Our summer neighbors had flowers too, but their gardens paled beside Grandma's.

Gardening was only one of her hobbies. She sewed and embroidered beautifully, and made copies of paintings that would have done credit to a professional. (One of these, a portrait of a lady in a powdered wig, in eighteenth-century dress and with an imperious expression on her face — I thought it was a picture of Mama — hung over Grandma's bed in the room I shared with her.) In her late sixties, Grandma took up English, and later she learned to make collages of dried flowers and straw. Once I started going to school, she helped me with my math homework, marveling at why I couldn't see how *interesting* a problem was.

At my clamorous insistence, Grandma never stayed up past my bedtime, because I was afraid of the dark. Sometimes she would try to sneak out after I fell asleep and go to the kitchen to read or talk to my parents, but I would usually wake up and trot out to fetch her. She often sang me to sleep. There was one song I especially loved, about the ghost of Napoleon rising from his grave at midnight once a year, going back to France on a ghost ship, and calling out to his faithful troops, only to find his soldiers dead and buried, so that he gloomily returns to St. Helena. An odd choice for a lullaby, but it had wondrously strange words like "Elba" and "marshals" and "gravestone." Sometimes Grandma would sing herself to sleep instead of me; in the middle of the song, her voice would trail off and turn into a peaceful snore — and I would heartlessly nudge her in the side to hear the rest.

On other nights, Grandma would tell me from memory the Uncle Remus tales about Br'er Rabbit, which she had read in an old Russian translation (and she made up some new ones for me, too). She would also tell me stories about her own past. My favorite ones had to do with her work in the late 1920s and early 1930s as a land surveyor, traveling with expeditions to Siberia and other vast expanses of virgin land to report on the quality of the soil and its suitability for agriculture. Her experiences were, I suppose, not unlike those of a pioneer in the 1880s American

West, only the Wild West might have been more civilized. Riding on horseback from one remote village to another, crossing rivers on a rickety raft, living in tents and cabins, buying food from gruff Siberian peasants who had never seen a car in their lives and gaped at a camera — what a life for a governess-reared young lady! Early in her first surveying trip, she had to make a long trek through a stretch of marshy woods to the area headquarters, in the company of a big, tough fellow. Macho Man apparently decided to teach a lesson to this uppity female who thought she could do a man's work, and took off in long strides, waiting for her to beg for a slower pace. Grandma, having changed from her pumps into rubber boots, walked cheerfully behind him; by the time the two got to headquarters, she was still striding briskly while her companion was huffing and puffing at her side.

She was one of two women in the group (three if you count the cook). The other was one Antonina, whose favorite pastime was gazing at herself in the mirror and murmuring, "My cheeks are like little red apples!" Unlike Grandma, who wanted nothing more than to be treated as an equal by the men, Antonina tried to use her weakness to her advantage. She demanded to be carried across streams in the strong arms of an obliging male instead of crossing on a raft like everyone else, and she pouted or cried when the men made fun of her — and did they ever. When changing into a nightgown, she always tried to hide behind a makeshift screen; the men would pretend to peek, calling out, "Oh boy! Guess what *I* just saw!" and Antonina would shriek in chaste dismay. Grandma would simply ask the men to look the other way when she undressed, and they complied with no fuss. I would listen, giggle, and ask to hear the story again a week later; I knew exactly what I *didn't* want to be like.

Grandma was eventually appointed to head her group of explorers. After she got married and settled down in Moscow, she continued to go on such expeditions, but reluctantly gave up the work after the birth of her second child, my mother. Then came the war, and Grandma never did go back to land surveying.

Grandpa, as a civilian in a defense-related job, was not drafted but stayed in Moscow, while Grandma and the two kids, twelve-year-old Yura and six-year-old Marina, were evacuated to a town in Siberia, having been given twenty-four hours to pack. Grandma described the journey in a crammed boxcar, with no sanitary facilities except a hole in the floor. Once in a while the train would stop, sometimes for hours, but no one dared to get off and stretch his legs or answer nature's call in the relative privacy of some shrubbery, because the train might start moving again at any moment, and it was *not* a good idea to get stranded.

Grandma returned to Moscow in 1943, and she told me about life then — about how my mother would find a piece of dried bread crust in the back of the cupboard and yell ecstatically, "Mama, look, look what I found!" (I had to hear this story every time I was fussy about food.) At that time, Grandma recalled, people would trade jewelry for a loaf of bread or a sack of sugar. A woman she knew gave her last money for a tub of butter; it turned out to be sand topped with a layer of butter. My mother was attending the Central Music School, the Soviet Union's premier school of music, where lunch consisted of black bread; on holidays, the students got white bread, made mostly from chaff, and candy, hard enough to chip a tooth. With no heat, the children sat in the classrooms huddled in their winter coats, their fingers nearly freezing to the piano keys in the music classes.

And there was more than the war. I'm sure Grandma never set out to talk politics to me; these were simply her memories. It was from her that I heard about the hunger of the early 1930s (around the time of the collectivization of agriculture): food shortages were bad even in Moscow, and once after she had finished her meal at a diner where she was entitled to eat because of her job, a man came up and asked, with a wild gleam in his eyes, if he could clean up the leftovers from her plate. It was also from Grandma that I heard about the law, issued a few years later, that mandated a jail term for those who were late for work: a man she knew overslept one day because his alarm clock was slow, rushed off to work in a panic, and collapsed with a fatal heart attack as he ran for a streetcar.

*

Grandma was the one who taught me to read, when I was not yet three years old, by a sight-reading method that most of her acquaintances regarded as quirky but that I now realize closely paralleled some of the techniques of American progressive education. Instead of first teaching me the alphabet, then having me put letters together into syllables, and only then going on to words (which was, and may still be, the standard teaching method in the Soviet Union, with the result that many children pause between syllables when reading aloud), she would draw an object and write its name underneath it, starting with simple monosyllabic words like "cat" (*kot*) and "house" (*dom*). Around the same time, Grandma also started to read to me in French and German; her knowledge of both languages was far from perfect, but good enough for me.

I don't mean to suggest that my parents took no part in my education. Mama recited children's verses to me when I was still an infant, and Papa read to me and told me stories on long walks. Despite his heavy workload, he shouldered a much greater share of domestic responsibilities than the average Soviet, or even American, male. He also dutifully went once a week to one of Moscow's two foreign-language bookstores in the hope that they might have children's books, and a few times he succeeded. One of Mama's favorite memories is of Papa trying to teach me how to count, using ducks in a picture book. I was only eighteen months old. I counted: "One, two, three, four." "Well," Papa pressed on, "how many are there?" I thought for a minute, and said, "Six." "Why six? You just said four! All right, count these." "One, two, three, four, five, six, seven, eight." "Well now, how many?" "Three." Papa was beginning to lose his temper: "Why three, you dope?" And so it went, Mama telling Papa to lay off, Papa standing his ground. I must have got tired of being yelled at, because I found an ingenious way out: when I counted the ducks in yet another picture and the inexorable "How many?" came, I snapped back, "A lot."

My father's reverence for books has always been nothing short of religious. Over the years he accumulated enough volumes to fill several walls of bookshelves. I knew even as a child that to handle a book with greasy fingers, or even to do something as innocuous as replacing a book on a shelf with the wrong end up, was just this side of a mortal sin. I cannot say that I developed the same reverent attitude early on — I covered the children's books that were bought for me with prolific doodles, and sometimes ripped the pages as well — but I did read avidly. In addition to more or less standard fare like the Brothers Grimm, Mother Goose, and Russian folk tales, I read just about anything at hand, including, at the age of four or five, a fat book on nutrition.

Some of the most popular books for Russian children are actually books by foreign authors, including *Tom Sawyer*, the novels of Jules Verne (best known in Russia for *Captain Grant's Children*, a moving adventure story about a young boy and girl who go off in search of their lost seafaring father), and *The Jungle Book*, by Rudyard Kipling (apparently forgiven his allegiance to British imperialism), which in the Russian translation bore the title *Mowgli*. There even were several pretty good Soviet-made animated film versions of the tale of the human child raised by wolves and befriended by panthers and bears. In the interests of decency, however, Mowgli did not run around in the buff as he does in the book but was provided with cherry-red briefs, which he was wearing when the wolves found him as a baby and which must have somehow miraculously grown with him through the years to fit him when he was a muscular young man.

Papa brought me another children's favorite, *The Magician of the Emerald City*, by one Sergei Volkov, in which a little girl and her dog, Toto, are carried away by a tornado from a Kansas farm to an enchanted land where her house crushes a wicked witch and. . . . If you think this sounds familiar, that's because the book was an "adaptation" of *The Wonderful Wizard of Oz*. The foreword, it's true, contained an acknowledgment, but rather haughtily implied that Volkov had in fact improved on L. Frank Baum. The only significant change I noticed, and I suppose it *was* an improvement, was that in Volkov's book Toto gains the gift of speech the moment he and the girl land in Oz ("the Enchanted Land" in Volkov's version). Dorothy became Ellie, the

ruby slippers turned silver, and that's about it — not a bad way
to dodge the issue of royalties. The movie *The Wizard of Oz* has
never been shown in the Soviet Union, but the Scarecrow, the
Cowardly Lion, and the Tin Woodsman are dear to the hearts of
millions of little Russians, who know them as creations of Sergei
Volkov.

Russian literature does have some delightful nonplagiarized
children's classics of its own, notably the poems of Kornei Chukovsky, which virtually every child from an educated family
knows by heart. Mama recited these verses to me before I could
speak. Indeed, I uttered my very first word when Mama once
paused before the last word of a Chukovsky line and I suddenly
filled it in. Before long I was reciting the poems myself, though
in a garbled language only my proud parents could understand.

Most of Chukovsky's poems are about very anthropomorphic
animals. A lovely lady fly finds a coin on the road and invites her
insect friends to a tea party, which is brutally interrupted by the
appearance of a murderous spider; just as the villain is about to
drag off poor Fly, he is slain by a valiant mosquito, who then
weds the damsel in distress. A crocodile sets out to devour the
sun but is thwarted by a brave bear. An army of African beasts
invade Petrograd to liberate their brothers and sisters from the
cages of zoos, and after a series of adventures reach an agreement
with humans that animals will no longer be mistreated.

Chukovsky, who lived from 1882 to 1969 and was already a
writer of some renown at the time of the 1917 Revolution, had
to wage a relentless fight to get his poems for children published
in the late thirties. Fairy tales and fantasy were then viewed as
useless, if not harmful, distractions from the proletarian struggle.
Children's literature was supposed to inculcate correct princi-
ples, not divert the tykes with some apolitical, and moreover
unscientifically depicted, flies and mosquitoes.

Around the same time, my grandmother tried her hand at
children's stories and ran into the same obstacle. She started out
writing charming, nonsensical little tales for her son, for the sole
reason that all the children's books she could find were so dreary.
Grandpa read one of her stories, about the friendship between a

hedgehog and a little girl, and prodded her to take it to a publisher. At the state publishing house, Grandma was told that her writing was good, very good, but it didn't reflect Soviet reality; she should by all means try again. If she had taken the advice — maybe made the little girl a member of the Pioneers, the children's Communist organization — who knows, she might have been a very successful children's writer. But although she was not antigovernment at the time, she recoiled from politics, and the endless sugary hype about the glories of Soviet life offended not so much her beliefs as her taste.

Some people, including Grandma, thought they could discern a heretical streak in Chukovsky's animal tales, especially in "The Cockroach." In this poem a community of animals is invaded by a cockroach who somehow cons everyone into believing that he is a dreadful monster. He sets himself up as king of the beasts, and tells the animals to bring him their cubs for dinner. The animals cower in terror, weeping over their young ones. At the last minute a sparrow appears and tells them they ought to be ashamed of themselves — scared of a miserable cockroach! One stroke of the sparrow's beak, and the "monster" is eliminated. Since the poem contains many references to the cockroach's feelers, and the Russian word for "feelers" is the same as that for "mustache," some saw the story as an allegory about Stalin: one puny little mustachioed man managing to keep a populace of millions in terrified subjection. (If only he had been as easy to get rid of as Chukovsky's cockroach!) Actually, the poem was written in 1922, when Stalin already had a mustache but was still a little-known Party functionary.

As far as I know, Kornei Chukovsky had little affection for the Soviet régime. The bad guys in his animal tales may or may not have been meant to symbolize the Bolsheviks; at any rate, his were among the few postrevolutionary children's books that were free of official propaganda. In part, that may have accounted for their popularity.

The American *Encyclopaedia Britannica*'s entry on children's literature waxes quite lyrical over the fact that "apparently Russian children read poetry with more passion and understanding than do English-speaking children. The mind of the Soviet child is carefully cultivated. He is provided with books, often beautifully illustrated, at prices that the West cannot match." Yet as far as I know, the *typical* Soviet child receives little more intellectual stimulation than does the proverbial American Johnny. With regard to the educated classes in Russia, the *Britannica* is probably right, at least as far as the reading of poetry is concerned, if only because poetry holds a more important and vital place in contemporary Russian culture than it does in most other modern societies. A Russian who considers himself truly well versed in literature must be able to quote easily from at least the better-known poems of Pushkin and Lermontov, as well as twentieth-century greats such as Blok, Akhmatova, and Pasternak. In general, children of the Russian intelligentsia may indeed get somewhat more exposure to quality reading than their American counterparts do; the situation of the average child, however, does not have much in common with the *Britannica* idyll. And although Soviet books for children may be beautifully illustrated and sell at low prices, they are often beyond the means of most parents, whose salaries are also quite low. Actually finding those books on sale is another matter — the quest consumes a great deal of time and energy in large cities like Moscow and Leningrad, and it may well be altogether futile outside them.

No one in my family shared the nearly obsessive fear of many Soviet parents that the little ones might read something they are too young to understand and never recover from the trauma. No one ever tried to keep books "for grown-ups" out of my hands, and even before I went to school I had an acquaintance of sorts with many classics of Russian and foreign literature. The images, the metaphors, the rhythms and cadences of speech, of poetry in particular, enthralled me even when I hadn't the slightest idea what it was all about, or interpreted what I read in my own highly peculiar fashion.

My favorite book for quite a while was an illustrated edition of *The Legends and Myths of Ancient Greece*. There were some things in it that I found baffling. For instance, in the legend of Perseus, the king, having been told by an oracle that he will die at the hand of his daughter's child, locks up the princess Danaë in a tower where no man can reach her. I could not for the life of me understand how keeping men away from Danaë would stop her from having a baby. I had never been fed stories about the stork or the cabbage patch, which are as common in Russia as elsewhere, but Aunt Olya had told me that babies were bought in department stores. This seemed dubious; a few times I had accompanied Mama to department stores, and surely I would have noticed if they had had babies on sale. I knew vaguely that a baby grew inside its mother's belly, and eventually concluded that all she had to do was wish to have one.

Despite such oddities (which Papa's evasive reply to my query did nothing to clarify), *Legends and Myths* was my constant companion. My pediatrician at the local children's clinic, a red-haired, sharp-nosed Jewish mother type named Galina Lvovna, once saw me reading it in her waiting room and was highly displeased. She told my parents that books inappropriate for my age should simply be taken away from me, and added, righteously indignant, that it was now perfectly obvious to her why I had trouble sleeping.

Characters from Greek legends, Hans Andersen tales, and other books I read showed up in my own writings. I began to write very early, at first in huge block letters, lavishly illustrating my *oeuvres* and even supplying footnotes. At the age of five or six, I composed a rather lengthy though unfinished tale about Aurora, a wise old mare at a king's court, and her colt Amour; I had them travel to the North Pole in the company of a reindeer, and then take in a cow who lived in abject poverty with her calf: "The king kicked out Aurora and told her to take the cow away into the woods. Aurora and the cow left. The king sold the calf to a neighbor. But soon everyone lost respect for him. Then the king went into the woods to look for Aurora and the cow."

Other stories reflected my own life. There was a series about a family of cats — Papa Cat, Mama Cat, and three girl kittens, Minet, Minou, and Matou (names taken from one of my French books) — who lived in an apartment, dressed like people, talked, and went skiing. The trio represented three sides of myself:

Minet, the superego-like goody-two-shoes, obedient, studious, and sweet; Minou, the rather bland ego, not ill-behaved but not stunningly virtuous like Minet; and finally Matou, the id, the bad apple whose peccadilloes were suspiciously like my own — she spilled her food on the table, nagged and threw tantrums, and was fresh and disrespectful to her elders. However, she eventually mended her ways, and I duly informed my father of this development in a letter while he was on a business trip: "Matou has become good — very good!"

It was in that essay on "Raising a Child," written in my first year of school, that I think I best summed up the first six years of my life. Speaking of a child very much like myself, I wrote: "My child understands from an early age that life is life and everyone has his own life to live. Since my cousin Dunya works in a kindergarten, she immediately suggested that I send Marina there. But I refused. The child grew up free in the home of her parents." Not being in kindergarten meant being free — something that I am sure no one had ever suggested to me. Growing up free with one's own life to live — where had I, a Soviet first-grader, picked up such an idea?

2

Off to School

ON A SPRING DAY in 1970 — probably in the middle of March, the season when the blackened snowdrifts that line the edges of every sidewalk in Moscow start melting, and water runs all over the street in rippling flows and rivulets, sparkling on sunny days — I found myself for the first time in the hallways of the building that was to be my school for the next ten years. I had passed by that four-story building of gray brick many times on walks with Papa or Aunt Olya, and had curiously and somewhat enviously watched the high-spirited kids emerge noisily from the doors and through the portico of elephantine white columns.

Escorted by Grandma, I was there for an admissions exam. In the lobby and the hallway, other parents and grandparents were hovering over little boys and girls spruced up for the occasion. One by one, the children were called in, and then it was my turn. A few people, mostly women, sat stiffly at a long cloth-covered table in the examination room. At their direction, I confidently read a couple of paragraphs from a large-print book of Leo Tolstoy's stories for children and breezed through a quiz in simple arithmetic. It was not for nothing that Mama, Papa, and Grandma had been drilling me for days before the test, patiently going over "two plus six equals eight" and "seven minus three equals four."

Then I made my only lapse. There were several large pictures on the wall, one showing a bunch of people at what was evidently an Arctic research station, waving their arms and otherwise expressing strong emotions at the sight of a polar bear who was waddling in the snow and had wandered too close. I thought the polar bear was a dog, and when told to make up a story based on the picture, I began to tell my story accordingly — only to be brusquely cut off by a heavyset, imperious-looking woman (the school principal, Nadezhda Pavlovna, I later found out): "What are you talking about? What dog? It's not a dog, it's a polar bear." As I stood there crushed, trying to regain my bearings, she added, "All right, you may go."

Usually a child in the Soviet Union is simply assigned automatically to an open-admissions district school, much as children are assigned in the public school system in the United States. But parents can also apply to a special school, which, in addition to teaching the usual disciplines, focuses on one subject — usually a language, sometimes math. School No. 1 of the Sokolniki district specialized in English. These schools require an admissions test in basic skills. (I am sure that many, perhaps most, students in district schools cannot read when they start first grade.) Other factors weigh as well: a very bright boy in our apartment building was denied admission to the school because he spoke with a slight lisp.

District schools have mandatory second-language classes too, but these classes do not start until the fifth grade and are not taken very seriously. We had English classes from the second grade on. The special schools follow the same nationwide curriculum as the district schools, but it is common knowledge that they provide a far superior education. Among the intelligentsia, district schools, known also as mass schools, evoke the same kind of sentiments that inner-city public schools often evoke in well-to-do suburban American parents. There are tales of abysmal academic standards, teachers with ungrammatical speech, fights in the hallways, hooligans bullying small children. When I was a child, schools in the new, mostly working-class districts on the outskirts of the city had an especially bad reputation that included harassment of Jewish students and even an occasional rape. These horror stories may have been generated partly by elitism, about which well-educated Soviets are far less bashful than their American counterparts. Still, many of them were probably true.

My neighbors Raya, the daughter of our building's concierge, and Tanya, the daughter of a military officer — both two or three years older than me — went to the local district school. When they started pestering me to do their English homework for them, I willy-nilly got a look at their grammar and spelling in Russian, which was not simply bad but atrocious. And they were both level 4 students; in our school, such writing would not have earned them anything higher than a 2. (Grades in the Soviet school system are given on a scale of 1 to 5, 1 being so low that even in our school hardly anyone ever got slapped with it, except when the teacher wanted to make a strong symbolic statement that your work was *beyond* bad.) Top students from mass schools who transferred to our school immediately saw their grades plummet to a 3 average. Some managed to readjust and pull back up; others continued to lag behind and eventually drifted back to district school.

Years later, at the end of the eighth grade, we were to face a far tougher exam, with tests in algebra, geometry, Russian, English, and writing, that was seen as a critical point in our lives. Eighth grade was the last year of compulsory schooling, the end of so-called middle school (roughly equivalent to junior high), after which a student either went on to high school or dropped out to attend training courses or vocational and trade school, known as PTU (an acronym for professional-technical school). More than a year before the critical point was upon us, rumors began to circulate about a mandatory new policy: only students with "excellent" and "good" grades, 5's and 4's, would be allowed to finish high school, while the rest would be channeled into PTUs (because of a labor shortage in the trades, they said). The word "PTU," the very combination of the letters, was enough to make us turn pale. To children of educated middle-class professionals, the prospect of being sent to a PTU had nightmarish implications, not just of low status but of frightening teenage yahoos, drunks, hoodlums, and sluts. I don't think the rumor was ever confirmed officially, but it was a bad scare.

During the writing exam in Russian, Masha Lyakhovskaya, a clumsy, overweight girl in glasses, was caught taking a furtive peek into a crib hidden under her desk — a long list, cleverly folded into an accordion shape, of difficult spellings. She was ignominiously booted out of the examination room, and though we weren't friends, a pang of horror and pity shot through me as I imagined the poor girl languishing in a PTU. She was very somber and puffy-eyed when I later saw her in the hallway; but when all was said and done, she showed up in school, safe and sound, on the first day of the next school year. Only a few floundering students were lost to PTUs or to mass schools.

But back to the entrance exam. Apparently, knowing a polar bear from a dog was not judged an absolutely essential skill in an applicant, for my parents were soon notified that I was admitted to School No. 1, group B. Each year's class in a school is divided into groups of no more than forty students; in our year, there were only two groups, A and B. I was to stay with that group until the end of my school years. In the Soviet Union, the separation between primary, junior high, and high school is largely nominal. Thus, unless a student transfers from one school to another, he spends his ten years of school in the same building, and since there are no electives, with the same classmates in virtually every class.

Classes began on the first of September. My family was still staying in the country, so on August 31 Mama took me to Moscow, where she spent all night making last-minute alterations to my uniform, pressing it, and otherwise grooming me for the big day. On the first day we were to wear the special ceremonial outfit: for girls, a brown dress with a frilly white pinafore (as opposed to the usual austere black one) and white knee-highs; for boys, a crisp white shirt with gray pants and jacket; for both, impeccably polished black shoes. My ponytail was neatly tied with a huge butterfly of white nylon ribbon. We also had to bring flowers, and Grandma outdid herself, cutting and arranging a splendid bouquet from her garden.

The schoolyard was bustling with children and parents. We excited, curious first-graders were lined up in front, our parents crowding the sidelines. A loudspeaker fixed on the top of the portico blared a solemn greeting from the principal, something about how this was to be a turning point in our lives and the beginning of our training as Soviet citizens. Important people were standing on the steps of the portico, and everyone was looking very dignified.

Then we were marched off to our classroom on the second floor, where all six primary school classrooms were. We laid our bouquets on the teacher's desk in a motley, dewy heap and were assigned desks. Each desk sat two students, and the rule was for boys to sit with girls, though the gender imbalance in the class — probably about twenty-two girls to fifteen boys — made for exceptions. (Gradually, as we grew older, we became free to choose our own seatmates, although teachers still expected each student to stay in the same seat at least throughout the term, and would reprimand us for seat-hopping.)

The woman in her mid-forties at the teacher's desk had a round, simple face with rather coarse features. Dressed in a plain outfit that was almost drab on so festive a day, she was the picture of a demure schoolmarm. She introduced herself as Lyudmila Alexandrovna Yefremova and read the roster, each of us getting up when his or her name was called. She was to be our guardian for the next three years, all through primary school.

Lyudmila Alexandrovna looked, and indeed was, even-tempered and somewhat passive. As I later learned, she had a good excuse for not brimming with vim and vigor. One day my mother met her on a streetcar a few stops away from our school, carrying the heavy bags that are the hallmark of the Soviet shopper. They struck up a conversation; when Lyudmila Alexandrovna said she was getting off at the next stop, Mama asked if she lived in the neighborhood. "Oh, no," said Lyudmila Alexandrovna with a sigh of quiet resignation, "this is where I do some private tutoring after I get off work." The poor woman was also raising two teenagers.

The moment our first class was over and we filed out into the hallway, most of the other kids clustered in groups, chatting like the best of friends. I marveled how they had gotten to know each other so well in so short a time. Then it dawned on me: they all knew each other from kindergarten. I felt a little lost. One of the few homegrown children, I knew no one. For the first time in my life, I was in the midst of strangers, with neither Mama nor Papa nor Grandma nor Aunt Olya in sight. What's more, I had to sit quietly in one place until the bell rang, and even worse, I wasn't allowed to sit with my legs tucked under me, the way I always did at home. When we were finally dismissed for the day, I rushed toward my waiting parents as if this reunion were coming after years of unbearable separation. They say the look in my eyes was unforgettable.

Lyudmila Alexandrovna, who had stopped to talk to the parents of her flock, turned to my parents and remarked, "I suppose your little girl has never been to kindergarten."

It took me a while to make friends, and perhaps it was not a coincidence that my best friend all through school, Rita Kuznetzova, had not been to kindergarten either. I didn't even know what her name was until one day in second grade, in September, when we were supposed to bring brightly colored maple leaves to school as models to use in our drawing lesson. I had forgotten all about it, and Rita generously lent me one of hers.

It turned out that this pallid-faced, silvery-blond girl lived only a ten-minute walk away from me, in a building I knew well because its first floor housed the local bakery. It seemed that she didn't have too many friends at school either, and we soon began to exchange visits. We walked home from school together, and sometimes her mother or someone from my family would take us to nearby Sokolniki Park.

Rita's mother, a good-natured, buxom lady with fuzzy red hair, was a member of the Communist Party and held some kind of midlevel management job. Her father, who held some job that was lower in status and pay than his wife's, sometimes came home drunk late at night and smashed things around the apartment, or even, Rita told me rather matter-of-factly, hit Rita's mom. To make things worse, Rita's mother and grandmother also fought constantly. (Rita's grandmother was a short, tubby woman, the very epitome of the Soviet *babushka*. A querulous creature, with her head wrapped in a long dark shawl, she had a nearly perpetual scowl of suspicious displeasure on her ruddy, beady-eyed face, except when she smiled fawningly at Rita.) All of this came as something of a shock. I had already realized that not everyone had a home as idyllic as mine, but that such things should be happening in the home of a girl I knew so well!

If I was something of a princess at home, Rita was a regular queen, and treated her elders like lowly servants. They doted on her, and only occasionally dared a mild rebuke. In third grade I was at Rita's place once helping her with her math homework (she wasn't, alas, too bright); she wouldn't listen to me, and I playfully gave her a little slap on the arm. She started squalling; her grandmother stormed in like a vengeful fury; and I, the stunned transgressor, was almost literally kicked out — told to gather my coat and hat and go home. "No one in this house has ever laid a finger on our Ritochka!" Babushka rumbled furiously to my back.

The nonviolence was not reciprocal. In junior high, Rita had great fun telling me how her grandma had imprudently washed the fashion knee-highs she was going to wear to a party, and she, Rita, had been so beside herself she had slapped Granny with the wet socks. Her parents took some rough treatment too. "The other day, my dad says to me, 'Rita, will you go down to the bakery and buy some bread?' and I just said, 'Aw, go to hell,' " she bragged.

Apparently Rita's parents, unlike those of the majority of our classmates, were not college educated. But they too reached after accouterments of culture, such as very hard-to-get subscriptions to the collected works of great writers, from Pushkin to Guy de Maupassant. I wouldn't be surprised if they never opened the fancy-looking volumes with gilt lettering after they ensconced them in the two lacquered bookcases in the living room, on display as a highly prized status symbol. The Kuznetzovs also owned the complete works of Lenin, the revered founder of the Soviet state — about fifty dark leather-bound volumes. But the collected works of Lenin, not being a status symbol, were discreetly shelved in Rita's parents' bedroom, along with the complete works of Stalin, a leftover from the days of the "personality cult," kept in the house either because no one ever got around to disposing of them or — who knows? — just in case such books ever became once again a token of good citizenship.

I suspect that despite the classics in the lacquered bookcases, the typical parents at the parent-teacher meetings probably looked down on the Kuznetzovs as not sufficiently *intelligentny*, a loaded adjective that comprises shades of "intellectual," "cultured," "well-mannered," and "genteel." These cultured ones were engineers, doctors, teachers, staff members of scientific research institutes. Of course there were nice, unassuming, and truly intelligent people among them. The rest read all the right books and went to all the right concerts and art exhibitions, especially those that were open for a short time only and thus the rage of Moscow. Rita's parents may have been more "common," but at least they weren't pretentious snobs and weren't trendily, unctuously artificial like so many ladies and gentlemen of the Soviet middle class — perfect examples of the bourgeois, in the Flaubertian sense of the word. (A factory worker, Flaubert remarked, can be a bourgeois in spirit, and so can a duke. So too — and with a vengeance — can the loyal employees of a Communist state.)

Far below Rita Kuznetzov, however, were the few kids in our class who came from working-class families, separated from the genteel by barriers that were informal but as implacable as those of the most rigid class structure. The sons and daughters of factory workers, dishwashers, cooks, and so on were tangibly different from the rest, much more likely to be coarse, brash, rowdy, messy, unsupervised at home. An extreme specimen, perhaps, was Borya Fedoseyev, a chubby runt with reddish-blond hair whose greatest pleasures were bullying others (preferably girls) and grossing them out. He made no bones about hating the school and especially English classes, and tried hard to get kicked out. He would not have stayed for a day had it not been for the over-my-dead-body protests of his harried, aging, single (or perhaps widowed) mother, a long-suffering woman with a tragic face. Someone later told me that children from working-class families were accepted into special schools under a quota system; after all, how would it look if the best schools in the workers' state had no working-class children in them? But the favor was a dubious one. Most of these kids, transplanted into an alien environment, never surmounted their academic and behavioral problems, and sooner or later dropped out to go to mass schools or PTUs.

From this lot I found myself a boyfriend. His name was Yegor Cher; he was one of our worst students and something of a little hoodlum, and it was for him that I developed a stubborn passion after I observed him being tormented by a bunch of bigger boys. My sympathy was misplaced: Yegor, small but wiry, was quite a bully himself. To say that he did not return my affection would be an understatement. When, after school, I would raise myself on my tiptoes, crane my neck, and shout "Goodbyyyye!" to him as we were leaving the schoolyard, the man of my dreams would yell back derisively, "Hellooooo!" Undaunted, I declared to my parents and to everyone else that I loved Yegor and was going to marry him.

Luckily, Lyudmila Alexandrovna took a rather indulgent attitude toward my infatuation, looking on it with amusement rather than disapproval. Many other teachers would have had a fit at the slightest suggestion of a budding "romance." At the school where Mama taught, a teacher intercepted a note from a ten-year-old girl to a boy that said simply "Let's be friends," and made a tremendous scene. She read the note aloud in class and bawled out the poor girl for taking such liberties. Then she called a parents' meeting and shouted that she would not allow "such things" to be carried on in her class: "What is all this talk about love at the age of ten!" When a parent timidly suggested that there hadn't been any talk about love in the note, only about friendship, she scoffed, "Oh sure! Some friendship! Actually writing a note — that's just like a billet-doux!"

It's only fair to say that even among Soviet teachers, such a degree of prudery is rarely matched. But it seems that my teacher's reaction was the more unusual one. Perhaps it came less from tolerance than from indifference. She only said to Mama a couple of times, "What a shame — Katya is such a nice girl, and this boy she likes is one of the worst kids in the class!" Yegor did come to the party for my tenth birthday; he made a mess of our apartment, rode our sofa cushions across the floor, and horrified Grandma by telling vulgar jokes about people losing their pants. At the end of that year he transferred to a different school, and I think even moved out of the neighborhood, putting an end to my romantic dreams.

Still essentially a homebody, I nevertheless adjusted to being a schoolgirl much more smoothly than my parents had expected. In first and second grade we spent only four hours a day in school, from eight-thirty to twelve-twenty, with four forty-five-minute periods and breaks in between. The few subjects we had were all taught by Lyudmila Alexandrovna, except for gym, singing, and, starting in second grade, English. For English we were split into three groups and assigned to different teachers. My early dabbling in French and German under Grandma's tutelage made learning a foreign language easier, and the summer before, Grandma and I had spent some time listening to educational English records. I quickly rose to the top of the class in English.

School discipline didn't bother me too much; I even got used to not sitting with my feet tucked under me. Our schoolwork was governed by strict requirements: we had to use standard-ruled, twelve-sheet notebooks (quad-ruled for math) and fountain pens, no ballpoints (a requirement that was not relaxed until sixth grade). A messy notebook, or even sloppy handwriting, meant a lower grade for writing. (Left-handedness, needless to say, was corrected.) I remember Mama sitting with me and patiently perfecting my handwriting ("Now, what about the loop of that *y*?"). Actually, my handwriting wasn't sloppy; I was just trying to write in very small letters, challenging myself to fit as many words as humanly possible onto one line. That sporting spirit was eventually driven out of me by Mama's persistence and a few bad grades.

Straight 5's entitled you to a fancy jacket for your notebook. Lyudmila Alexandrovna recruited some of the parents to make these jackets, with colorful drawings that had to include a red 5. My grandmother volunteered too, and used a special high-quality thin cardboard she got from her engineer brother. For one of the jackets she copied the Scarecrow and Ellie/Dorothy on the yellow brick road from a picture in my much-read copy of *The Magician of the Emerald City*, and added a big scarlet 5, which the Scarecrow was handing over to Ellie. (A jacket designed by another parent featured Donald Duck; American imagery was all over the place.) The jackets were then collected by our teacher and given out to the deserving few. I finished my first year with straight 5's and got a special award: a book called *The Icebreaker Lenin*, a nonfiction account, adapted for a youthful audience, of the first Soviet nuclear icebreaking ship. It was inscribed by Lyudmila Alexandrovna.

These were the occasional carrots; the sticks were of far greater concern to most of us.

In the second half of our first year, each pupil was issued a journal, which signified that we were now serious students. The journal, an innocuous-looking thick notebook with a blue cover, was the principal stick. Each two-page spread was allotted to the records of one week, divided horizontally into six sections (Saturday was a schoolday, too) and vertically into three columns, the one on the left for the class schedules, the one in the middle for the homework assignments, and the one on the right for the teacher to put grades in. The bottom of the page was reserved for such uncomplimentary remarks as "fidgeted in class," "talked in class," "misbehaved during the break," or even stronger criticisms. The journal had to be kept in perfect order. If you wrote down a homework assignment in your notebook but not in the journal, you had to copy it into the journal by the time of the next inspection by the teacher; doing the homework wouldn't get you off the hook for not writing it down in the right place. We were also graded on "keeping the journal."

At the end of each week, the journal had to be signed by the teacher and by the child's mother or father, and many children submitted theirs to their parents with fear and trembling. ("Please don't write in my journal that I behaved badly in class!" one of my mother's piano students — a very high-strung one, it's true — would plead tearfully. "You cannot *imagine* what my daddy is going to do to me!" This was quite an exaggeration, as far as Mama knew.)

A journal was more than a daily report card; it was a record of all your school activities, as well as an ID of sorts, which you had to be able to present whenever you were in school — a sort of schoolchildren's equivalent of the Soviet passport. I remember how my heart would sink when I plopped down at my desk in the first class period of the day, opened my schoolbag, and found that the journal was not in it — I had left it on the table where I'd been doing my homework. Losing a journal was even worse, and for a teacher to take away a student's journal temporarily was a very serious and unpleasant punishment.

On the positive side, the journal did develop our organizational skills. Recently a friend of my mother's, now a Bostonian, formerly a Muscovite, was complaining that her twelve-year-old son was not doing his homework and she was getting flak from his teachers. But she couldn't monitor his homework all that easily: "It's not like back there, where they had a journal and you could look into it and see what their assignments were and everything. Here they have no journal, no notebooks, nothing — just some loose pages in a folder!"

My mother's experience illustrates a related difference between the Soviet and the American approaches to education. At the Gnesin school in Moscow, she was regarded as a flaming liberal because she not only pointed out the faults in her students' performance but also praised them when they did a good job. With her American students, she has all too often found that the mildest criticism — and mindful of the habits of the natives, she makes an extra effort to respect the pupils' dignity — provokes resentment in both children and parents. Of course it is hideous to humiliate a child who has made an error, the way our principal did when I mistook that polar bear for a dog. But why go to the opposite extreme, to the point where you almost can't tell a child he is doing something wrong for fear of discouraging him or "hurting his feelings"? How will a person so raised ever cope with criticism — or with real life, for that matter?

The most memorable ordeal of my first years of school had to do not with rude teachers, or with the journal, or with grades, or with other children, but with school lunches.

At the tender age of seven, we must have been considered too young to be exposed to the dangers of the school cafeteria. Instead, during the twenty-minute "big break" after the third period, we had lunch right in our classroom — tea or coffee and a sweet roll. We were served by our mothers, who had to take turns coming to school to bring the trays with our meals from the cafeteria to the classroom, distribute the glasses and the rolls, and then wash the emptied glasses in a basin of warm water, right in the hallway outside the room. With almost forty mothers to the class, this was a less-than-once-a-month duty, but it was bothersome nevertheless, considering the fact that all of them were working mothers. They had to take time off their jobs to come to school and spend at least an hour serving trays and washing glasses. The lucky ones got to do it on Saturdays, a day off for most adults. Things would get quite heated, Mama recalls, when lunch-duty schedules were being worked out at the parents' meetings. Sometimes, predictably, grannies would come instead of mothers. (Aunt Olya once went as a substitute for Mama, although Mama was a little embarrassed at the thought that people would take Olya, with her accent and rough manners, to be my grandmother). There never was any question of a male family member taking time off *his* job to perform this duty.

In third grade we were finally deemed mature enough to eat lunch at the school cafeteria, to which we were solemnly marched, single file, by Lyudmila Alexandrovna. That was when the trouble started. I simply could not bring myself to eat most of the food. I still shudder when I remember the oatmeal — so cold and thick that it was congealed into a solid, lumpy mass. It seemed to me then that I would rather die than put a piece of that oatmeal in my mouth, and my parents' admonitions about starving children in Africa or in India, or about their own hungry wartime days, failed to have much effect on me. "All right, don't eat the food," Mama would tell me. "Just go to the cafeteria with everyone else and leave it on your plate." "But they'll scold me!" I would wail, driving her to exasperation. This went on until eating at the cafeteria became optional, in sixth grade.

Many of my classmates simply scooped the food off their plates when no teacher or attendant was looking and dumped it into their cups of coffee or cocoa. A few, however, obtained a note from a doctor stating that they could not eat at the school cafeteria because of health problems; when everyone else went to lunch, these lucky few stayed in the classroom and ate the sandwiches and apples they had brought from home. I pleaded with my parents to allow me to get such a note, which shouldn't have been difficult. However, my parents did not believe in coddling oneself so conspicuously or setting oneself up as privileged. I would just have to grin and bear it, like most others.

3

Grandfather Lenin
and Other Facts of Life

In kindergarten, a supervisor is entertaining her wards with animal riddles. "He lies in the grass and moves his long, long ears. What is he?" The children look perplexed; no one seems to know the answer. "Oh, come, come," the teacher goads them. "It's someone we all like a lot, someone very, very sweet — someone we've sung songs and read stories about . . ." The children exchange bewildered glances. Then one ventures timorously, "Could it really be Grandfather Lenin?"

This, of course, is a joke, but not a very far-fetched one. To get even close to the image of "Grandfather Lenin" as most Soviet children know him, you have to think of someone who combines traits of George Washington, Jesus, and maybe Santa Claus, and is more ubiquitous than all three put together. In kindergarten and in grade school, children still too young to digest any political slogans, even the most simplistic sort, get large doses of the saintly Grandfather Lenin, whose bountiful virtues and kindly squint they can learn to love on a personal level.

Unlike most of my kindergarten-reared classmates, I had not been exposed to any political indoctrination before I went to school. Oh, I had seen huge posters with slogans — white letters printed on red cloth — proclaiming THE PARTY AND THE PEOPLE ARE ONE and things like that; but these slogans, and the huge banners with pictures of Lenin and Marx that adorned the streets, were simply a part of the urban landscape to me, with no more ideological meaning than a bakery or grocery sign, or a traffic light, or a bus stop. A picture book I used to pore over at the age of five or six introduced me to subjects like the Revolution (the usual army and navy men with red banners and bayonets storming the Winter Palace) and elections (a two-page spread depicting a huge Soviet banner, red with yellow hammer and sickle, and a dignified-looking couple standing stiffly in front of a ballot box). But the shocking truth is that only a short time before going off to school, I did not even know who Lenin was.

As a result, I made a rather singular faux pas when I was five. Grandma and I went into a food store of some kind, where I spotted a bronze bust of Lenin surveying the place. "Grandma, Grandma!" I shouted. "Who is that weird little guy and why did they put him up here?" Grandma quickly pulled me outside. If this had happened thirty years earlier, and particularly if — perish the thought — I had referred to *Stalin* as a "weird little guy," it's quite probable that Grandma would have ended up in a labor camp and I in some sort of reform school.

I don't remember exactly how I lost my innocence. One thing, however, is certain: once I started school, it did not take me long to find out about Grandfather Lenin, also known as Vladimir Ilyich (first name and patronymic), or simply by the affectionate Ilyich (connoting both intimacy and filial respect). There was a portrait of Lenin in our classroom, and, tacked up on the wall, a quotation from a speech Lenin gave before a group of students: "To learn, to learn, and once again to learn!" In the third-floor hallway was a huge sign that read LENIN LIVED, LENIN LIVES, LENIN WILL LIVE FOREVER. (This reminds me of another joke: *An elderly man writes a letter to Lenin asking for a new apartment, and mails it to the Kremlin. A few days later he is summoned by the KGB: "What do you think you're doing, comrade? Don't you know Lenin died fifty years ago?" "Aha — so that's it!" says the man. "When you people want him, he lives forever. When I want him, he's dead!"*)

In the very first week of school, we read a story about a group of small children visiting Grandfather Lenin at his retreat in

Gorki, a country place (the name means "little hills," and is not to be confused with the city of Gorky). The leader of the Revolution is very busy, of course, but he takes the time to receive the little ones, chats with them lovingly, and gives them candy and gifts.

In another story, a delegation of petitioners comes to Lenin with some comestibles as a gift — nothing fancy, but the story takes place during the postrevolutionary years of terrible hardship, and of course Lenin suffers privations along with everyone else. (That part is true: Lenin seems to have had rather an ascetic bent and was known to scorn all material privileges.) And what does good Grandfather Lenin do? He has all the food sent to hungry village children instead of taking it for himself.

In our singing class, we learned a song about a little girl who wakes up every morning to the portrait of Lenin on her wall and finds Lenin's smile sunnier than the sunlight. Like Protestant Sunday-school songs about Jesus, the lyrics said: "All the children in the world love Lenin, / Because Lenin loved them all so much." And for a while I actually believed that Lenin was a universally beloved figure, a sort of Santa Claus, for millions of children everywhere. It would have come as a shock to me to find out that children in America or France bore him no particular affection.

The pious mush about Lenin and the children was parodied in a horribly nasty joke: *An old Bolshevik reminisces about Lenin before a group of youngsters. Asked for an anecdote illustrating the leader's legendary affection for children, the old man says, "One day Vladimir Ilyich was shaving, and this little boy who was playing in the room kept bothering him. So Vladimir Ilyich said, 'Little boy, you'd better get out of here fast or you'll be sorry.' And the boy ran away. Just think: Vladimir Ilyich could have slit his throat!"*

In addition to the pages upon pages of Leniniana in our readers, we were also assigned books about Lenin. Most of them were about the leader's childhood as little Volodya Ulyanov (his real name; "Lenin" was a *nom de guerre*). One episode, whether apocryphal or not, was a near-exact replica of the story about George Washington and the cherry tree, except for its middle-class urban setting: while playing with other children at an aunt's home, little Volodya accidentally knocks over and shatters a crystal decanter, and later makes a voluntary confession. We had stories about Lenin as a schoolboy, resisting the mindless tyranny of the school inspectors; about the teenage Volodya, comforting his sisters after their eldest brother, Sasha, was executed for an attempt on the czar's life, and uttering the famous phrase "We shall go a different way"; about Volodya Ulyanov as a university student; about Lenin as a revolutionary, in Siberian exile, cheerfully outwitting the czarist police to smuggle out his writings and keep forbidden books in his home.

Lenin the Holy Child had a Holy Family as well. There was the noble, long-suffering mother (named, by an apt coincidence, Maria), who played the piano exquisitely and confronted the czarist secret police with quiet, sorrowful dignity after Sasha's execution. There was the father, Ilya Nikolayevich, a big-hearted, wise humanist who instilled in Volodya a passion for social justice. There were the younger brother, Mitya, and the sisters, Olya, Maria, and Anna, who followed in Volodya's footsteps and devoted themselves to the happiness of the people. We had to get intimately acquainted with them all, the entire Ulyanov family.

Some of the stories about this household had little if anything to do with ideology. One was a vignette of the family spending a winter evening together by the fireplace; the father arranges some chairs in a row to suggest a sleigh and takes the future revolutionaries for an imaginary ride in the snowy woods, imitating the neighing of horses and the howling of the wind and of wolves. Of course such tales could have been about any children and any family. But they were not. Even a feel-good little story about playing games with good old Papa by the fireplace had to drag in the Ulyanovs. Perhaps no mere mortals could be shown enjoying such a perfect evening.

Most of the other materials in our grade-school books dealt with the Great October Socialist Revolution, the horrors of life before the Revolution, the horrors of life in capitalist countries, our great Motherland, and so on. Our third-grade reader was divided into more than a dozen sections by topic, and of these, only four were apolitical: "Autumn," "Winter," "Spring," and "Summer." I'm not at all sure they didn't smuggle something about May Day into the section about spring, in case the special section on May Day was not enough. The nonideological texts were few and far between, and for some reason always seemed to be about animals: delightful short stories by the prerevolution-ary writer Kuprin, with dogs, cats, and zoo animals as central characters; Chekhov's *Kashtanka*, a novelette about the adven-tures of a dog that has lost its master (an immensely popular piece of children's literature in Russia); "Tyoma and Zhuchka" (an excerpt from the early twentieth-century novel *Tyoma's Child-hood*), a poignant, suspenseful and similarly popular story about a boy rescuing his dog from a well where it has been thrown by a thuggish peasant. In other words, we were always reading either about Communists or about animals. I suppose animals — and the four seasons — could be allowed the luxury of being politically neutral.

The same third-grade reader contained a remarkable poem by Sergei Mikhalkov, "Them and Us," which we all had to learn by heart. Here is what I remember of it:

> Their every dollar they will put to use
> To furnish murderers with deadly tools;
> We, on the other hand, our rubles choose
> To give for better hospitals and schools.

And the concluding stanza:

> Forward we go, into a realm of light;
> Backward they go, into the dark of night.
> In the whole world, there's Us and Them today,
> And surely we're the stronger ones, not they.

Just in case someone missed the point about the precise iden-tity of "Us" and "Them," the drawing on the page juxtaposed a big, blond, muscular worker in overalls and a little man with a hawklike nose who was wearing a top hat, a tuxedo, and dark glasses and clutching a bag with a dollar sign on it in one hand and a missile in the other. That, mind you, was in 1973, when détente was in full bloom — and when we were still too young to know the word.

With ideology came "social responsibilities." It so happened, thanks to Lyudmila Alexandrovna — not through any good intentions on her part, but probably owing to her exhausted passivity — that my first three years of school were not filled with civic activities quite as much as most of my peers' were. The students in the A group, under the leadership of their small, slim, beaming dynamo of a teacher, the curly-haired, sixtyish Ariadna Vladimirovna, were always busy doing something edifying. They decorated their "class corner," a bulletin board, with displays glorifying Soviet astronauts, Soviet warriors, or Soviet mothers. They had readings of stories about Lenin; they took trips to patriotic landmarks, sites, and museums. Sometimes we were graciously invited to join them. I felt a twinge of envy: they were doing so many interesting things, while our Lyudmila Alexandrovna . . .

Our Lyudmila Alexandrovna, bless her heart, pretty much left us alone. I don't recall any rousing pep talks from her about the good fortune and the awesome responsibilities of being future Soviet citizens. For the time being, our biggest social responsibility was to take turns being "on duty," which meant wiping the blackboard before the beginning of each class, collecting notebooks after a test, sweeping the floor and dusting the desks after classes, and so on. You got to wear a red armband, which of course made being on duty much more exciting. In the first year of school, our "public service" also included taking turns being the "class nurse" (white armband with red cross), which meant checking the cleanliness of the other kids' hands and fingernails and asking them, politely but firmly, whether they had brushed their teeth in the morning before leaving for school.

In the middle of our first year, we all automatically joined our

first Communist organization: the Little Octobrists, named for
the October Revolution. On the day of our induction, we wore
our special uniforms and were given Octobrist badges. The
badge was a five-pointed red tin star with a tiny engraving of a
little boy in the middle: the smiling, cherubic Volodya Ulyanov.
We also had to memorize "the code of Little Octobrists." I remember only one of the rules: "Little Octobrists have lots of fun:
they draw, they sing, they dance, they read — a very happy life
they lead," which was true if your idea of fun happened to be
listening to sermons and singing songs about Lenin and the Soviet Motherland.

As for other social activities, we had one school party in each
of the three years of primary school. That was for New Year's
Day, the secular Soviet version of Christmas, with a tree and a
Santa Claus called *Ded Moroz,* "Grandfather Frost." We wore
costumes for our parts in the holiday show; in first grade I wore
a sparkling frilly dress of white gauze and a headband with imitation pearls, made by Grandma, to be one of the snowflakes
dancing in a circle around the tree. Another time, in third grade,
we put on a modest stage version (with no sets) of Chukovsky's
tale about the fly, in which I played Fly in a green dress, with a
green kerchief on my head and wings (again made by Grandma).

Our big move up the ladder of membership in Communist
organizations came in third grade: that was Young Pioneer time,
much more serious business than the Little Octobrists. The code
of the Pioneers didn't say anything about having fun, only about
being committed to communism, being a friend and protector to
Little Octobrists, and so on. Our class joined the Pioneers in
three batches, in order of birth. My birthday was in February,
fairly late in the school year, and so I went with the third batch,
in spring.

Before each induction, Lyudmila Alexandrovna presided over
a meeting at which each candidate for the Pioneers was "discussed" by the entire class, to determine whether he or she was
worthy of admission to that organization. The discussions were
carried on right in the presence of the candidate-victims, with

comments like "He copies his homework," "She doesn't wash her hands," and "He starts fights." In the spirit of the occasion, I felt duty-bound to expose a classmate who had sometimes tried to peek into my notebook during tests and quizzes. I actually had something important to report! When I proudly announced this to my parents a few days before the meeting, they were horrified.

"Katya, you don't understand!" shouted my mother. "Decent people simply don't *do* such things!"

"But they told us it's the right thing to do!" I protested furiously, almost in tears with frustration at my thick-headed parents. After much arguing and screaming, my parents talked me out of my patriotic obligation.

Of course all of us, faults or no faults, were accepted into the ranks of the Pioneers. Not being a Pioneer by the time you were in fourth grade would have been as extraordinary as being educated at home by your parents in the United States — and would almost certainly carry a much greater stigma. I never heard of anyone who stayed out of the Young Pioneers, although I know that children of practicing Christians sometimes didn't join. And once you were in, you were suspended or expelled only for very gross misconduct, usually of the kind that crossed the line into juvenile delinquency: vandalism, assault, stealing. The two or three chronic malefactors in our class were regularly threatened with this penalty, but kept their ties and badges no matter what they did.

And so on a soggy day in spring I became a Pioneer, along with ten other girls and two boys, at the Kalinin Museum (Kalinin was a revolutionary and a big shot in the Soviet government in the early years). We were taken from school, wearing the ceremonial Pioneer uniform of blue skirt or pants and white top, and given a tour of the museum (Kalinin's desk, inkstand, papers, armchair, and other such edifying things). Then we were ushered into the hall of ceremonies for the solemn event.

The "Pioneer master" of our school, a stocky woman in her midtwenties named Lyuda, with a bad complexion, a perpetual scowl, and a brusque manner, pinned Pioneer badges (red banner and head of Lenin in profile, this time as an adult) on our immaculate white shirts and tied red ties around our necks while we stood at full attention. The "Internationale" was played on the piano. Then Lyuda barked, "For labor and defense of the Soviet Union — be ready!" and we responded briskly, "Always ready!" adding a military-style salute. (We had rehearsed the ritual with Lyudmila Alexandrovna. In my parents' schooldays, the formula had been slightly different: "To fight for the cause of Lenin and Stalin — be ready!") Then Lyuda said, "At ease," and it was over.

I had been waiting eagerly for this event. Membership in the Pioneers was a milestone of maturity. "Pioneer" was a word that connoted courage, integrity, goodness; we used to say "Pioneer's honor" for a solemn promise. This is not to imply that I was a zealot; my interests at the time ran to something more exotic. Having read a collection of stories about the harsh and dangerous life of explorers and hunters in the far east of Russia, I had decided that I was going to travel to Siberia — to *walk*, for maximum thrills — and spend a few years living in a cabin in the northern wilderness. Still, I began to feel at home in the world of slogans and paeans to Lenin, to the Revolution, and to the Socialist Motherland, and cheerfully accepted it all as a part of life.

At mealtimes at home, I would remark with utter conviction that "most children in capitalist countries have probably never tasted such delicious chicken noodle soup." One Sunday morning, I grabbed hold of Papa and insisted that he listen to me read an inspiring story from the Russian civil war era about a teenager's courageous devotion to his Pioneer tie in the face of jeers and dirty looks and finally death itself. My father turned very somber and curtly said he didn't want to listen. It was as if he had suddenly hit me for no reason at all.

"Katya, you must never tell anyone at school that we talk about these things at home," my mother would say to me. "You remember, don't you?" And I, an earnest ten-year-old, would nod wisely and say, "Of course I remember. If I tell anyone, Papa will go to jail, right?"

"These things" were heretical counterpoints to the orthodoxies I was being taught at school. Shortly after I became a Young Pioneer, my father took my political education into his own hands and began to let on to me that Soviet society was not in fact the best and freest in the world, Lenin was not the best friend children had ever had, and so on. I later learned that the decision to tell me these facts had not been an easy one. My parents fought many a battle when I started to show the first signs of at least a mild case of brainwashing. Should I be told that I was being fed lies at school? Mama had mixed feelings about it, and not just because she was afraid I would blab to someone. Why teach a child, she would say, to mistrust grown-ups? Why make her feel she is living in a terrible society, perhaps traumatize her permanently? She did not want to keep me in the dark for the rest of my life; she was just in favor of opening my eyes gradually, carefully, not all at once as my father preferred. But her resistance was rather halfhearted, especially since I kept sorely testing her concern for my peace of mind by saying things like "What do you mean, nobody's perfect? What about Lenin?"

How lucky I was to have my parents. (As my Uncle Yura used to say, "One should choose one's parents very carefully.") Even among the freethinking intelligentsia my parents hobnobbed with, very few ever said anything critical of the Soviet system in front of, let alone *to*, their young children. I knew kids who, at the ripe age of fifteen or sixteen, believed everything the papers said and spoke indignantly of the "anti-Soviet propaganda" in the West, while their parents read Solzhenitsyn, regularly listened to foreign radio broadcasts, and acted like closet dissidents. And these were not cases of kids rebelling against their parents; no one had ever taught them the facts of life.

Many people rationalized their lack of candor with their children with the same kind of logic my mother wasn't able to stick to, that is, "Why traumatize their immature little psyches?" But whether that was an excuse or a genuine anxiety, the acknowledged or unacknowledged fear that the kids would spill the beans and get the whole family into trouble was always present. The un-usually outspoken husband of a friend of my mother's once said in the presence of his three-year-old son that Lenin was a liar. The boy promptly repeated the terrible charge to his kindergar-ten supervisor, who (presumably after regaining the gift of speech) demanded to speak to his father. "Listen, I don't care what you talk about at home," she said, "but would you please be more careful in front of the boy?" The supervisor acted quite decently, too; someone else might have reported the incident to "the right people," as the saying goes in Russia, and then the boy's father would have had to face a much more unpleasant talk.

Mama, who seemed cautious compared to Papa, was in fact not all that docile. She went so far as to talk illicit politics with a few of her trusted older students; she even lent them banned literature, or let them come to our apartment to read it. My father, however, had such a propensity for candor that in retro-spect I am surprised he did not end up in hot water (or in the cold snows of Siberia). For instance, during the Twenty-fifth Congress of the Communist Party in 1971, everyone at the State Radio Broadcasting and Sound Recording House was issued a "25th Party Congress" button to wear; my father was one of two employees who did not wear it.

He was not one to keep his opinions to himself. One night he was standing at a bus stop with a pal who more or less shared his attitude toward the Soviet régime. The conversation turned to a mutual acquaintance, of whom my father said, "Can you imagine — that bastard has joined the Party!" He added a few other choice words, after which his companion, cowering slightly, mumbled, "You know, Alik . . . I've got something to tell you . . . I joined the Party, too. You know that's the only way to get ahead." Oblivious of all the people around them, my father yelled at the top of his voice, "Borya! I can't believe it! *You* joined the Party! How could you!"

Somewhat later, my father, one of the top sound engineers in the outfit, was himself under pressure to accept a promotion to an administrative post — low-level, but with excellent pay and benefits. Like any executive position, it required Party membership. For some time the resident Party organizer was on Papa's back, badgering him to join the Party. Finally, to put an end to the man's efforts, my father looked him in the eye and said with a straight face, "I can't join the Party because I have moral failings. I'm a gambler, a womanizer, and a heavy drinker." The stunned Party organizer, who was surely used to hearing reports of such failings in someone who wanted to join the Party but had almost certainly never encountered anyone who ratted on himself, haltingly tried to convince Papa that he had a chance to reform — but Papa insisted that he was quite hopeless, and was thereafter left alone.

He once played a wicked, though basically harmless, joke on a department head. The executive was mingling with some fellow Party members in a hallway outside a conference room where a Party meeting was about to begin. Passing by, Papa stopped and casually inquired, "Tell me, Yevgeny Solomonovich, do you know what the initials CPSU stand for?" (The initials of the Communist Party of the Soviet Union, KPSS in Russian, are deciphered in a number of facetious ways — among others, as *Kampaniya Protiv Sakharova i Solzhenitsyna*, "Campaign Against Sakharov and Solzhenitsyn.") Yevgeny Solomonovich was especially keen on staying out of trouble because he was Jewish. Knowing my father's sense of humor well, he blanched and muttered with trembling lips, "I don't know and I don't want to hear it! Don't tell me!" Papa looked him straight in the eye and deadpanned, "Why, Yevgeny Solomonovich, it stands for 'Communist Party of the Soviet Union.' You ought to be ashamed of yourself — a Party member, and you don't know a simple thing like that!"

Whatever verbal inhibitions my father did have vanished completely whenever he had a bit too much to drink — which, fortunately for him and for us, did not happen often. God only knows what he said while in a state of intoxication, since he never remembered anything the next day and learned about these incidents only if others (such as Mama) told him. For instance, one time Papa was on a tour of Lithuania with an orchestra. After a concert in Tallin, a banquet was held in honor of the players, and liquor flowed freely. The next morning Papa woke up to hear Mama say, "Do you know what you did last night? You were raising toasts to the liberation of Lithuania from the yoke of Soviet communism!" Just what you want to hear when you're hung over!

I don't mean to suggest that my father's behavior was uniquely courageous, or reckless; sometimes Papa was the voice of reason, trying to restrain a drunken anti-Communist buddy. Yet his outspokenness was unusual enough to backfire in a hilarious way: as Papa later found out, many people thought he was an *agent provocateur*, working for the KGB. They simply could not imagine that someone would say the things he said unless he had a good reason not to fear the consequences.

It was only here in the United States that Papa learned from a fellow émigré of a little comedy of errors in which he was an unknowing participant. At a party to which he was invited, someone said just before he showed up, "Listen, this guy Alik Jung is coming, and of course I don't know anything for sure, but better be careful — they say he might be a *stukach*." (*Stukach*, "stoolie," literally means "someone who knocks"; the verb *stuchat'*, "to knock" or "to rap," is also a slang word meaning "to inform on someone." This double meaning has given rise to jokes about a sign on the front door of the KBG saying "Please knock," or "The office is closed — knock by phone.") A few minutes later, Papa came in and opened the conversation by saying, "Does anyone know where I can get some *samizdat* books bound?" The guests exchanged meaningful glances, their suspicions now fully confirmed. Some people must have said to themselves, "What a jerk! He's just too obvious, starting right off the bat like this!"

This was the man who undertook my consciousness-raising. Before long, I was eagerly seeking out especially pompous propaganda in my fourth-grade reader and choking with laughter as I read the florid passages to my father — "Just listen to this one!" — while Mama was cautioning me to keep my mouth shut. Frankly, I don't think that one or two slips of the tongue on my part would have had such dire consequences as jail for my father;

we were not, after all, living in Stalin's times. But there could
have been trouble. And my mother wasn't just conjuring up a
boogyman to scare me; she was not at all sure what might happen.

In any case, one lesson I learned well was that I should not
mention our talks at home to anyone at school. I didn't mind; the
conspiratorial aura made it all the more exciting. Nor was I
traumatized or overwhelmed by my newfound knowledge. On
the contrary, I felt thrilled, as if I had finally been let in on some
huge, secret, immensely funny joke. After a while, after hearing
so many people, even at school, privately indulging in risky wit,
I began to believe that everyone was in on it, that everyone was
consciously playing the game of doublethink. I remember my
shock, at the age of twelve or thirteen, when I heard our country
neighbor Masha quite earnestly say something about Brezhnev
being a great fighter for peace. *Wow*, I said to myself, *there actually are people who take the stuff seriously.*

Meanwhile, at school I was learning how to fit in as a member of
Soviet society. We fourth-graders were now officially full-
fledged members of the Pioneer body of the school. This meant,
first of all, that we were to wear the red Pioneer tie to school
every day. Leaving it at home (which I did quite often, since I
was always late and frantically grabbed my things at the last
minute) meant that you were lacking in patriotic vigilance (which
I was). You could get a chewing out, or even have a reprimand
written down in your journal. Even a messy-looking tie could
earn you a reprimand. The tie was supposed to be an object of
profound reverence. A poem in our third-grade reader said:

> Once you begin to wear your tie,
> It must be worn with pride;
> Its color is the same as that
> Of the banner by our side.

It went on about how red was also the color of the blood of the
workers and peasants who had died fighting for the Revolution.

But few, if any, kids felt much reverence for the Pioneer tie

— or if they did, it wore off pretty fast. Some used it for so sacrilegious a purpose as surreptitiously wiping a leaky fountain pen. The tie even became an instrument for a popular prank. Someone would come up to you and ask, "Does Mommy love you?" Your yes was the cue for the mischief-maker to say, "Well, then she won't mind untying this," and pull violently on the two ends of your tie, tightening the knot so that it was impossible to pry apart without tearing the silky synthetic fabric or breaking your fingernails. Or else, after making sure that no teacher or other authority was in sight, someone would wave the tie in your face like a toreador's red cape and taunt, "Toro, toro!"

We also had a Pioneer salute, very much like an ordinary military salute, only invested with a ponderous symbolism: the five fingers tightly pressed together, we were told, symbolized the unity of the world's five continents, and the position of the hand slightly above the forehead symbolized the priority of the public over the personal. This catchphrase, "the public above the personal," was the standard reply whenever someone complained about being late for a music lesson or for sports practice because we had been detained for an hour after school for a "class meeting" — an hour-long brainwashing session which even the most right-minded among us detested. I cringed every time this happened, seething with helpless revulsion. All right, I would think, let's say the public good is more important than a music lesson, but how would the public good suffer if one kid missed a boring class meeting?

Along with tie, uniform, and salute, the Pioneers had an official anthem:

> Fires in the blue night,
> Rise to our cheers!
> We're children of workers,
> We're young Pioneers.
>
> Near is the era
> Of bright, happy years.
> "Ready!" the motto
> Of Young Pioneers.

Our glorious banner
Proudly we wave.
Children of workers,
Onward! Be brave!

Near is the era
Of bright happy years.
"Ready!" the motto
Of Young Pioneers.

Anyone with an ear for the absurd should have appreciated the
irony of the students of Special School No. 1 belting out "We're
children of workers," when as a matter of fact not even one tenth
of us came from working-class families, and most looked on the
proletariat with hearty contempt.

We now attended ceremonial meetings on Soviet holidays with
the entire secondary and high school student body. These meetings were held either in the large performance hall on the fourth
floor or, on less solemn occasions, in the large gym in the basement. In our ceremonial Pioneer outfits, we lined up in files
and marched like good little soldiers, to commands of "Li-ine
UP!" and "Atten-SHUN!" Lyuda-the-Pioneer-master reviewed her
troops (not always to her satisfaction), then snapped, "Ready for
labor and defense of the Soviet Union?" and we saluted and
replied with the obligatory "Always ready!"

Sometimes the ritual was more complicated: turn right, turn
left, step forward, form a double file. We trained for this in our
gym classes, but if an important event was coming up, and especially if some VIPs were going to be there, we also had special
rehearsals in the hallways. We didn't mind that at all; practice
interrupted regular classes, a possible lifesaver if you hadn't done
your homework.

At every meeting we stood at full attention while the Soviet
flag was brought out in proper military fashion, the standard-
bearer preceded by another goose-stepping Young Pioneer whose
right hand was frozen in the unity-of-all-continents/public-

above-the-personal salute. The flag was then placed on the stage, with a change of honorary guard every half-hour.

At some of the longer meetings, we were allowed to sit down while listening to the speeches. Very little of the speeches themselves lingers in my memory; I don't think anyone paid much attention to what was being said. We occupied ourselves with doing our homework, solving crossword puzzles, or reading, our schoolmates' backs shielding us from the watchful eyes of teachers and school administrators. (If you happened to sit in the front row, well, it was just your tough luck.) The important thing was to clap your hands at the right time (indicated by the especially solemn, hyped-up inflections of the speaker's voice) and to raise your hands on cue (the cue being "Everyone voting for, raise your hand!"). In this respect, the meetings were indeed very good training for Soviet citizens, who have to attend such meetings at least until retirement — at school, at college, at the office or factory. (*A man comes home from a Party meeting* — so goes a well-known Soviet joke — *and his wife asks him, "Do you want some borscht?" He raises his hand. "Would you like some beef chops?" Up goes the hand again. The wife's getting worried: "Are you all right, dear? Maybe you want a shot of vodka?" The man bursts into applause.*)

It was in fourth grade that our class had to elect a Pioneer leader. Also, the class was divided into three teams — the Russian word was *zveno*, meaning "link," as in a chain — and a leader was elected by each. The teams were supposed to compete for best grades (in a spirit of camaraderie, of course — none of that dog-eat-dog Western stuff!), but no one ever paid much attention to anyone's grades except his or her own. Perhaps things had been somewhat different in more enthusiastic (which is not to say better) days; Grandma told me that when my mother was a Young Pioneer, she and a couple of other girls used to chase the dimwits, slackers, and other academic underachievers in their team around the hallways, chiding them and urging them to shape up and stop being a blot on the reputation of the collective. As a result of these efforts, no one's grades improved but a lot of people began to hate my mother.

Our class, however, came from a generation that was short on zeal. No matter how many times we heard the motto "one for all, all for one," its only practical application in our lives was the one lampooned in a shockingly irreverent cartoon in the newspaper for students, *The Pioneers' Pravda*, in which a single student, evidently the brain of the class, labors over a test while all the rest crane their necks to peek into his notebook. The caption read "One for All . . ."

The duties of the Pioneer leader and the three team leaders consisted of organizing class meetings and other public-spirited activities. Come to think of it, the elections we held for these positions were very bad preparation for a future of Soviet citizenship. Unlike the grown-ups, we could choose among several candidates, whom anyone in the class could nominate at will!

For the most part, the students who took these positions had public service thrust upon them, sometimes for the least civic-minded of motives. In fifth grade, I myself conspired with a couple of other girls to get Galya Malinovskaya, a tomboyish mischief-maker from a working-class family, elected team leader, very much against her will — to get back at her for some inconsequential prank she had played on us. I even engaged in some electoral fraud, buying a few votes for a pledge to do the voters' English homework. At election time, at a Pioneer meeting after class, a sullen Malinovskaya was nominated. Just before the voting began, I decided to do a little more election-rigging. I leaned over to Borya Fedoseyev, who sat right in front of me, and hissed into his ear, "Hey, Fedoseyev, vote for Malinovskaya and I'll do your English homework!" Fedoseyev, who couldn't have cared less about his homework or his grades, ventured to expose me, howling, "This is unfair! She's agitating! Unfair! Agitation!" There was a commotion as I violently tugged at Fedoseyev's jacket to shut him up while he shoved me back. The presiding teacher called for quiet and pronounced that agitation wasn't necessarily a bad thing; after all, he pointed out, agitation is always conducted before an election. (He meant the tired, bored men and women who shuffled from door to door, taking down the names of citizens and asking whether they were going to cast their votes. One could hardly think of an activity more incongruous with the word "agitation," which, after all, connotes some measure of excitement.) Luckily, he didn't know just what kind of agitation I was engaged in. Malinovskaya was all but literally dragged kicking and screaming into the post of team leader.

Those who volunteered for such work were usually regarded by others as a little suspect and were derided as teachers' pets who wanted to suck up to the powers that be because it would be good for their future careers. (We all knew, and were occasionally reminded by our teachers, how important a good public service record would be come college admissions time.) They were quickly labeled "activists," a word that acquired unmistakably derogatory connotations ("Oh, she's such an activist!" meant "She's such a toady!"). To see this contempt as a conscious rejection of the Soviet régime would be a sad case of wishful thinking. It was more an adolescent rebellion against the phony pieties of the adult world.

There were other official positions in the class, notably member of the council of the *druzhina*. (*Druzhina*, a lofty epithet for the school's Pioneer body — grades four through eight — actually had very little to do with communism; it is an old Slavic word for "army.") The council was made up of two representatives from each class, and met for forty-five minutes every Tuesday afternoon. In fourth grade, some jokers nominated me for council of the *druzhina*; declining a nomination would have been bad citizenship, and to my chagrin, I got elected, no more willingly than Malinovskaya was to be a year later.

And so for a year I was a member of the council, along with a lanky boy from my class, Sasha Skorupsky, who used to walk me home from school and even carried my schoolbag sometimes. The weekly meetings were a pain in the neck, especially since we had to hang around for an hour after our last class before the meeting started. We usually spent the time doing our homework or chatting; we were both ancient history buffs, and Sasha, who had rather impractically chosen Julius Caesar and Alexander the Great as his role models, talked on and on about Greece and Rome and told me that if he ever became an emperor, he would make me the empress. Even at the meetings, we would often find an opportunity to converse in a whisper. These sessions were held in the school's "Pioneer room," around a table covered with a crimson tablecloth that had a yellow fringe. If I couldn't chat with Sasha, I amused myself by twisting the fringe into neat little braids. As the youngest members of the council, the two of us hardly ever took part in any discussions and were never asked for our opinions; we just voted for whatever resolutions had been proposed.

We did have one uncommonly lively discussion on a topic not devoid of originality. It seems that some students, mostly thirteen- and fourteen-year-olds, were in the habit of yanking their Pioneer ties off their necks the moment they emerged from the school building after classes, at least in spring, when we wore no overcoats. Political defiance was the very last thing on their minds. Being normal teenagers, the kids simply wanted to look older — say, sixteen or seventeen. Since one could join the Komsomol from the age of fourteen, and most did, the Pioneer tie was a dead giveaway, a great embarrassment to girls trying to pick up older boys and to those boys who tried to pick up older girls.

Lyuda-the-Pioneer-master, who presided over the council meetings in her humorless, snappish way, expressed her outrage and distress at this lack of reverence. Just think — to take off one's Pioneer tie! "There were Pioneers in the 1920s who wore red ties even when they knew they were exposing themselves to the danger of being killed by counterrevolutionaries!" fumed Lyuda, supported by a couple of hard-driving "activist" older girls. "There were days, you know, when Pioneers wore their ties all day, even after coming home from school." She switched to a more elegiac tone (*Ah, the golden days of Stalin, when that fine custom existed*). "Now that would be a good tradition to bring back! And also, you know, it used to be that when two Pioneers met in the street, they gave each other the salute. We should bring that back, too."

Everyone talked about it a great deal, even though we all knew — including, in all likelihood, Lyuda — that there was about as much chance of restoring those fine Soviet traditions as there was of going back to hoop skirts (barring a special Politburo decree and a special KGB vice squad to enforce it). We probably ended up unanimously approving a righteous resolution, and needless to say, the tie-doffing continued.

In secondary and high school, the barrage of cute Grandfather Lenin stories, crude slogans, and jingles about the Revolution and the Pioneer tie dwindled considerably. Still, every classroom had to have a slogan, in huge letters cut out of paper and tacked to the wall. Even the hard sciences could not be left alone. A wall-to-wall quotation from Lenin in the physics classroom said, "Communism equals Soviet power plus the electrification of the whole country"; another proclaimed, "Matter is objective reality we experience through sensation." The Lenin quotation in the chemistry classroom was "The electron is just as inexhaustible as the atom."

Every English textbook, too, had to have at least one reading about Lenin and the Revolution, maybe something about Marx and Engels, and a heavy dose of selections about oppressed workers and blacks (from which we got the impression that "white" and "colored" restaurants were still the order of the day in America). The rest of the space — perhaps as much as two thirds — was occupied by refreshingly neutral stuff: adventure tales, short stories by British and American writers, a piece about Shakespeare and the theater of his time, a reading about Trafalgar Square, and so on.

We moved on from Lenin's generosity to children to Lenin's generosity to adults. In fourth grade, we read a poem, "Lenin and the Stoveman," by Alexander Tvardovsky, an outstanding poet who was in the forefront of cultural liberalization under Khrushchev. He was the author of an anti-Stalinist epic poem, "Horizons Beyond Horizons," and as editor-in-chief of the literary magazine *Novy Mir* ("The New World") was responsible for the publication of Solzhenitsyn's *One Day in the Life of Ivan Denisovich*.

"Lenin and the Stoveman" was obviously not the product of one of his finer moments. The poem retells in verse a supposedly authentic episode from Lenin's life: one day in the early 1920s, Vladimir Ilyich, already the head of the Soviet state, takes a stroll near his country house and sees a neighbor, the stoveman of the title, walking on a freshly cut lawn. Vladimir Ilyich gently reprimands him. The stoveman, uncouth working guy that he is, tells Lenin to go to hell. Only later does he realize whom he bawled out, and he 'trembles for his life, expecting at the very least to be carted off to Siberia. A few days later, two government agents knock on his door. *That's it for me*, the poor man thinks in resignation. He bids farewell to his distraught wife and follows the agents, who take him straight to Lenin's house. But lo and behold, Lenin just wants him to fix the stove, and the only reason for having him fetched in such an unusual way has been to give him a little scare, in order to teach him good manners. In fact, once the job is done, Lenin cordially invites the stoveman to stay for a cup of tea.

Well, wasn't Vladimir Ilyich one hell of a nice guy? we were supposed to marvel. *Big deal*, I, the budding dissident, testily said to myself. But it never occurred to us, not even to me, just how the stoveman's abject fear characterized the system, or what twisted standards of human behavior this little fable actually reflected. The assumption was that it would have been perfectly normal to send the stoveman up the river for the crime of being rude to Lenin, and that not doing so was somehow a sign of most superior magnanimity on Lenin's part. Pretty much like the joke: "Just think — he could've cut that little boy's throat!"

In the same year I got a chance to see another Soviet joke come almost literally true. *A contest is held for the best monument to Pushkin. The third prize goes to a statue of Pushkin reading a book by Lenin.* (Pushkin, of course, died about a hundred years too early for that pleasure.) *The second prize is awarded to a statue of Lenin reading a book by Pushkin. And the first prize goes to a statue of Lenin, period.*

That's the joke; now, the reality. Our school held a poetry-reciting contest to commemorate the hundred and seventy-fifth anniversary of Pushkin's birth. I decided to enter and spent a whole evening carefully memorizing, with Grandma's help, a moving passage from Pushkin's "The Bronze Horseman," learning to recite it with just enough feeling. I placed second. The first place went to my friend Anya, a demure, earnest girl with big misty eyes. The poem she had recited, however, was not a Pushkin poem. The program of the recitation contest, you see, included *two* poems by Pushkin and *six* poems about Lenin.

4

Public Service
and Its Stewards

IT WAS SEPTEMBER 1, 1975, our first day of classes in fourth grade and our first day at school outside the sheltered world of Lyudmila Alexandrovna's second-floor classroom. On that fine, gently glowing day in early autumn, we were marched into a large classroom with geographical maps on the walls, where we were greeted by a portly, bespectacled man in his sixties, with short-cropped graying hair and a mustache that made him look like an aging Cossack. After a few brief words of welcome, he launched into a long, impassioned diatribe against Western imperialism and the arms race, unhurriedly pacing back and forth between the rows of seats. "They say, 'Let's cut back on this kind of weapons but keep that kind,'" he drawled, mimicking the sly tone of the imperialists. "Well!" he went on with a theatrical flourish. "What difference does it make to *me* if I am killed with a nuclear missile" — he arched his eyebrows and rolled his eyes — "or an ordinary bomb that *plops* down on me from an airplane?"

This orator was our newly assigned *klassny rukovoditel*, or "class guide," who would oversee our performance of public service and generally provide us with guidance — moral, ideological, and any other kind we might need — now that we were no

longer wards of Lyudmila Alexandrovna. That colorful welcoming speech turned out to be a preview of coming attractions.

Gennady Nikolayevich Poliakin, who taught geography, was
considered the toughest grader in the school, which earned him
the nickname "Gena the Crocodile." "Gena" (with a hard *G*, as
in "give") is an informal diminutive of "Gennady," and Gena the
Crocodile was a character in an immensely popular cartoon. I
heard from a woman who graduated from the Special School
No. 1 about ten years before my time that the creator of that
cartoon was also an alumnus of our school, and that Gennady
Nikolayevich had in fact been a prototype for Gena the Crocodile. I don't see that they had much in common, though, since
the cartoon Gena was a harmless beast who played an accordion
and sang a cute little song ("Isn't it too bad that birthdays come
only once a year?"). *Our* Gena the Crocodile had the well-earned
reputation for being a man-eating animal.

To be fair, he was an excellent teacher, and as far as geography
went, he tried to make us use our heads (which hardly made him
any more popular). He had traveled a great deal in foreign expeditions, and could tell captivating stories about tropical forests
with their exotic and sometimes deadly flowers, about cyclones
and typhoons. His grading, however, was not only tough but
capricious. Once, in fifth or sixth grade, just before the end of a
semester, he quizzed us without warning on some material we
had covered two months before. Everyone in the class got a big
fat 2, and consequently, no matter how good our grades had
been through the entire term, a 3 for the semester. Academic
standing was not determined by a grade-point average; one 3 in
a semester meant that even if your grades in all other subjects
were impeccable 5's, you tumbled from "excellent" or "good" to
the status of "fair" and the mortifying label of *troyechnik* (from
troyka, "three"). On the last day of the semester, when we received our journals with our term grades in them, the mood in
the class was very somber. In the cloakroom, as we were leaving
for our marred vacation, some of the girls started to cry.

Gennady Nikolayevich took his responsibilities as moral

guardian to budding Soviet citizens extremely seriously. Weekly class meetings weren't enough for him. At least once a week we also had to convene before our first class, coming to school at eight instead of eight-thirty for "political information time." A student had to prepare a report on current events and read it to the class. I once did a report on the struggle for the release of Luis Corvalan, the Chilean Communist Party activist imprisoned under Pinochet. A couple of times we all had to sign petitions for his release; a few years earlier, schoolchildren had signed petitions in support of Angela Davis. (Corvalan was eventually traded for Soviet dissident Vladimir Bukovsky, whom the Soviet press had on many occasions described as "a common hooligan." This prompted the sarcastic couplet "Now we've had a hooligan / Swapped for Luis Corvalan.")

When, in fifth grade, we began to have geography lessons with Gena the Crocodile, he would often get carried away and use the classes as a forum for his political sermons. I must say that those speeches were fun to hear. They were colorful and alive with sincere, genuine, raging emotion. Gennady Nikolayevich spoke slowly and solemnly, even when beside himself with righteous fury. Every clearly enunciated word fell like a stone, with only the rising and falling inflections of his basso revealing emotion as the heavy voice built up slowly to a shattering crescendo. Berating someone who was falling behind in his grades, he would thunder, "BORISOV! Aren't you ASHAMED of yourself? Look at everything our country has done for you! Maybe you live in a capitalist country where you have to go hungry, pay for your education, and work for a living? No, you live in the USSR and our Motherland is giving you a free education! And you are GOOFING OFF!"

He had other, more unusual pet peeves. A partisan in World War II, he railed against, of all things, Soviet war movies, in which the Nazis were almost invariably portrayed as cowardly, pompous jerks. "If the Germans were morons," Gennady Nikolayevich intoned, pacing around heavily, "how come it took us four years to beat them? If they were just a bunch of asses, how come they killed twenty million of us?" While the latest victim of his wrath cringed and squirmed under the avalanche of Gena's eloquence, he would exclaim, "I am an old Communist! I am an *ex-partisan!* And here you are MONKEYING AROUND in front of me!"

On the occasion of Solzhenitsyn's expulsion from the USSR in 1974, our flamboyant class guide exhausted his supply of printable epithets and even ventured a little beyond the printable, calling the writer a son of a bitch — very shocking language in a Soviet classroom. "About fifteen years ago, he published this book" — Gennady Nikolayevich spit out the word "book" as if it were unutterably obscene and might sully him just by passing his lips — "*One Day in the Life of Ivan Denisovich.*" His glasses sparkled and his mustache bristled angrily. "It's a *revolting,* slanderous little book! I simply don't understand how the authorities could allow that rubbish to be printed. It shows a Soviet man as someone who would sell his dignity for a herring!" (It must never have occurred to Gennady Nikolayevich that life in one of Stalin's labor camps could be expected to reduce a man to something rather undignified.) He grandly declared, his voice crisp with contempt, that no one abroad was going to be interested in Solzhenitsyn once he lost his value as a thorn in the Soviets' side, and that the writer would spend the rest of his life "panhandling at the doorsteps of publishing houses." Despite this grim prognosis, Gena the Crocodile was disappointed at the state's leniency toward Solzhenitsyn and flatly declared that "they ought to have hanged him."

In his own way, Gennady Nikolayevich seemed to have an original, even fiercely independent mind. He certainly broke every mold, and found many faults with the Soviet society of the 1970s. The worst fault of all was that our society had gone too soft. No matter how hard he tried to rule us with an iron hand, nothing he did could alter the fact that we lacked, as he pointed out more than once, a true, staunch, fiery Communist spirit — the kind that people had had in the days of his youth. Still, he tried. He waged a relentless, losing battle against decadent bourgeois Western influence.

In my fifth year of school, the police caught a boy from our class standing in front of a swank hotel trying to get chewing gum from foreign tourists. Enterprising boys and girls often staked out such hotels, hoping to exchange souvenirs (mostly badges and buttons with views of Moscow) for packs of gum, or, if they had a lot to offer, for blue jeans. If they had nothing to offer, they weren't above panhandling.

The passion for chewing gum — which I got to try a few times in my Soviet years, putting a piece of Wrigley's Doublemint in my mouth as reverently as if it were caviar — led to at least one tragic incident. It happened right in my neighborhood, at the Sokolniki Sports Palace, during a Soviet-Canadian hockey game. After the game, the Canadian guests began to give out packs of chewing gum to an eager public, and some of the public got a little *too* eager and stormed the generous Canadians in a mad stampede. Foreign correspondents began snapping pictures, and someone in the management of the Sports Palace decided that this sight was injurious to the image and dignity of Soviet Man. All of a sudden, without warning, the lights were shut off, just as crowds of people were trying to elbow their way to the rink. Naturally, a panic ensued. At least five or six people were trampled to death in the commotion, and many more were hurt. For the next few days this disaster was the talk of the neighborhood and of our school. Not one word appeared in print or on the airwaves.

My classmate who was caught panhandling for gum (fortunately, under far less dramatic circumstances) gave Gennady Nikolayevich a great opportunity to exercise his eloquence. The culprit, his face crimson, was on the verge of tears as he received the verbal lashing, standing before the class like a traitor before a tribunal. I don't believe that anyone in the class felt even a twinge of the required outrage; more likely, the majority felt sorry for the poor fellow, and I, for one, squirmed in my seat at the sight of this public flogging. Gena the Crocodile's voice was tremulous with indignation as he spoke, yet he seemed to relish every word of his tirade: "There are people who will go and suck up to foreigners, who will exchange *our Soviet badges* for the Americans' tattered jeans . . . [pause for effect] . . . and stinking UNDERPANTS!"

Because of Gennady Nikolayevich's spontaneous and often very long-winded outbursts, our weekly class meetings, scheduled for forty-five minutes, would last much longer, and we would sit there starving and silently cursing him. Once a student's father, just back from an official trip abroad, came to one of our class meetings to show some color slides he had brought back. Gennady Nikolayevich must have feared that the pictures of magnificent shop windows and other luxuries would make the wrong impression on our susceptible fourth-grade minds: once the show was over, he launched into a harangue about the evils of life under capitalism, focusing on the cost of medical care in the United States. For some reason, he was especially galled by the fact that a pair of glasses cost as much as a man's suit. He brandished his own plastic-framed glasses and announced that he, a Soviet man, had simply gone to an eye doctor — "for FREE," he boomed — gotten a prescription ("for FREE"), gone to a pharmacy, and bought his glasses "for THREE RUBLES AND FIFTY KOPECKS!" A boy raised his hand and asked, "Is it true that you can buy a car with a month's wages in America but only with a year's wages in the Soviet Union?" (No, it isn't; it would take at least five years' wages, on the average salary, to buy a car in the Soviet Union.) "That," rumbled the Crocodile, "is *hogwash!* And whoever told you this, tell him he's a SUBVERSIVE!" (or, literally, "a pest," *vredityel* — the common term for "enemies of the people" in the Stalin era).

At meetings to which our parents were periodically summoned for talks with the class guide and other teachers, Gennady Nikolayevich would rail against excessive TV watching and Western-style dancing. He once gave a particularly vivid description of the latter: "The girl has *grabbed* the guy . . . and he's got his hands on her back — BELOW THE WAIST!" In his battle against bourgeois decadence, he was particularly intolerant of short skirts on girls (the miniskirt rage had just reached the Soviet Union) and long hair on boys, though even the most strait-laced American would not have found either the shortness of the skirts or the length of the hair particularly daring. Gena the Crocodile was always threatening to cut the hair of male offenders with his own hand. We all thought he was kidding, until he actually did it once, when we were in sixth grade. The victim emerged from the classroom with his hair shorn in zigzags and his face flushed and tear-stained. Gennady Nikolayevich also made frequent threats to cut into shreds the skirts of the female offenders. He never went that far (I don't believe he would have gotten away with it, even with public decency as the ultimate goal); but it was humiliating enough when he bellowed, "Next time, Andreyeva, I'll take your skirt off and cut it up into ribbons!" and all the boys snickered. A few times he smacked students on the forehead with a ruler for misbehaving in class.

My brushes with Gennady Nikolayevich, though none too pleasant, never got as far as corporal punishment. I was a good student and generally well behaved, at least in school; but he must have instinctively sensed an enemy. I incurred his anger very early on, in the middle of his first year as our class guide. The issue was a New Year's Eve party at school.

Grandma and I had a tradition of going to Leningrad every year for part of my winter vacation, to stay with her brother and sister. December 29 was the last day of classes, and by the time Gennady Nikolayevich announced that a New Year's Eve party would be held at school on the thirtieth, we had already bought tickets for that date. Tickets always had to be reserved a few weeks in advance; Grandma spent hours making the reservations and listening to a recording intone every five seconds, "Wait for an answer. . . . Wait for an answer. . . ." To return the tickets and get new ones for the last day of the month was virtually impossible. I tried to explain all that to Gena the Crocodile, to tell him that I would not be able to attend the party. He told me to cut out all that individualistic nonsense — I *had* to attend. I ignored him, and we left the morning of the thirtieth. If I had said nothing at all to Gennady Nikolayevich and just skipped the party, he probably would never have noticed my absence, and even if he had asked me about it later, I could have told him I'd been sick. This show of willfulness, however, called for swift and effective retribution.

As soon as I returned from my vacation and classes resumed,

the Crocodile somberly demanded to see my mother, and lectured her as if she too were a ten-year-old. "You are raising your daughter as an antisocial element!" he thundered. In his eyes, I had neglected the public interest for my own little private affairs. (I was never able to understand why my presence at a New Year's Eve party was so essential to the public interest.) Apparently, to Gennady Nikolayevich, having fun when the authorities wanted you to have fun and with the collective of which you were a member was a kind of social duty. He was angry because my family was interfering with his plans for my education, and in particular because I was being given too much freedom at home.

"Well, what am I supposed to do — lead her by the hand?" Mama asked.

"That's right!" said the Crocodile. "Exactly! Lead her by the hand!"

"Until when?" Mama asked hopelessly.

"Until she gets married! After that, her husband will lead her by the hand."

Another unpleasantness had to do with a very important social duty: the collection of wastepaper. On collection days, four or five times a year, everyone had to bring in three to five kilos of old newspapers and notebooks and the like, supposedly to be turned over for recycling. (Most of it, I've heard, actually rotted in warehouses, never making it to the recycling factories.) Quite a few students shirked this duty, not only out of negligence. In the 1970s, despite all the rumors that the collected paper usually went to waste, the authorities decided to provide incentives for recycling. Citizens who turned in twenty kilos of wastepaper received coupons entitling them either to a few rolls of toilet paper — definitely a prize — or, more commonly, to fashionable and therefore hard-to-get new editions of popular books, usually translations of novels by Alexandre Dumas and Wilkie Collins. Understandably, many parents resented the sacrifice of the now-precious wastepaper for school collections. My parents never cared for the coupons, because they weren't particularly interested in the books that were offered and because the lines to turn in the wastepaper were just about as long as the lines to buy toilet paper.

Normally, coming to school empty-handed on collection day was no big deal. The worst one risked was a verbal slap on the wrist. But one day Gena the Crocodile got fed up and decided to rectify the matter. All those who failed to bring in the requisite three kilos of wastepaper got a "severe reprimand" written down in their daily journals, with a predictable effect on their term grade for behavior. The ax fell on me; I had simply forgotten all about collection day. The text of the reprimand in my journal, written in Gennady Nikolayevich's bold hand, said, "Put on notice for sabotaging the collection of wastepaper."

Gena the Crocodile retired after we had completed the sixth grade under his stormy stewardship; he died about a year later, and we were all bused from school to his funeral. I was astounded to see my classmates, the same ones who had so heartily hated him and made fun of him behind his back, get all tearful, the girls sobbing aloud and the boys sniffling and wiping their eyes. I can't say that I missed him much; I got nothing but trouble from the old curmudgeon. But he had personality — too much personality for anyone's good — and his presence added a certain zest to life at school. How often on my way home had I savored the anticipation of doing an impression of the Crocodile's latest spiel for Grandma and my parents!

Since I had at least that reason not to wish Gennady Nikolayevich ill, I am sincerely glad he did not live to see the Gorbachev changes; *glasnost* and *perestroika* would have cast a pall over the last years of his life. If he had survived the shock of seeing "ideologically alien views" given so broad a leeway for expression, his letters decrying "the denigration of our glorious past" probably would have piled up on the desk of many a newspaper editor.

I wonder, too, what he would have become if he had been born in America, not in Russia. Perhaps a crusty old radical, always grumbling about the evils of capitalism and greedy bankers and tycoons ripping off the common man. Or perhaps a flag-waving fundamentalist, writing letters to the editor of the local paper castigating our society for having grown too soft, fondly recalling the good old days when kids used to pray in school and men were men and women were women, and crusading against the menace of rock and roll.

In the book *Timur and His Crew*, written in 1941 by the Soviet writer Arkady Gaidar, a group of Young Pioneers led by a spunky boy named Timur perform all sorts of community services in their small rural town. They rout a gang of teenage toughs who steal apples and break windows; they carry water and hew wood for old people, and do other Boy Scout–type things. Pious though it is, this wonderful, sweet, and supremely sincere little story instantly became a children's classic, and the idea of "Timur crews," *Timurovtsy*, became very popular. Even my father, about eight years old at the time, helped organize such a team at his school, to visit elderly men and women at home, help them with their chores, and so on. He doubts, though, that even in the heyday of the *Timurovtsy* movement more than a handful of kids were involved in it; mostly it existed in the papers, on TV, and in high school textbooks. By the time I was in school, we heard a great deal about how the *Timurovtsy* Pioneers were helping make the world a better place, but not one of us knew of a single teenager doing such volunteer work in real life.

"Public service" (*obshestvennaya rabota*, literally "social work" or "social activism") took up a lot of our time in school, but very little of what we did was of any service to anyone. Most of the "activism" had to do with performing the rituals and repeating the incantations of the state religion. Other social duties were not explicitly ideological but were regarded as a general service to society. One such duty was the wastepaper collection that got me into such trouble with Gena the Crocodile. Occasionally, schoolchildren were also sent to collect scrap metal, in total disregard of fretting parents not at all pleased with the idea of their children hanging around junkyards and picking up God knows what off the ground. Our class was dispatched on a scrap metal hunt once in my school years, but I happened to be out sick. Often college students were sent to collective farms for three or

four weeks in the fall to help harvest potatoes. Music professors
Mama knew shuddered at the thought of their students' delicate
hands plunging into the freezing mud. But Rita said that her
cousin had had a great time: she spent the evenings carousing
with boys, and everyone spent the days digging up potatoes and
putting most of them back in the ground, so they would have
lighter sacks to lug to the warehouse.

Two or three times a year, there were the *subbotniks*, which
originated in the 1920s when workers, we were told, volunteered
to work without pay on Saturdays (hence the word *subbotnik*,
from *subbota*, Russian for Saturday) to help rebuild the economy
of the Soviet Union. In keeping with that alleged tradition, periodic "volunteer work" on Saturdays is mandatory for every man,
woman, and school-age child in the USSR; in fact, the Saturday
before Lenin's April 22 birthday is celebrated with an All-Union
(that is, national) Lenin Subbotnik. For us, the work consisted of
scrubbing floors, stairs, and windows in the school, raking leaves
in the schoolyard in the fall, and doing other work the cleaning
woman was ostensibly paid to do. Since we had classes on Saturdays, we did the "volunteer work" after classes.

The extent of hardship the *subbotniks* inflicted on adults de-
pended on the adults' own conscientiousness or docility. At my
mother's school, the teachers had to wash the windows, and they
did it diligently, bringing their own buckets of water, washrags,
and soap (there were no bourgeois luxuries like Windex) and
standing in a draft as they scrubbed the open windows. Many,
especially the older ones, came down with colds or even pneu-
monia afterward. At the State Radio Broadcasting and Sound
Recording House, where Papa worked, a lot of people got sick
the day after the *subbotnik* as well — from drinking too much.
They dutifully showed up at the office for the *subbotnik* but prov-
idently brought bottles with them, and a supply of jokes to kill
the time. My father usually worked a full day on Saturdays
anyway, and thus managed to avoid *subbotniks* altogether.

Some of our social duties did have a degree of actual util-
ity. Starting with seventh grade, each class had to be "on watch"
for a week once in every eight weeks. Split into pairs, with red

armbands as symbols of our authority, we patrolled designated areas of the school hallways during the breaks. Our job was to put an immediate end to all misbehavior — to break up fights, to stop any student who was running through the hallway, and generally to preserve law and order.

Of course, a student's authority was limited compared to that of a teacher or any other school employee. You could, however, tell a misbehaving student in your jurisdiction to stand in a corner or at the wall until the end of the break, and in extreme cases you could even write down a reprimand in the miscreant's journal (a teacher had to co-sign). Whatever your formal prerogatives, your power was purely nominal if the populace you were appointed to control was your own age or older; there isn't much a fourteen-year-old girl can do to break up a fight between hulking sixteen-year-old tenth-graders. Those who patrolled the second floor, allocated to grades one through three, were the luckiest; bossing around seven-, eight-, and nine-year-olds was a piece of cake.

There were ample opportunities, too, for abuses of power. In fourth grade, I often had the misfortune of being in the territory of two girls who picked on everyone but seemed to take a special pleasure in tormenting me. A few times they spotted me running through the hallway, grabbed me by the collar, and told me to stand at the wall until the end of the break. One would stand by, arms folded, to make sure I didn't get away, and tell me not to fidget. I would be close to tears with sheer helplessness, humiliation, and a feeling of monstrous injustice. That spring I bumped into one of the girls, an ash blonde with icy gray eyes, in the schoolyard during a break; she had no red armband, no authority whatsoever, but I was momentarily gripped with shameful, paralyzing terror. She looked at me with a wry, gloating little smile.

When your time came to assume the responsibilities of patrolling the hallways, you were graciously allowed to choose your own partner. Rita and I got lucky: we were assigned to the wing of the second floor where Lyudmila Alexandrovna's classroom was. I had a tough time with a sassy little girl in her class who looked chubby and clumsy but was always fighting and making trouble. I also remember wondering if perhaps I was picking on her just to get a taste of exercising my newfound power.

Students on duty had to come to school every morning of the week at seven-thirty, one hour before classes started, to do some perfunctory dusting and cleaning. For all the inconvenience, I managed to see something romantic about being in the school building at such an early hour, almost all alone. The tidying up done in a few minutes, we would sit on a windowsill reading, or stroll up and down the empty hallway, our voices reverberating eerily. In winter the mornings were dark, and the fluorescent lights weren't on yet, so the dusk in the hallways made it all the more exotic. Then, around a quarter past eight, the faint din of voices would well up as the lights went on . . .

After classes we had to clean up the floor and dust the radiators on our beat once again. And before going home on Saturday, the on-duty class had to give the building a thorough scrubbing — floors, walls, windowsills, stairs — with mops and brooms and washrags. It wasn't pleasant, but we took it in stride, our minds much more on the chatter and jokes we exchanged than on the work. I sometimes wondered whether the place got any cleaner by our efforts.

Come to think of it, we spent a great deal of time at school with mops and brooms in hand: sweeping the hallways, washing the tiled floor in the lobby, cleaning up the Pioneer room where the council of the *druzhina* met, cleaning up this or that classroom at the end of a semester. The gray burlap rags we were issued on these occasions were old, saturated with so much accumulated dust that the moment they were dipped into a bucket, the water turned a disgusting yellow. As you wrung out the rag over the bucket, streaks of yellowish water smelling of dirt ran down your hands and under your cuffs.

None of this, mind you, counted as public service. Being on watch, scrubbing floors and stairs and windows — all this was just a part of our regular responsibilities. Nothing to be entered into our public service records, nothing to be considered by a college admissions committee — not like blathering at a meeting of the council of the *druzhina*.

After I completed my term in that noble capacity, I was harnessed into another, fortunately less time-consuming "social activity": writing for the "wall gazette" (*stengazeta*), which had five or six issues in a school year. Tacked to the bulletin board in our class guide's classroom, this gazette consisted of propaganda clichés recycled from textbooks, newspapers, and posters, notes on school events, and even a humor section — very tame jokes satirizing truants and goof-offs. The wall gazette was entirely handwritten. There was exactly one typewriter — a rather antediluvian one to boot — in the entire school, and that was in the principal's office. (The first time I saw a copying machine was in 1980, in New York.) As for a high school gazette or bulletin being *printed* — the idea would have struck us as utterly preposterous.

I was known to have a knack for writing and even rhyming — a reputation I had had ever since second grade, when Lyudmila Alexandrovna had read to the class a short poem I had written about swans. (Only a few days later, Petya Mogilevsky had also presented our teacher with a poem, but he had promptly been exposed as a plagiarist; Lyudmila Alexandrovna recognized the verses as Alexander Blok's "The Crow," a piece often anthologized in primary-school textbooks.) Thanks to my mother's efforts, I had neat handwriting as well. So I was recruited to serve on the board of the *stengazeta*, mostly to write poems for Soviet holidays. There was a schoolwide wall gazette as well, posted in the hallway outside the Pioneer room. Once or twice, the implacable Lyuda-the-Pioneer-master managed to collar me and keep me after school to work on the *stengazeta*. Crouched over the stiff white paper, I painstakingly penned the text and colored the headlines, sacrificing the personal desire to go home and have dinner to the public cause of putting out a sheet no one had the slightest interest in reading.

One of my classmates, Misha Belikov, shocked everybody by refusing to work on our class's wall gazette. Misha, a stubby, snub-nosed kid with a round face and short white hair, had the look of a very simple, very Slavic farm boy — nothing to suggest a rebel or an individualist. He also had the makings of a very talented graphic artist. He was not exactly an academic achiever (although I heard that he wrote exceptionally interesting essays), but he was the best in art classes; his pencil sketches showed not only an ability to draw good likenesses of things but imagination and even the beginnings of mastery. Our new class guide, Ksenia Stepanovna, struggled again and again to get him to design and illustrate the *stengazeta*, to draw red banners and strutting soldiers on parade and fiery-eyed Pioneers giving the salute. But Misha just kept saying curtly and sullenly, with an I-don't-care-what-you-do-to-me undertone, "I don't want to do it." Ksenia Stepanovna was outraged, upset, and plain puzzled by his anti-social attitudes, but as hard as she tried to shame him into changing his mind, the boy never budged. He would only draw for himself, the way *he* wanted to draw.

I admired him and wished I had the guts to act the same way. I had a vague feeling that the rest of the boys and girls, much as they might have resented "public service" themselves, looked at Belikov's recalcitrance with faint disapproval, or at least with incomprehension.

The following summer, I drove my parents to distraction one otherwise perfect day on the beach in Latvia, where we were vacationing, by whining on and on about how all of us, upon graduation from high school, would be drafted to work on the construction of the Baikal-Amur Transcontinental Railroad (known as BAM) in Siberia. Rumors had been creeping around the school. My parents tried to tell me, patiently at first, that it was silly to be in despair over a distant and merely rumored calamity. Indeed (aside from the fact that we emigrated before I finished school), it never did happen. Still, it was not easy to shrug off such fears. There had been so much hype at school about the heroic self-sacrifice of Komsomol volunteers working on the BAM, including classroom displays of the beaming heroes, that one was bound to get suspicious: they might volunteer you all the way to Siberia.

5

Teachers

I THINK I FOREVER LOST my reverence for teachers as a class at the age of twelve, when Papa and I stopped by to pick up Mama at a faculty party at the Gnesin music school. One of the first things I saw upon entering the large room where the party was held was a huge, not very young woman in a tight, low-cut dress, dancing in a circle, her breasts bobbing and rolling like mounds of jelly as she jumped up and down and kicked up her legs with ebullient girlish squeals — "Eeeee-aaah!" — meant to show what a great time she was having. Just as we were about to leave, a man with graying hair and a crimson face hobbled up to us. Stumbling over words and exhaling noxious fumes, he insisted on making the acquaintance of "Marina's little girl," who was all the while thinking to herself in shock, *These people are teachers!*

Whatever suspicions I might have had thereafter about the behavior of our own teachers when we couldn't see them, I got along pretty well with most of them. Some — our priggish algebra and geometry instructor, Nina Ivanovna, for one — stayed with us from fourth through tenth grade.

We had a few ogres, none as entertaining as Gennady Nikolayevich. Among them was Nadezhda Pavlovna, the school principal and our first teacher for literature and Russian (which replaced reading and writing in fourth grade). A huge, tall, stout matron with a heavy jaw and a triple chin, she always wore stolid business suits and carried herself with an air of ironclad, all-knowing authority. I don't remember her ever smiling. With a little more polish, she could have been the epitome of a strict boarding-school headmistress.

Her heavy stare presumed you guilty — of loafing, cheating on exams, talking in class, misbehaving on breaks — until (if ever) you could prove yourself innocent. Inspecting our notebooks at the end of a semester to grade them on spelling and general neatness, she convicted sweet, demure, studious Anya Petrosyan of having switched from blue to violet ink midway through the term. That made her notebook look sloppy, decreed Nadezhda Pavlovna, her lips scornfully curving downward as she gave Anya a 2. The girl was in tears; she took her grades very seriously, and so did her mother.

Doing well in Russian and literature did not keep me from getting into trouble with Nadezhda Pavlovna. Once, in my rush to school in the morning, I left at home the composition I had spent hours writing the night before. In a steely voice, Nadezhda Pavlovna demanded my journal. It turned out that I had forgotten the journal, too. "All right," said the frustrated but inventive Nadezhda Pavlovna, "give me your schoolbag." *That* was a form of punishment I had never heard of before. She made me take all my things out of my red imitation-leather schoolbag — all my books, notebooks, pens, pencils, and the apple I had brought with me for lunch, the sight of which, for some reason, sent bubbles of laughter through the classroom — and impounded the bag. I was beside myself with humiliation and confusion. What was I going to do with an armload of books, trying at the same time to hold on to my pens and pencils and my apple? Fortunately, a few friends, including Rita, were kind enough to carry some of my things. During the break, I scampered frantically to the one pay phone in the school building, called home, and begged Grandma to bring my composition to school. She did, and on the next break I breathlessly handed in the ill-starred essay to Nadezhda Pavlovna. "You have to bring it on time," she said icily. "I'm not going to accept something you've scribbled on your break." A look at the five or six pages of my neatly written essay must have convinced her that I couldn't have scribbled it on my break, though. She took the essay and let me have my schoolbag back.

After two years of this formidable lady, we got a new Russian and literature teacher, a very nice woman named Alla Maximovna, who quit after only one year because of health problems. All I remember about her — besides that she was nice — is that she sometimes wore pants, which was very unusual for a woman teacher. (In my mother's school, dress regulations for teachers absolutely prohibited pants on females, although an exception was made for a woman who had had a serious operation on her leg.) Nor do I remember much at all about our fourth-grade history teacher, Maria Petrovna, a lovely lady of sixty or so, slender and trim, and a marvelous storyteller. Unfortunately, the disagreeable ones were usually by far the more colorful and memorable characters.

Most of our teachers were in their fifties or sixties; a few were in their forties, and only a couple seemed younger. One, Tamara Petrovna, taught English in my group from fifth through seventh grade. Whether or not she was at all representative of the younger generation of Russian teachers, she probably got as close to an American teaching style, at its worst, as anyone could in the Soviet school system. A platinum blonde in her early thirties, she wore flashy dresses and tons of makeup. She clearly considered herself a sexpot, and a very chic one at that. She went through three last names in her two and a half years with our group, and often shared her marital problems — jealous husband, ugly scene, that sort of thing — with us in class. These rap sessions about the private life of our English teacher were all the more devoid of educational value because they were conducted entirely in Russian. Her friendliness soon began to rankle and to seem phony to me. Tamara Petrovna was nothing if not easygoing; at her desk during class, she would apply her makeup or eat her lunch, pouring coffee with cream from a thermos and munching on cheese sandwiches. Some of the students, the boys especially, helped themselves to her lunch once in a while, while she rolled her eyes and shrugged in a show of helpless dismay.

Since I was far ahead of everyone else in the group, reading the ninth-grade textbook on my own in seventh grade, Tamara Petrovna apparently believed that there was nothing more to teach me. So I enjoyed a near-complete freedom during her lessons and could use the time to do my homework for other subjects, to read, or to work on my literary compositions. (At the time I was into writing tragedies that I thought were Shakespearean, in blank iambic verse, with each scene ending in a rhymed distich, prose dialogue between servants or soldiers for low humor, and piles of dead bodies in the finale.)

The rest of the class, for better or worse, muddled through the curriculum in between talks about jealous husbands, jokes, and occasional total breakdowns of whatever semblance of discipline remained in Tamara Petrovna's classroom: the girls giggled and chattered, the boys tussled and jumped over the desks with hoots and whoops. My mother met Tamara Petrovna once, and did not like her. Affected and effusive as usual, she whined about being stuck in this horrid school with these horrid children (children of present company presumably excepted).

Tamara Petrovna's familiarity with students was quite anomalous, but this is not to say that all the other teachers were stuffed shirts. We even had one of the type that is so familiar to American students and much more of a pleasant (though eventually tiresome) surprise in a Soviet high school: the standup comedian. That was our physics teacher from eighth grade on, Valery Vasilyevich, a fortyish, nearly bald, neatly dressed man with a sly wink who was always cracking jokes. When he once intercepted a paper on which I had written a humorous sonnet beginning with the words "I'm in the physics class, and anguish fills my soul," all he did was grin at me and make some quip about finding a better use for my talents. We had eccentric teachers and we had friendly teachers: one of the other English groups in our class had Olga Nikolayevna, a middle-aged woman of wide girth and warm smile, whom some of the girls trusted enough to ask ticklish questions like "Does a woman get pregnant every time she has sex?"

*

American observers who have visited Soviet schools tend to find that Soviet schoolchildren, while usually ahead of American students in knowledge of their subjects, are much less likely to be able to think for themselves and to have their own opinions. Today, in the changed climate in the Soviet Union, both educators and students openly complain in newspaper and magazine articles that the Soviet educational system is geared toward producing obedient robots who do what they are told to do and think what they are told to think.

I do not mean to say that this educational system does not encourage students, in some ways, to develop logical skills. But whereas a typical assignment in an American high school social science or literature class may ask the students to state their positions on a certain issue and to defend them — "Tell us what you think about this and why" — our typical essay or oral report assignment *gave* us a position to defend — "This is what you think; tell us why." Even when an essay question was formulated in an ostensibly open-ended way, the appearance of open-endedness was deceptive. If we were asked to "analyze the conflict between Bazarov and Pavel Petrovich in Turgenev's *Fathers and Sons*," our textbook and our teacher had already told us that Bazarov represented the progressive, antiauthoritarian Russian youth of the 1860s and Pavel Petrovich stood for the dying aristocracy; it would hardly have occurred to any of us that the conflict could, much less should, be interpreted in any other framework.

Occasionally a shoot of individual opinion would push through a crack and disturb the peace. It happened once at the school where Mama taught piano. In an ironic twist that surely went unnoticed, the hubbub broke out over an essay on the 1824 comedy *Wit Works Woe* (the meaning of the Russian title can perhaps be best rendered as "Too smart for his own good"), by Alexander Griboyedov. The hero of the play, Chatsky, a young man of independent mind and mordant wit, scandalizes high society at a Moscow ball by his political and personal frankness, and the assembled guests unanimously decide that Chatsky must be insane (strange that I should have missed an obvious parallel to certain popular methods of dealing with dissidents in my own time). The eighth-grade author of the essay refused to see Chatsky as a hero. How would you like it, he wrote, if somebody came to a party at your house and started insulting all your guests, even if he was merely telling them the truth about themselves? The boy received just a reprimand, but the uproar at the school was second only to the one that erupted a couple of years later when a male student hopelessly in love with a girl took up her challenge to prove his passion by striding through the hallway stark naked.

Of course, it is true that in American high schools and even in colleges, the students' views, at least to the extent that they are expressed in the classroom, are often heavily influenced by the outlook of the textbook and/or the instructor. I had my own run-ins with dogmatic professors during my American college years, and on occasion hesitated to express contrary opinion because the air was so heavy with communal self-righteousness. But at least American students are likely to be exposed to a variety of biases, from teachers and textbooks alike. More important, perhaps, it is at least theoretically considered a virtue in the United States — except, I suppose, in fundamentalist Christian schools and the like — for the teacher to bring out the students' own views, and students even grade their instructors on this ability in evaluation sheets at the end of the semester. The very idea of students evaluating teachers or professors is something that would seem ludicrous to anyone, student or instructor, in a Soviet high school or college.

In the monolith of the Soviet educational system, where every child from Moscow to Vladivostok learns the same things from the same textbooks, breathing room is a matter of some teachers sticking to the dogma less rigidly than others. For people like Gennady Nikolayevich, enforcing the required orthodoxy is a labor of love; others halfheartedly play by the rules, trying to stay away from ideology as much as they possibly can. But to challenge that orthodoxy, however subtly or timidly, is to put oneself on the line.

The most heretical words ever spoken by any of our instructors came not from a heretically inclined intellectual but from a silly, gushy woman with cowlike eyes, the geography teacher we had in ninth grade, after Gena the Crocodile was gone. She once confided to some of our girls that she didn't think our country would ever achieve communism — quite a discovery to make in your midforties. (Soviet society, according to official doctrine, is socialist, not communist; communism is the ideological base of the system, as well as the eventual goal of perfection toward which it is supposedly evolving.)

I heard from Mama of one teacher who did put herself on the line to offer her students an alternative viewpoint. I got a glimpse of her once when Mama took me to some event at the Gnesin school, where Yevgenia Pavlovna taught literature. She stood out in the crowd: a woman in her sixties, with short, moon-white hair, in a white shirt and a sleeveless black robe — almost nun-like in appearance — with a vulnerable and confused, even frightened, look. She was rumored to be a churchgoer (very scandalous), and she taught literature her own way, not challenging the textbooks but largely ignoring them, mostly staying away from Soviet books and treating the nineteenth-century classics — Pushkin, Tolstoy, Dostoyevsky — from a humanistic perspective rather than that of the prescribed Marxist dogma. Most of the students, to their credit, adored her. A few complained that she wasn't preparing them for the official questions on the exams at the end of eighth and tenth grade, which was true. Some of these malcontents must have taken their unhappiness to the school administration, because all of a sudden monitors showed up two or three times to sit in on her classes. Yevgenia Pavlovna was taken to task for not following the curriculum and for her "outmoded" analysis of the classics. Soon afterward she was more or less bullied into retiring.

In eighth grade, just as we were getting into more serious study of literature, we blessedly got a replacement for the querulous woman who had succeeded Alla Maximovna. The new teacher, Lydia Davydovna, who also happened to be Jewish, was not a great intellectual, perhaps, but she was an intelligent, nice, cultured woman. She looked bookish yet friendly in her plain brown or navy blue suits and wire-rimmed glasses. She stunned us all by addressing us in the polite second-person plural form of "you," *vy* (pronounced *vee*), instead of the familiar *ty;* the equivalent in America would be to call students Miss Jones and Mr. Smith. We were not used to such civilities from the teaching staff.

Our literature curriculum by then included Pushkin and Turgenev — interpreted whenever possible so as to fit one or another aspect of Soviet doctrine. Since the thrust of prerevolutionary Russian literature was strongly critical of the existing social order, getting some propagandistic mileage out of it usually wasn't difficult. Where no such opportunities existed, they could be made. For example, witness the highly inventive treatment of Pushkin's poetic tale *The Gypsies.*

The story goes as follows: Aleco, a young aristocrat, flees the stifling artificiality of urban life to wander with a tribe of gypsies, among whom he finds himself a wild and beautiful wife, Zemphira. A year later, Zemphira has grown noticeably bored with married bliss, and Aleco suspects her of infidelity. Her father, the wise Old Gypsy, tells Aleco that Zemphira's mother loved and left him, but he didn't try to get her back, because hearts must be free. Instead of heeding this useful advice, Aleco catches Zemphira at a rendezvous with a young gypsy and stabs them both to death, after which he is banished by the shocked tribe. It is the Old Gypsy who pronounces the verdict on Aleco: "You would have freedom for yourself alone."

This line, we were told, showed that Pushkin was challenging the ideal of the individualistic romantic hero. I felt instinctively that this was not what Pushkin had had in mind, and racked my brains to understand where the interpretation went wrong. Only much later did I realize something that ought to have been obvious: Aleco's sin is not individualism but failure to respect the individualism of others, and *The Gypsies* is a plea for a sort of communal individualism, not collectivism. (Zemphira, whom Pushkin clearly admires, was a rather poor collectivist.) Yet for the past thirty years or so, every Soviet schoolchild has been taught to read the poem as a scathing indictment of the romantic hero's individualism.

An even sadder fate befell Dostoyevsky (who, not so long before my time, had been deemed too much of a reactionary to be in the high school curriculum at all) when we got to *Crime and Punishment* in ninth grade. It turned out that the problem with Raskolnikov's idea of killing the old woman to prove that he was strong enough to be one of the chosen was not that it involved murder. No, poor Raskolnikov's fatal mistake was that he decided to act *on his own* and set *himself* above humanity. (If you butcher old women while you're at the head of a revolutionary government, that's a different matter.)

Somehow, I doubt that Lydia Davydovna wholeheartedly embraced such interpretations. Whether she passively accepted them or quietly rebelled inside, it seems to me that she encouraged us as best she could to express our opinions and venture our own views. It's true that such largesse applied only to minor and nonideological issues: a hero's psychological motivation in a particular scene in *War and Peace;* Tolstoy's treatment of female characters in the novel; the question of whether a minor character in *Fathers and Sons* was presented in a sympathetic or a sarcastic way.

A few times she allowed me to do oral reports on topics of my own choosing, more or less loosely tied to the curriculum. I did French classical drama when we were covering Russian classicism (what there is of it), German romanticism when we were on the Russian Romantics, "decadent" Russian poets of the first quarter of the twentieth century when we were studying their more ideologically palatable contemporaries. The first couple of times I got up in front of the classroom, with sweating palms and a stomach tied in knots, trying hard to keep my voice steady, I was nearly finished off by the sudden awareness that my classmates did not care a fig about what I had to say about Racine's *Andromaque* or the dramas of Heinrich von Kleist. Some were whispering, others were reading something hidden under the desk, and perhaps the most conscientious ones were furtively

doing homework for other classes. Some must have been listening to me, though; when I got to the part where I said that
although von Kleist's comedy *The Broken Jug* was set in Holland,
the characters, mores, and customs portrayed by the playwright
actually came straight from his native Germany, titters bubbled
up in several corners of the classroom. Lydia Davydovna came
to the rescue: "Well, what's so funny about that? Shakespeare set
Hamlet in ninth-century Denmark, but he was really writing
about sixteenth-century England." Grateful for the interference,
I recouped a little and somehow muddled through the rest of my
report. And then I came to a wonderful conclusion: it didn't
matter to me whether my classmates cared to listen to my reports
or not. I got to speak my piece and I got my 5 from Lydia
Davydovna.

The latitude she gave me emboldened me. In my oral report
on Russian poets of the first quarter of the century, I ventured to
do something — in all humility — truly unusual. Not only did
I talk about Nikolai Gumilev, shot for alleged involvement in a
counterrevolutionary conspiracy in 1921, and Georgi Ivanov,
who emigrated after the 1917 Revolution and held a very unflat-
tering view of the Soviet régime — neither of them accorded any
mention at all in our textbook — I even recited some of their
poems, copied from smuggled, foreign-published books. I wonder whether anyone in my class — or Lydia Davydovna, for that
matter — had any inkling that the stuff they were hearing was
illegal. A couple of girls later came up to me to ask for a copy of
the poems, and so did Lydia Davydovna. I gladly obliged, putting my typewriter to an outlaw use and adding my schoolgirl's
mite to the samizdat network. Today, with Gorbachev and *glasnost*, Gumilev and Ivanov are foremost among the previously
taboo cultural figures received, to the joy of nearly everyone,
back into the bosom of Russian literature (though not without a
bit of cosmetic work, designed to polish off the rough edges of
their embarrassing politics and to show that there wasn't really
anything anti-Soviet about them).

I don't know if I was a special favorite of Lydia Davydovna's,
but at least in dealing with me, she more than once showed

herself not at all inclined to sniff out ideological lapses. In eighth grade, we were assigned, as part of our extracurricular reading, a work by the writer and poet Marietta Shaginyan called *Four Lessons with Lenin*. I was able to rouse myself to no greater effort than to check it out of the library and bring it with me on the very day when we were supposed to write an essay on the book in class. The question was "What lessons can you learn from Lenin on the basis of the Shaginyan memoir?" The bell rang; settled down at our desks, we opened the notebooks, and I felt the onrush of helpless anxiety that must be familiar to every student in the world who has ever come to a test totally unprepared. All right — there was nothing to lose, so why not give it a try? *Let's see*, I said to myself, *what's Lenin supposed to be like? Hard-working, committed to his ideals, generous . . . What else? Understanding, wise, modest, unpretentious, always willing to listen to people's problems . . . that should be enough.* I leafed through the book searching for quotations to illustrate all these qualities, and sure enough, I found them. I set about writing my essay, squeezing a few paragraphs out of every virtue. By the end of the hour and a half we had for the assignment, I was in high spirits and ready to hand in my work. A week later, I got it back graded 4 on content, 5 on style and grammar. As I picked up my notebook, Lydia Davydovna looked up at me from her table with a hint of a kindly smile and, I fancied, a slightly mischievous sparkle behind her thick eyeglasses, and remarked in a confidential tone, "Katya, I can see you haven't read the book. But you've still written an excellent essay, so I gave you a four."

In ninth grade, Lydia Davydovna came up with a surprise treat for us (her own idea, I'm sure): a taste of what a polemic was like. This one was over a hundred years old and therefore safe, but a remarkable experience all the same.

We were reading *The Thunderstorm*, by Nikolai Ostrovsky, a classic of nineteenth-century Russian theater. The heroine of this social drama is a small-town woman married to a kind but weak man and terrorized by a wealthy, authoritarian mother-in-law. The beautiful and passionate Katerina, whom we might describe in contemporary American lingo as unfulfilled, has an affair with

Boris, a freethinking local clerk; then, tormented by guilt, she betrays her secret. Boris leaves town, fearing scandal, and Katerina drowns herself in the Volga.

Our readings also included the critical essay "A Ray of Sunlight in a Dark Kingdom," by a famed critic of the time, the liberal thinker Dobrolyubov. In Dobrolyubov's interpretation, officially canonized in the school curriculum, Katerina (the ray of sunlight) is a rebel against the stifling social order of provincial czarist Russia. In our last class on Ostrovsky, Lydia Davydovna read to us from a polemic against Dobrolyubov's essay, written by another critic of the time, the radical Pisarev (like Dobrolyubov, held in high esteem by official Soviet historiography and scholarship). Pisarev argued that Katerina was no rebel and no sunbeam, just an insipid, hysterical, impulsive housewife. A fierce-tempered, acid-tongued young cynic, he ripped Dobrolyubov to shreds and shot wickedly funny barbs at poor Katerina. Everyone in our class had a terrific time.

Having read the excerpts, Lydia Davydovna asked us what we thought. Most of us sided with Dobrolyubov and defended Katerina against the mean-spirited Pisarev — partly, I suppose, because that clearly was the politically correct position. My own entirely honest opinion was that Pisarev had been extremely unfair. And yet, for myself, and I suspect for quite a few others, there was a perverse pleasure in listening to someone not just dispute but completely destroy the correct view of the play that we had been taught — and in listening to it *in class*.

The most original mind among our teachers, however, was the English instructor we got after Tamara Petrovna. Tall and heavyset, he limped and walked with a cane, but as far as we could tell was not lacking in vigor. He had a funny name: Cheburashkin, funny not only because it is derived from a colloquial verb meaning "to tumble" but because there was a very popular cartoon character named Cheburashka, a monkeyish creature with huge round ears. It was like having a teacher named Mr. Bugsbunny. Needless to say, he was plain Cheburashka behind his back.

Cheburashkin did not hesitate to attack the school administration. His complaint was that for all intents and purposes, teachers were not allowed to fail students. He left little doubt (and perhaps even said outright) that if it were only up to him, some of us would have gotten 2's for the semester, but the higher-ups thought it made the school look bad if any students got failing grades, and now he, an abused and humiliated teacher, was completely at our mercy; we could do whatever the hell we wanted and we'd still get at least a 3.

At the end of eighth grade, when the big exams that would determine our further schooling were coming up, Cheburashkin gave us tips on what we needed to do to get a 5 and what to get a 4. "And to get a 3?" inquired Fedoseyev, his swaggering tone implying that he wasn't going to exert himself to get anything higher than that. "To get a 3, you can just come into the examination room, lie down on the floor, and wiggle your arms and legs in the air," Cheburashkin shot back. "No matter what, nobody gets a 2."

Fittingly for a person with a funny name, he was as much of a character as Gennady Nikolayevich, only he was not a willful tyrant but a benevolent despot. He gave us assignments that made everybody groan, like translating into Russian a John Mansfield poem in our English textbook, preserving rhyme and meter, or a short story in which the humor relied heavily on wordplay. He got impatient with the students who gave him a straight word-for-word translation of such a story; our task, he blustered, was to find Russian equivalents for the puns. He suggested some that sounded pretty far-fetched. We exchanged glances that silently said, *What a nut.* Nevertheless, we had an odd sort of respectful affection for Cheburashkin. When he turned fifty, we raised a modest amount of money to buy him a gold-tipped fountain pen for a gift. (As we were about to write the standard message on the greeting card — "Wishing you good health, happiness, many joys, success in everything you do" — a protest came from a girl in our group. "How can you wish happiness and many joys to a man who's fifty years old?" Natasha Timina scoffed, pursing her lips. "It's ridiculous. He might even think it's insulting, like we're making fun of him." After some argument, we decided to stick to the original, insulting version.)

Cheburashkin could raise his voice and inspire awe, but he managed to command respect, and even some fear, without browbeating and degrading his subjects. He could be scathing, but he couched his ire in witty and inventive terms. He detested loafers and those who didn't like to use their brains. The décor of his classroom included an aphorism, in large blue paper letters tacked to the wall, that went something like "The only way not to make mistakes is to do nothing." This was a quotation from Lenin, no less, which rather surprised me, because a Lenin who admitted the possibility of error did not jibe with the image sanctified by our textbooks.

6

All in the Family

AT AGE TWELVE I became a commuter, if only for a very small portion of the school year: we now moved out to Kryukovo in early May, about a month before the end of school, and stayed there until mid-September. Breathing the healthful country air was so important that for the sake of it Mama agreed (not without trepidation) to let me travel alone by train from Kryukovo. That meant getting up at six o'clock and scampering in the fresh morning breeze to catch the bus to the train station. The chugging, puffing train was often packed by the time it got to Kryukovo, and I sometimes had to stand the whole way, for about forty minutes, trying to keep steady on my feet, surrounded by somewhat rumpled men and women with serious faces. I truly believed, or at least told myself I believed, that if I wore a white blouse and a blue skirt instead of the school uniform, had no Pioneer tie around my neck, and carried a bag that didn't look too conspicuously like a schoolbag, maybe these people would think I was a grown-up on my way to work, or at least to college. Every time someone addressed me as *devushka* ("girl," roughly equivalent to "young lady") instead of *devochka* ("little girl"), or said *vy* instead of the familiar *ty*, it gave me a thrill of pride: I had just received a seal of approval.

I also began to make occasional trips to the city in summer, to go to the library, and while I was at it to stop by at our eerily stripped-down apartment and take a shower. At the country house, all we had was a faucet with cold running water. About once a week we would heat up water in buckets and lug them to a small wood cabin in the far corner of the garden, rather mis-leadingly known as the shower. Eventually, it was rebuilt to be a bit more consistent with its name: we had a shower nozzle installed and connected to the bottom of a large bowl fixed up on the roof of the cabin. All one had to do was climb up a ladder with a bucket of steaming water in hand (which Grandma often uncomplainingly did, despite her crippled hands and feet), pour the water into the bowl, and then turn the water on or shut it off by turning the nozzle. We owed the ingenious design of this shower to my restless grandmother, though she was not quite up to wielding hammer and saw herself. For such purposes, we had to hire a handyman from the surrounding settlement.

When I was very little, one of the fixtures of summer life in Kryukovo was a character named Uncle Sasha, also known in our household by the explanatory nickname Sasha the Drunk. For three to five rubles — a contribution to the then-mammoth state revenues from sales of vodka and cheap liquor — he would do all sorts of odd jobs around the house and the garden for us and other local summer residents. He even put up a little ply-wood house for me to play in, with a real door and a window too, and painted it bright red. He was a jolly, good-natured fellow and seemed quite fond of me, although my mother, who couldn't stand drunks, later told me that her heart sank every time he came close to me.

When he needed cash for his fix, Sasha the Drunk could be intimidating enough. If mooching didn't work, he would demand the money, bellowing, "I am a sick man!" I was not yet five years old when Sasha the Drunk unexpectedly met a sad end: he was run over by a car while stumbling across a road in an alcoholic daze.

He soon had a successor, a fellow named Kostya, who might have been just as appropriately nicknamed Kostya the Drunk. He did the same jobs for us, for the same pay, for the same purposes. He lived a five-minute walk away from us with his wife, Raya, a plump redhead who probably took quite a few beatings from her man but was feisty enough to keep money away from him. Sometimes she came over for a kaffee klatsch, minus the coffee, to talk about her problems. "I'd divorce him, of course," she would say to Grandma, "but where am I going to find another guy? Leastwise I got a man around."

Raya wielded enough clout for Kostya to be afraid to come home to her when he was sloshed. It was better to sleep it off in the street — nothing unusual in those days, even in Moscow, to say nothing of the outlying areas. According to recent émigrés and people who have traveled to the Soviet Union, public drunkenness has all but vanished since Mikhail Gorbachev launched his antidrinking campaign. Even though the Soviet press admits that drinking has only been driven underground and may have actually gotten worse, this still might be an improvement in the overall quality of life. In my day, men and occasionally women in various stages of inebriation were as ubiquitous as are derelicts in train stations in large American cities. I remember getting off the bus in Kryukovo and almost stepping on a fellow sprawled by the curb — a fellow in a three-piece suit, his hand feebly clutching a briefcase. The public got so used to the sight that people who collapsed in the street because of sudden illness often received no medical assistance and died; everyone passed them by, assuming they were just drunk. A friend of my father's once found an apparent hit-and-run victim on the highway; it took him some time to persuade the police to come down ("Just leave him by the roadside and he'll wake up in a few hours," the dispatcher assured him).

But sleeping in the street was not without its hazards. Once Kostya woke up to find a rather expensive watch gone from his wrist; another time he lost his fur hat in the same way. (By then he was in bad shape, his face red and haggard, the skin taut over the skull, the eyes sunken and red.) So he got into the habit of seeking refuge at our place. Not in the house, of course — he would just stumble into the garden, collapse on the grass under the apple trees, and pass out for a few hours. There was nothing we could do about it, at least not without losing his services, which we needed — and finding a handyman who did not suffer from the same vice would have been difficult indeed.

Most of the locals, like Kostya and his wife, were factory employees allotted small pieces of land to build their homes in Kryukovo, where they lived year round. Many of them raised chickens; someone had a flock of geese; there was also a menacing-looking goat roped to a peg, and a brown cow that belonged to Aunt Dusya, known to us as "the dairywoman" because we bought milk from her. I was no more than six when my parents began to send me alone to Aunt Dusya's, a five-minute walk, with an aluminum container dangling in my hand; I felt very important because they were entrusting me with money and with the fresh, warm, foamy milk. The dairywoman, in her wide calico skirts and kerchief, with her tawny face as wrinkled as a baked apple, looked just like the peasant women I was later to see in photo albums of prerevolutionary Russia. She also shared the hard-working habits of these women. Her small but well-tended piece of land had tidy rows of vegetable beds and apple and cherry trees. Like many old Russian women, Aunt Dusya fussed over small children, and often slipped me a chocolate bar or a piece of candy.

Life in Kryukovo went by uneventfully, except for frequent visits from prowlers. How many times we woke up in the morning to find that some of the most beautiful flowers in the garden were gone, the flower beds mercilessly trampled! "If only they would cut the flowers neatly instead of pulling them out, roots and all," Grandma would say with a sigh. Sometimes she had to cut the flowers and put them in a vase in the house, leaving the garden less attractive to our eyes but also to intruders.

The prowlers, known as thieves among Kryukovo residents, were mostly teenage boys after berries, apples, and flowers, which could be sold at the train station or at a farm market. Every now and then, as we sat in the glass-enclosed front room of our cottage having a late-night snack, there would be a sudden rustling in the garden, and my intrepid grandmother would grab a flashlight, firmly determined to go out and get them despite

Mama's desperate pleas that she not go. Sometimes the intruders would shamelessly sneak into our garden in broad daylight. We fixed some barbed wire around our picket fence, but that didn't help much. Complaining to the police was useless.

We resorted to borrowing dogs from Kryukovo locals for the summer — shaggy mutts of indeterminate color who usually turned out to be friendly, tail-wagging creatures far too good-hearted to be even minimally efficient at warding off the prowlers. They were far less alert to strangers than they were to harmless hedgehogs. Every so often, at dusk or late at night, we would hear an instantly recognizable anguished yapping: the stupid mutt was trying to uncurl a hedgehog and was getting stung in the nose by its needles. Grandma (or Papa if he was home) would have to go to the rescue and take the hedgehog away. About an hour later, the prowlers would go to work undisturbed.

Another bit of uninvited excitement was added to our country life by the appearance of a Pioneer camp — a children's summer camp — separated from our garden by nothing more than a fence. The land had been owned (rented, strictly speaking; you don't own land in the Soviet Union) by the family of a famous aerospace engineer, Semyon Lavochkin, who had joined his less distinguished ancestors in the midfifties. Their plot was at least four times the size of the gardens of other summer-home owners; most of it was uncultivated, the dark evergreen woods intact. As for the Lavochkins' house, it looked more like a castle — just like the castles in my picture books, I thought, with a looming spire and a dainty weathervane, and a portico with white plaster columns (marble in my eyes), and a terrace with ivy and two spacious balconies. In the midseventies, with Zelenograd moving in on us and rumors of the impending eviction of all summer-home owners in the area more and more persistent, Lavochkin's widow sold the house and the lease on the land. A year later, the place reopened as a Pioneer camp. Crude wooden shacks, the children's living quarters, sprang up all over the Lavochkins' huge garden.

Who could have known that we would ever come to regret the absence of the hoity-toity Lavochkin dowager, the richest and the most pathologically miserly person I ever knew in the Soviet Union? However annoying the Lavochkins might have been, at least they didn't wake up to a bugle at eight o'clock in the morning, and they didn't have a raspy bullhorn blaring announcements like "Attention! Pick up the trash on the campgrounds!"

Reveille at the Pioneer camp was followed every day with a military-style exercise which was heard all over the area. At eight-thirty a coarse voice (sometimes a man's, sometimes a woman's) would bellow through the amplifier, "*Li-ine up!*" and then, "*As you were!*" which meant that the Young Pioneers hadn't done a very good job of lining up and presented a rather ragtag file. Then they went through the whole thing again: "*Li-ine up!* . . . As you were. . . . *Li-ine up!* . . . As you were . . ." and so on, sometimes for about five minutes, through ten or more repetitions of the incantation. Finally the campers would get it reasonably right and "*Li-ine up!*" would be followed by "*Atten-shun! Pioneers, for labor and defense of the Motherland — be ready!*" and the familiar chorus of "*Always ready!*" and the merciful "At ease." And so it was every morning, except perhaps for Sundays, from mid-June to mid-August.

Pioneer camps were supposed to be exciting, dynamic centers of wholesome group fun and athletic, character-building, creative, and of course patriotic activities: hiking through the woods, swimming and boating, playing basketball, and then at night gathering around a campfire under the deep blue star-studded canopy of the pure country sky to sing the Pioneer anthem:

> Fires in the blue night,
> Rise to our cheers!
> We're children of workers,
> We're Young Pioneers . . .

In fact, the endless line-up every morning was just about the only character-building activity the Pioneer camp visibly, or rather audibly, had to offer, unless perhaps you counted the occasional collective cleanups of the grounds. What went on during the day may have been fun, but there was nothing athletic or patriotic or very wholesome about it. It was, however, loud.

Mostly the campers listened to a somewhat limited selection of records of Soviet pop tunes, resembling nothing so much as Muzak. The songs — sometimes the same tune three or four times a day — blared through an amplifier at such a volume that we had to shout over the music to hear one another. The one I remember best, intended no doubt to be witty, described the tribulations of prehistoric man prior to the invention of the wheel: "He had to walk on foot to drugstores / And maybe also to the zoo — *to the zoo!*" The records, old and overplayed, sometimes got stuck — "He had to walk on foot to drugst- to drugst- to drugst-" — until someone bothered to remedy the situation. Once it went on like this for about ten minutes, and Mama and Grandma ran to the camp in sheer desperation. The supervisor with the key to the room where the records were played was nowhere to be found; blind drunk since the morning, he had collapsed somewhere on the campgrounds.

My mother had headaches. My father, being a sound engineer who recorded music all day long on the job, greatly treasured quiet and had always seen our summer home as a serene refuge from the noise of the big city. He soon gloomily declared that he wasn't going to come to Kryukovo anymore, though I don't think he really meant anything that radical. Trying to talk to the usually tipsy supervisors was hopeless.

My reaction to this calamity was a sudden passion to join the Pioneer camp. It sounded like so much fun on the other side of the fence, with the outdoor dances and movie showings at night! (Not once did I hear a campfire chorus belting out "Fires in the blue night.") Maybe all that preaching about the joys of collectivism had caught up with me after all. I begged my parents to put me in the camp. Even if they had not been utterly aghast at the idea, it wouldn't have been easy. Summer camps were attached to the workplaces of the parents, and I doubt that an outsider who just happened to live in a local dacha had any chance of being accepted. In any event, my parents wisely did not worry too much about my yearnings for collective summer living. They were confident that if I ever got a taste of it, my infatuation would evaporate.

I got my chance when I made the acquaintance of two spunky, brassy, and friendly girls from the camp who were about twelve like myself. They told me to come over for the movies, and I went twice, for a Captain Nemo film, *The Mysterious Island*, and a very funny comedy, *The Gentlemen of Fortune*, about the tribulations of a mild-mannered day-care teacher improbably asked by the police to infiltrate a gang of hoodlums on a jailbreak. The hoodlums on the screen were not the only ones I got to see. The Pioneer boys and girls in the audience pelted each other with wads of paper; there was taunting and jostling and yelling, and shrieks of laughter at gross jokes. My dampened enthusiasm took another severe blow when I visited the bathroom and found it to be an assault on all the senses at once.

A few days later, my new friends showed up to invite me for a dance; I declined, saying I wanted to finish a book. They gave me a look as if I had said something utterly idiotic, and one remarked, "If you were with us in the camp, you think anyone would let you sit by yourself and read some book?" I never said another word to my parents about going to the Pioneer camp.

Incidentally, the Young Pioneers added to the ranks of the young prowlers violating our garden. One fine summer day as I was busy doing something outdoors, I heard the sound of wood boards creaking, and then a terrific crash. A board in the fence had been broken. Right away, two or three big teenage louts made their way into our garden through the new opening and headed straight for the strawberry patch. I ran to the house yelling for Papa; by the time he showed up on the scene, the boys were gone. He went over to the camp and tried to talk to the bored Pioneer master, who insisted the prowlers couldn't have come from the camp. The fence was mended, and nothing much changed.

Every year in July, when Papa had a month off, my parents packed their bags and took a train to some place with an exotic-sounding name like Piarnu or Vilyandi, in conformance with the hallowed Soviet middle-class ritual of going away on a summer vacation.

For the masses, there were vacation homes — out-of-town places, often in picturesque locations, providing room, board, and usually some sort of entertainment as well. People normally got spaces in vacation homes, as a rule for one person only, through their jobs, so that the husband went one way and the wife another. Mama ventured out to such a place once on a ticket offered by her school. She found herself lodged with two young and merry roommates (one just discharged from a mental hospital), who stayed up into the wee hours of the morning entertaining male guests with booze and songs.

People of finer sensibilities vacationed as "savages" — the nickname, not as pejorative as it seems, for citizens "resting" on their own by renting a room. This was done on a legally murky basis (the residence laws require you to be registered at any place where you stay more than a few days) and mostly, I suspect, with the connivance of officials paid off by locals who took in summer lodgers. Homeowners in the summer hot spots could undoubtedly afford bribes: they rented out everything they could, including, according to one joke not so far removed from reality, the doghouse. Rooms were divided into two with partitions of paper-thin wood, which usually left one side windowless and with no access except through the other side. These lodgings went for sixty to seventy-five rubles a month, about half the salary of the average engineer or doctor.

The most famed vacation spot was probably Koktebel, a resort town on the Black Sea with sunlight-flooded beaches and rugged cliffs and rocks looming high and austere cypresses. To me, the name Koktebel, with its shades of "cocktail" and "belle," shimmered with romance. The spring after I turned thirteen, Mama's college friend Zina Petrova, who vacationed there every year, called to announce that a small but very nice room was available for me and Mama. There was a restaurant nearby, too, though of course eating there all the time would be too expensive — but the landlady had kitchen facilities, and there was no problem with food if you came to the store early enough ("You know, the store opens at eight and you have to be there by six to line up"). Well, Zina admitted, sometimes you might go to the store and

wait for two hours until it opened and then it would turn out
that you didn't get anything because deliveries hadn't arrived;
but it really wasn't so bad, she and her daughter and Mama and
I could take turns going. . . . And then, just as Mama started to
waver, she added, "Oh, I'd better tell you this, because I know
you are really difficult and finicky about such things. I mean the
toilet facilities. You see, there's just an outhouse in the yard,
basically a hole in the ground, and there are going to be about
twenty-five lodgers using it, and sometimes, well, the hole kind
of overflows, and, in a word, when you go in you just have to
shut your nose very tight and get out of there as quickly as
possible. And you have to watch your step when you're coming
up to the outhouse, because a lot of people do their thing right
outside, and . . ." End of the romantic Koktebel fantasy.

At least life in the Baltic was more sanitary, and more affordable. That very summer my parents took me to Engure, the quiet
Latvian village where they had vacationed the year before.
(Grandma stayed behind to tend to her garden.) An overnight
sleeper train took us from Moscow to Riga, and then it was off
to a town called Tukums by a local train. (All the names here
sounded exotic: Ragaziems, Tukums, Kalgari, Dubulty — and
for the first time in my life, I was looking at signs spelled in a
Latin alphabet, though all had Russian translations.) We went on
to Engure by bus, along the highway, then a country road, and
as I peered out the window I got my first glimpse of the sea,
though it was only the humble Riga Bay of the Baltic: through
an opening in the pine trees beside the road, a great glittering
veil spread out, a bright, piercing blue.

And then there was Engure and our home for the next three
weeks: a large, two-story brick house, painted buff, with a tidy
little garden in front — bushes of glowing crimson roses. It was
almost like the pictures of country houses I had seen in my
French books. Perhaps the most striking thing of all was something that was *not* there: no fence, not even a picket fence, around
the garden, and no guard dog either — nothing to protect those
gorgeous roses or the currant bushes. And no one making off

with the flowers and trampling the flower bed after nightfall. This place was different, all right.

Of the three second-floor rooms the owners rented out for the summer, ours was the smallest, six by seven feet at best, but cozy nonetheless. It had a couch, a bed, a small three-legged table on which our stout middle-aged landlady, Valentina, had put flowers to welcome us, and even a decoration — a ceramic plate — on the wall over the couch. All of this left just enough space to set up a folding bed graciously provided for me. When we turned in for the night, we always made sure everything had been taken care of before my bed was unfolded, because once it was in place, getting up was all but impossible. At least we had access to a decent bathroom, *inside* the house — no indoor plumbing, but a makeshift toilet bowl built around a hole in the floor over a very deep pit. Instead of toilet paper, which was near-mythical in these parts, there were stacks of cut-up newspaper sheets; but the place was always kept clean, and even the smell was only a faint one.

One thing that gave Engure a Garden of Eden aura was the very low density of the vacationing population. One of the other two rooms on the second floor of the house was occupied every summer by our friends the Matskins, Mama's little student Yulya with her mother and grandmother; the family in the other room changed from year to year. Apart from them, there were hardly any summer lodgers in the vicinity. The beach across the road, a strip of silky pale gray sand, was so deserted nearly all the time that it was almost like having a private beach. We would sit there reading, having snacks, getting a bit of sun (a bit was all my mother, having heard all about the sun and skin cancer, would stand for), going into the water, exercising — my parents regularly and diligently, I usually under duress. Every evening when the weather was pleasant, we went for a stroll on the beach; the sea was all pearly, with shades of pink and blue and gray, and then (if we stayed out late) it turned a deep dark blue, with a rippling strip of moonlight running from the horizon toward the shore.

The other major pastime in Engure was going into the woods — in a long-sleeved jacket, no matter how hot it was, for protection from insects, and high boots, for protection from snakes. We also each took a stick and tapped it on the ground in front of us to ward off the snakes. Most Engure natives counted at least one snakebite during their lifetime, although they usually got off with only a few days of fever. There were some stories of deaths, but people seemed to take a rather casual view of the whole thing.

We were not just idle strollers in these woods, but gatherers, indulging in a much-loved leisure activity of the Russian intelligentsia: picking wild berries and mushrooms. This was, as far as I could tell, far more popular even than fishing. Moreover, fishing was for the most part a male preserve, but a serene equality of the sexes reigned in the gentler art of gathering.

Blackberries grew in abundance here, and the ground under the pines and firs was carpeted with stiff little shrubs heavy with clusters of big, dark, juicy berries. Any picturesque forest clearing with mossy tree stumps and bushes and fallen branches could suddenly turn out to be a strawberry field, though the wild strawberries, rosy, small, and delectable, played hard to get, hiding under leaves and in the grass.

Among the riches of the wild, mushrooms held top rank. True mushroom lovers (which my parents were not) would get up at the crack of dawn to beat out competing gatherers at carefully chosen spots. All the culinary uses of mushrooms aside, it was the sport that counted, and the art as well: mushrooms hid in the tall grass and under fallen leaves even more cleverly than wild strawberries did. If you were a real pro, you never yanked a mushroom out of the ground but carefully, lovingly sliced it off at the foot of the stem, leaving the root. You needed a lot of patience and dedication, good intuition and a sharp, well-trained eye, and the knowledge to tell good mushrooms from bad ones. The best of the good ones was the white mushroom (which actually had a brown cap and a grayish stem, and an immaculately white and rich inside) — the coveted prize, the crowning glory of every mushroom enthusiast. "A white one! A white one!" the lucky member of the mushroom-picking party would cry out in triumph.

During our holiday, my parents and I did all our cooking and eating in a shack in the yard. Once we went to the one and only local restaurant, a fifteen-minute walk away, and I greatly enjoyed the dessert, a fruity mush with a dab of whipped cream. The only time I had seen whipped cream before was in a picture in a French children's book. The rest of the meal, however, was such that once we were finished, my father grimly announced he wanted to walk home instead of taking the bus; when you've had such a dinner, he said, the sooner it wears off and you're ready for another meal, the better. We never went back. On one very hot day I stepped in for a lemonade, but was shooed away by a couple of elderly female Russian vacationers who loudly rebuked me for being clad in shorts ("Where do you think you are, the beach?").

The store right next to the restaurant was very decent, though; it had great farmer cheese. The Baltic, Latvia in particular, is renowned for the quality of its dairy products, and we even bought a kilo or two of butter in Riga before heading back to Moscow (except on our last trip, when we couldn't find any). We also bought homemade cream and sour cream from Engure locals. And there was another delicious local specialty: smoked fish, *kopchushki*, so tender it melted in your mouth. We got it once in a while from our landlord, who worked for the state-owned fisheries but also made some money for himself on the side. He told us that to stop the villagers from making smoked fish for private trade, the authorities sent helicopters to circle overhead, on the lookout for suspicious-looking smoke. But these tenacious Latvians must have found a way to outsmart the fish police, because we had *kopchushki* on our table five or six times in the three weeks we spent in Engure.

Maybe, as my father suggested, the people in the Baltic, not having lived "under the Bolsheviks" for quite so long as the rest of the Soviet people, had not had their private-sector instincts beaten out of them quite so thoroughly. The Latvian countryside was a vision of neatness and what then looked like affluence to my eyes: pretty houses and well-groomed orchards and gardens, and velvety, geometrically quilted fields, and bright pastures with grazing cows — and everything, down to the haystacks and the piles of firewood, was so tidy, so well kept.

Our landlord, Sigurd, and our landlady, Valentina (he tall and rugged, a man of few words who, with his weathered, rigid face, could well have passed for a midwestern farmer; she rotund but agile, far more sociable, fussy, and sentimental), kept a large vegetable patch, flowers and berries, and a cow and two sheep in a barn. Every morning, if we got up early enough, we could see our landlord's son, Andres, a Germanic-looking youth with curly blond hair — a Wagnerian hero in blue jeans and with a portable radio in hand — taking the animals out to pasture. What an amusing sight it was. For us, blue jeans and portable radios just didn't mix with farms and barnyards. Cows were supposed to be tended by wizened, sturdy old women in kerchiefs, long cotton skirts, and woolen sweaters (even on sweltering summer days).

When Andres's sister, Anita, a tall and robust Valkyrie, came home for a few days on a break from summer school, she did not lounge about or get herself a suntan on the beach but energetically took to scrubbing the house, picking berries, taking care of the cow, working in the vegetable patch. My parents and our Russian neighbors never ceased to marvel not only at Anita's stamina — hardly a day's rest after a long trip home from college! — but also at the Latvians' strange notions of parent-child relations. Why, any Russian parents whose daughter was home on a break would have been waiting on her hand and foot. If the girl got the weird idea into her head that she wanted to do some *work* around the house, the parents would not have heard of it. Yes indeed, the people here were a different sort.

It was an open secret that Russians were not looked upon kindly in the Baltic. Whether or not you were Jewish mattered little. You came from Moscow, you spoke Russian — that was enough: you were of the same stock as the soldiers who had invaded the Baltic in 1940, installing a régime not only despotic but foreign. Too many people here still remembered what life

had been like before the Soviets came along, and the memories
didn't make them feel any better about the present system.
("Back then, we used to think we had problems," the landlady of
a vacationing family my parents knew used to say nostalgically
about the bourgeois days.) And there were many more people
here than in Russia who didn't bother to hold their tongues —
politically, that is (most of the Latvians we came across seemed
generally reserved and not often verbose). Mama's fellow teacher
Nadya Berkovich, who also made a trip to the Baltic every summer, recalled that one of her landladies used to come out in the
courtyard every morning, stare pensively in front of her, and
then pronounce, as if in response to some inner thought, "Boy,
are the Communists in deep shit!"

On my very first day in Latvia, right after we got off the train
in Riga, an elderly man in the train station scowled at us and
muttered something in Latvian as we passed by, speaking an
animated Russian. Judging by the scowl and the tone of his
voice, we were better off for not understanding the words. People gave us sideways looks in the stores, in the streets, on the
bus, the moment they identified us as Russian. Once, heading
back from a shopping trip into town, Papa asked a Latvian at the
bus terminal which bus went to Engure, and the man sent him
to the wrong bus, which cost him five hours of time and Mama
five hours of frantic worry. For a Russian in Latvia, there was a
natural temptation to see this not as an innocent mistake but as
premeditated retribution. My father, however, was so thoroughly sympathetic with the Latvians' grudges that he couldn't
get too mad at the fellow.

Going on vacation and knowing that the indigenous population
tends to see you as part of an occupying force, as a foreign
oppressor, can be perturbing. In all honesty, though, I cannot
say that I was plagued by feelings of guilt or remorse. We never
noticed the slightest hint of resentment on the part of Sigurd,
Valentina, or their children. And whatever blame my parents
and I shared for the Soviet occupation of the Baltic, it could not
be much; we didn't even like the Soviet system. The moments of
acute discomfort we did experience may have helped raise my

political consciousness, but they were not enough to cast a pall over the golden days we spent in Engure.

Back at home, my parents had had the apartment redecorated when I was eleven years old. Papa now enjoyed a luxury he had wanted for a long time: a wall-to-wall bookcase *cum* entertainment center, custom-built in the spare room. Nearly all of the old furniture, long overdue for the trash heap, was finally doomed to go there. I had set my heart on a Baroque living room set, white with flowery blue upholstery, called, of all things, a Louis XVI set. It caught my eye in a furniture store to which my parents had imprudently taken me. They rolled their eyes and tried to explain that, first of all, the set was utterly tasteless, and second, it cost two thousand rubles, which we couldn't afford unless I was willing to live on nothing but potatoes and sauerkraut for a year, as some acquaintances of theirs did when they bought new furniture. The room I shared with Grandma ended up with a thoroughly modern, angular, but quite attractive wood-finish bedroom set. Finally our apartment no longer looked like it was furnished from a junk shop.

The renovations were completed over the summer, when Grandma and I were safely away at the dacha. My parents wisely decided to splurge and hire *chastniki*, or "privateers" — illegal moonlighters — instead of turning to a state Bureau of Household Services for a smaller charge and a bigger headache. They had heard too many horror stories about the state company workers, who gabbed and boozed more than they worked and then got transferred to another job, perhaps for someone who had been better at greasing palms, leaving your apartment looking war-ravaged until they came back.

This is not to say that the two fellows Mama and Papa hired "on the left," a father- and son-in-law team, were perfect. Employed by a government-run outfit during the day, they really got down to business after putting in their legal hours. Still, the men took turns recovering from bad drinking bouts, and when sober, bullied my mother into buying from them a few rolls of garish wallpaper (no doubt stolen from one of their legitimate jobs, just as the paint and the brushes they used were). Later, when the time came to do the walls, Mama felt awkward telling them we weren't going to use their wallpaper. They must have had a good laugh at the expense of these milquetoast eggheads who were getting ripped off and being so polite about it. All in all, they took about two months to paint the ceiling and the doors and paper the walls. (Whatever one can say about the miseries of home repair in America, a comparable operation took slightly over two days in the larger New Jersey apartment we have occupied since 1981.)

Fate had a way of making up for the improvements in our interior. Fate's instrument was the telephone station, which notified us of a slight change in our phone service that fall. This remarkable new amenity, which quite a few people had to endure, was known as a paired telephone. This meant that we shared the line with neighbors; they had a different number, but if we picked up our phone while they were using theirs, we got dead silence instead of a tone, and anyone calling us got a busy signal.

Mercifully, the neighbors across the hall with whom we had a joint line were not quite as talkative as we were, and they probably were the ones who suffered most from this arrangement — except on the few occasions when they tied up the phone for a long time, which happened, wouldn't you know it, just when we badly needed to use it. My parents could never work up the nerve to walk over and knock on their door and ask them to get off the line. They were bound by no such scruples and angrily banged on our door every once in a while (the only contact we ever had).

Whether it was because of our own unsociability or the kind of people who lived in the building, my parents had only the most minimal contacts with most of our neighbors. Among the kids I occasionally played with in the back yard was Raya, three years my senior, the youngest daughter of our building's concierge, Valya, who lived next door to us. A few times I visited their apartment, where a thick, sweetish smell of cabbage soup always hung in the air; with chintzy curtains and embroidered bedspreads, the place looked gaudy and somehow squalid at the same time. It seemed inhabited by so many people that I could never figure out how they were all related to one another, until I realized that these were two families sharing a communal apartment. Two none-too-spacious rooms, considerably smaller than our two bedrooms, were occupied by Valya, her husband, Raya, and Raya's divorced sister and her two children. Raya's father, a surly, silent man with the rumpled face and the reddened, swollen eyes of a heavy drinker, bred yellow and orange canaries, which he kept in ten cages stacked on top of one another. The family had periodic brawls that we could hear perfectly through the wall. If I had slept in the bedroom adjoining their apartment, I would have learned a rich vocabulary of swear words.

I lost my favorite preschool playmate, pretty, plump, dark-haired Vika, when her mother walked out on her father, taking Vika with her. Vika's father, Zhenya Froyants, had a cushy job at the Soviet foreign trade agency Vneshtorg, traded extensively on the black market (they had a very posh apartment), and drank "like a shoemaker," as the expression goes in Russia. He went through three Volga automobiles, buying each new one after wrecking its predecessor (there's no need to explain why his license was not revoked). One night, coming home from work, Papa spotted him curled up by his door, peacefully snoring; he had apparently passed out just as he was about to ring the doorbell. My parents felt that we should somehow alert his parents, who lived with him — but how? Finally a very embarrassed Grandma dialed their number and diplomatically said to Zhenya's mother, "Pardon me, there's a man sleeping on your doorstep."

The most pleasant member of the family living next door to Zhenya was a huge, sad-eyed St. Bernard. My father came home heartbroken one night after seeing the animal standing ruefully over its heavily intoxicated master, who was sleeping it off by the curb outside the building. The lady of the house, a haggard lush with matted dyed hair, often made the rounds a day or two before payday, seeking to borrow three rubles, even though her pretty but bitchy daughter was wearing expensive boots and earrings at the age of twelve.

We had a few nice neighbors. In a tiny, cluttered room on the first floor lived Sukhachova, a sweet old lady, shriveled, wrinkled, and stooped, often seen in the street in a long, shapeless black coat and with a woolen kerchief wrapped around her head. She never forgot to give me a chocolate bar on a holiday, and once gave me five rubles, which probably amounted to about one tenth of her monthly pension, for my birthday. My parents were always reminding me to give her flowers and greeting cards. Sukhachova was a true believer, actively involved in the block Party committee for retired people; when she died, she was buried according to her wishes, in a red coffin with the "Internationale" for a funeral march.

The entire first floor of our building was occupied by old women who lived in cramped communal-apartment rooms and dressed in the same monastic way as Sukhachova, but who did not have her kindly disposition. These were the semilegendary Soviet *babushki*, the scowling grannies serving as volunteer watchdogs of public morality. Around the building, they were known less affectionately as *babki*, roughly translatable as "crones." A few could always be found sitting on a bench outside, chattering and keeping an eye on anyone who passed by, looking out for transgression. When I was small, my parents did not want to keep me too bundled up in cold weather, the way most people bundled up their children. Whenever I was taken for a walk, the crones moved in for the kill: "What do you think you're doing, taking the child out dressed like that? Just look at you! I suppose *you're* dressed up warm enough!" An adult venturing outside underdressed, in the crones' opinion, was in for some nagging as well: "Where do you think you're going without a hat, young man? Want to catch a cold?"

That was perhaps only the most extreme expression of the basic Soviet social custom of butting in — collectivist ideology lived out on a popular level. My mother got a taste of it every time I, as a toddler, threw a tantrum on a bus or a trolley, provoking a barrage of comments: "That's some way to raise a kid!" "You'll see, this one's gonna give you nothing but trouble when she grows up!" The Greek chorus was prone to spring into action too if a husband and wife had an argument aboard a vehicle of public transportation; other passengers would take sides and give advice. The basic motive was certainly not to help or to show concern for the well-being of others, but to make a fellow citizen feel utterly worthless — there was nothing benevolent about the interference. And yet I sometimes think that American society, at least in the Northeast, tends toward the opposite extreme: an all but total atrophy of all mechanisms of social control over public behavior. Often on a suburban train from New Jersey to New York, a group of teenagers will get rowdy, yelling or laughing or singing at the top of their lungs. If this were a train from Kryukovo to Moscow, you could count on a few adults to come up and tell them they ought to be ashamed of themselves (though the teens might respond with a "Get lost!" accompanied by peals of brazen laughter). I am all for respecting a person's privacy. But aren't the noisy teenagers violating the privacy of other passengers by making their ride extremely uncomfortable? Why shouldn't an adult come up to them and politely tell them to quiet down a bit? At the most, people will sigh conspicuously, roll their eyes, and exchange meaningful glances. Perhaps there is something here for Americans to borrow (in a very, *very* small dose, please!) from the Russians.

Old men, fewer than the women for historical as well as demographic reasons (far more men than women perished in World War II and in the Stalin state terror), were also far less conspicuous; I guess they just kept to themselves more. In parks or courtyards where crude wooden tables and benches had been set up for the benefit of the public, they would spend their days absorbed in their favorite pastime: playing dominoes. As you passed by, you could hear the loud, sharp clacking of chips brought down on the table with a flourish. The men, though, never butted into anyone else's business.

The *babki* meanwhile terrorized kids playing in the courtyard, chewing us out for being too rowdy or too messy and threatening to complain to our parents. The very sight of a crone shuffling out of the front door with a walking stick was enough to cast a pall over a game of hopscotch or catch. On rare occasions, children would work up the nerve to attempt a counterstrike, sticking out their tongues at one of these holy terrors or taking their frustration out on the innocent pigeons (the only creatures for whom these ladies ever showed affection) by shooing them away from the breadcrumbs dotingly scattered by the *babki*.

Quite a few people asked whether we weren't scared to walk on our street after dark. Our guests often wanted to be walked at least to the corner if they stayed late. The district where we lived wasn't bad at all — not too far from the center of the city. But on our block and the surrounding streets, there were very few residential buildings. There was an office building, a tuberculosis hospital, a tramway depot, a welding factory, a few stores. This meant that in the evening, the streets were virtually deserted. Mama always called home to ask Papa to come out to the Sokolniki metro station (a walk of about ten minutes) and pick her up if she was coming home late. On those rare occasions when I went out on my own, I was to do the same. One night I called and called and called — I was stuck at the metro station for about half an hour. I kept getting a busy signal; it turned out that our neighbors across the hall were using the phone.

When my parents began to consider me adult enough to come home alone and to open the door with my own key if no one was around, my mother devised a precautionary measure. She would leave a shoe or a piece of paper inconspicuously lying on the doorstep, in such a way that if anyone opened the door, he would disturb it and I would notice the moment I came in. If there were any signs of prior entry, I was to run downstairs as quickly as possible and get help.

Perhaps my mother's fears were exaggerated, but groundless they were not. One of her co-workers had been scared out of her wits when she opened her door and a man with a nylon stocking pulled over his face ran out of her bedroom. She froze in her tracks. The ghostly shape raced past her, out the door, and down the stairs. Some of the woman's jewelry was gone, but she felt so lucky to be alive and unhurt that she couldn't get all that upset over it.

Crime in the United States, and especially in New York, has always been a topic dear to the hearts of Soviet newspaper editors. Needless to say, the underlying assumption is that there is none to speak of in the Soviet Union. Compared to New York, especially certain sections of it, Moscow indeed seems almost a crime-free haven. But if Moscow had tabloids with full latitude to report and sensationalize violent crimes, they would not be at a loss for headlines. I can think of a few based just on the stories I heard firsthand: GIRL SNATCHED AS KID BROTHER WATCHES — FOUND DEAD; WOMAN SLASHED TO DEATH, THROWN FROM WINDOW.

None of that ever showed up in the newspapers or on television. When crime stories did make an appearance, it was usually some time after the event, when the courts had had their say and the story could conclude on the positive note that justice had been done and the social order restored. In addition, the tale usually had to have a moral. The prestigious weekly *Literaturnaya Gazeta* devoted a lengthy article to a grisly incident of which we had already heard a great deal because it took place near Zelenograd, in the woods that lay across the road from our dacha. A group of high school students, mostly children of executives of various local organizations, regularly got together for parties involving drugs and group sex; when a girl wanted to drop out, they lured her into the forest and would have beaten her to death if some strollers passing by had not scared them off. The girl was left permanently disabled and blinded in one eye. Her assailants received substantial jail terms, and it was only after the sentence that the newspaper story came out, saying all the right things about the evils of spoiling young people and leaving them without proper guidance, with a void inside where Communist ideals should be.

The TV program *Man and the Law* occasionally dealt with criminal law, and therefore with crime. The only time I ever watched it (by sheer chance), the topic was how cruelty to animals is a frequent prelude to cruelty to people. The show described in repulsive detail the case histories of several young men who had started their careers by disemboweling cats, immolating dogs, and so on, and then had gone on to do pretty much the same to humans. The host, or one of the panelists, spoke indignantly of an incident in which a boy sitting by a window in class noticed several boys torturing a dog in the schoolyard; he asked the teacher's permission to step outside and interfere, but the teacher wouldn't let him leave the classroom. Parents and teachers were exhorted to be watchful and to stop their children from abusing animals the moment they saw any signs of such proclivities. (When I told my father about the program, he wryly pointed out that the Soviet Union was the only developed country in the world that had no legislation against or penalties for cruelty to animals, and that the government had rejected all requests from citizens for permission to form a society for the prevention of cruelty to animals because "they just don't like any initiatives that come from below.")

Instead of news reports, we had the good old grapevine, the rumor mill of Moscow, which seemed never to take a moment's rest. Through the grapevine, we heard stories that would ring familiar to any jaded New Yorker — stories of violence, of the brazen self-assurance of criminals, of the helplessness and cowardice of the populace. These stories were exchanged at school, at work, at dinner parties and other get-togethers. There was much talk of an incident in which two men armed with razor blades allegedly held up a bus full of people, relieving them of all their money and jewelry. It was said that two military men armed with handguns were among the passengers; apparently, neither felt an urge to pull a Clint Eastwood.

My mother's older colleagues talked ruefully about how people were so afraid of criminals nowadays and how criminals were getting more vicious: "You know, just ten years ago, I was coming into the entrance of my building and this young fellow jerked at my handbag and said, 'Give it up!' And I said, 'No I won't!' And I didn't. Today, I suppose, I would have let him take it." It was in Moscow, not in New York, that my mother first instructed me that if someone tried to rob me, I was not to fight but to give up whatever he wanted.

An epidemic of persistent rumors broke out in 1977 or '78 about a maniac running around Moscow knifing women, often in broad daylight and on busy streets. Women in red were reputed to be his preferred targets — and I had a red winter coat. The serial killer was said to be of medium build, with chestnut-brown hair, and to wear a blue jacket. In our school, rumors about stabbings multiplied, with very specific references to the time of the day and the place where the latest victim had met her fate. One day, as my friend Anya and I were lounging about in the lobby of my building, I suddenly yelled, "The man in the blue jacket! Right behind you!" Anya screeched and whirled around. For my poor choice of a practical joke, I was punished by a nightmare. In my dream, I was coming out of Rita Kuznetzova's apartment, which was on the top floor of her six-story building, so there was no way out but to go downstairs from the very narrow landing in front of her door. And then I saw the man in the blue jacket sauntering up the stairs, holding a knife with a long glistening blade behind his back. Just as I realized that I was quite hopelessly trapped, I woke up in a cold sweat, my heart pounding.

The rumors eventually died down. If the serial killer actually existed, perhaps they got him. However, it didn't take long for the next rumor to sweep the city: a whole bunch of very dangerous criminals, killers and rapists, were supposedly running loose on the streets after breaking out of a train that was to take them to a labor camp. There was talk of gangs who played gambling games in which the loser had to go out and cut the throat of a random passerby. We heard of gangs who used children as decoys to ring a doorbell and ask for help, so some poor sucker would open the door, only to find himself face to face with a bunch of thugs. Rumors about crimes in our own neighborhood also abounded. In a mammoth high-rise two blocks away from us, a woman was coming down the stairs and a drunk asked her for three rubles; she said no, and he smashed her head with a brick.

In addition to the rumors and sensational cases, there were incidents of which we came to know more or less firsthand. One of Mama's students was robbed *every day* for a couple of years on his way to school: a gang of teenage toughs waylaid the poor boy and took his lunch money, threatening to kill him if he told anyone. Two married couples, good friends of my parents, were assaulted by two knife-wielding fellows in a park just outside Moscow, and were saved only by the quick thinking of one of the men, who picked up a long, heavy tree limb from the ground and began to swing it around so that the attackers couldn't come any closer. The women were able to break away from the group and find a cop; the public responded to their screams for help by running in the opposite direction.

A co-worker of my father's lost an eye and a kidney after being worked over by two young men who approached him in the street and asked for a cigarette. (The two men were apprehended and turned out to be Komsomol members highly rated for "moral character and political awareness" by their Komsomol section.) In the building where a friend of Grandma's lived, two elderly sisters were beaten, tied up, and robbed by a bunch of female gypsy fortunetellers they had imprudently let into the apartment. In Leningrad, my mother's cousin Zhenya, a tall, husky fellow who hauled in loads of money working as a taxi driver, eventually decided to find another job because too many cabbies were being robbed, assaulted, even murdered.

People said that crime was much worse in small towns, and that was probably true, if only because of the widespread practice of dumping criminals there. A Soviet prison sentence often includes the stipulation that for a period of time after a convict's release, he cannot live within a certain radius of a large metropolitan center, or in a town with a population over a certain limit. People convicted of felonies are routinely stripped of their Moscow or Leningrad residence registration, which is virtually impossible to get back.

Large Soviet cities also have their good and bad neighbor-hoods, though the contrast is not as stark as in New York. The bad ones are for the most part the new housing projects growing on the outskirts of the metropolis — clinical white high-rises populated by the working class. These outlying areas are known as *Cheryomushki* ("bird-cherry trees"), after the name of the first such district built in Moscow. A friend of Grandma's sister in Leningrad, who had been living with his wife in a cramped room in a communal apartment, was finally given a new, modern apartment in a *Cheryomushki* part of the city. Grandma's sister mentioned in one of her letters that "Mikhail Vasilyevich never stays late now when he's over, because he's afraid to go home after dark."

I had heard enough horror tales of abductions and assaults and gangs to break out in a cold sweat every time I passed by a lone male or a group of youths on a deserted Moscow street. But it was at the Latvian seaside, of all places, that I had my most unnerving brush with the threat of violence. At fifteen, I was staying overnight with Mama's colleague Nadya Berkovich, who had the good fortune to rent an apartment in a local town, with indoor plumbing and other conveniences. Her son and another teenage girl invited me for a stroll on the beach around nine o'clock at night, when it was naturally quite deserted. As we passed through a strip of pine trees on our way to the beach, we glimpsed a bunch of teenage boys on bicycles. There were shrill whistles and calls of "Hey, gals! Come on over and let's have a good time!" In a stupid show of bravado, I turned around and yelled, "Arrivederci, bambino!" — an Italian expression I had picked up from some very chic girls.

Moments later we saw the boys following us on their bikes. We quickened our pace and they sped up too, and then they were right on our heels. We were now walking at the very edge of the water, the tide lapping at our feet, and the four or five guys, with guffaws and wolfcalls, were nearly tripping us up with the bike wheels, jostling us, reaching out to grab and pinch at our breasts and behinds. The fact that we were in the company of a boy in glasses who did not look like a very effective protector probably spurred them on. Along with all of this, they were cursing a blue streak, mixing sexual threats with anti-Semitic taunting. (How is it that anti-Semites can smell Jews with a nearly unerring instinct?) One of the boys kidded another, "Hey, cool it — you know, the new constitution says one ought to be nice to Jews." (That was the summer of 1977, the year the Soviet Union formally adopted a constitution that contained some lofty language absolutely and positively prohibiting any expressions of ethnic or national hostility or acts demeaning to anyone's dignity on the basis of ethnic origin.)

Not allowing myself to think about what might happen next — as if, in a way, I shut off my mind — I concentrated on only one thing: walking fast. And we kept walking, until all of a sudden we saw a lifeguard patrol boat coming up. Our tormentors saw it too, and bicycled off to the pine trees. With a sigh of relief, we headed home. But even back in town, we kept looking over our shoulders to make sure *they* were not behind us. Having caught our breath, we decided that we were not going to tell the adults about this, or they'd never let us go anywhere unescorted again.

For myself and my family and the people around us, the threat of violent crime was certainly a reality, and it *was* on our minds, though not on the front burner. But I readily concede that this threat had far less of an impact on our lives than it does in many large American cities. Being mugged or assaulted is not, in Russia, the ultimate urban trauma it is in the United States. One might say that the ultimate trauma of Soviet life, urban and to an even greater extent small-town, is a far more routine and far less avoidable experience: shopping.

7

Born to Shop

ONE NOT-SO-FINE November day, just as she had to throw together a birthday party for her son Sasha, Mama's cousin Vega came down with a bad cold. My mother offered to do the shopping for her. "All right," Aunt Vega said. "I'll call the better stores to find out where they have ham and liver pâté," two delicacies considered gourmet enough for a festive occasion and still within the horizons of a realist.

Aunt Vega called store after store and kept getting a curt no followed by a click. Finally she called Mama. "Look, I haven't been able to find ham, but they'll have liver pâté later today at the deli in the high-rise on Vosstaniye Square. And also, if you see a Polyot cake [meringue and cream]; would you please buy it? It's Sasha's favorite cake. They have it sometimes at the bakery on the Kalininsky Prospect."

Mama trudged halfway across the city to Vosstaniye ("Rebellion") Square. She and the pâté arrived at the same time. Just as Mama entered the store, a saleswoman called out, "We have pâté at the deli!" In the wild stampede that ensued, quite a few people beat her to the deli counter, and before her turn came, the first batch of pâté was sold out. Mama stood there dejectedly; had she braved the chilly wind and sleet to go back empty-handed? But here was the saleswoman coming with another announcement . . . they were bringing out more pâté!

Having bagged the pâté, Mama headed for the bakery on the

Kalininsky Prospect (Moscow's poor relation to New York's Fifth Avenue). The first thing she saw was a store employee pushing a cart with a stack of Polyot cake cartons on it. A moment later a saleswoman loudly heralded its arrival. Hardly believing her luck, Mama went over to the cash register — you had to pay first, as in most Soviet stores — and said, "Four twenty-five, please."

"What are you getting?"

"The Polyot cake."

Suddenly, from behind Mama's back came a shrill cry: "Where's your number?"

Mama looked around to find at least a hundred and fifty people standing to one side of the bakery. They had all been waiting.

"I don't have a number," she stammered, the mirage of a lucky break dissipating before her eyes.

"Well, forget about that cake!" exploded dozens of voices. "We've been standing here since six o'clock in the morning, waiting for them to bring this cake! You can't just cut in without a number!" They all had numbers written on the palms of their hands with a ballpoint pen. "She thinks she's smarter than everybody else — just coming in here and saying she wants a Polyot cake!"

"Sorry," Mama muttered, "I didn't know there was a line." Meanwhile, the saleswoman announced there were only ninety cakes. Getting in line now made no sense.

On the way home, Mama stopped at a neighborhood meat store, and once again couldn't believe her luck. There, stacked up on the counter, were turkeys. Mama asked for one, and was told she couldn't have it because there was a limit of one kilo per customer. "All right, then, cut it and give me a kilo," said Mama. "Can't do that," the saleswoman snarled. "The butcher isn't in today."

Just another day in a shopper's life.

My first confrontations with the harsh realities of shopping occurred when my mother began to take me along, when I was four or five, in the hope that I might be of some help by holding a place for her in a line while she was buying something else or paying the cashier. On one of these trips, I almost made a terrible, innocence-shattering discovery: I saw some chickens piled up on the counter, complete with heads, feet, and even some feathers, which is the way chickens are usually sold in the Soviet Union (except for imported frozen chicken). "Mama! Mama! Look!" I shouted. Mama looked, and her heart sank. I had never yet made the connection between the meat we ate and actual animals ("Why should people go fishing and kill a real fish when you can go to a store and buy one?"), and knowing how I always got upset at the killing of even a fly, my mother expected nothing less than a full-blown tantrum. Instead, I continued, "Look at this — they're made up to look just like real chickens, with heads and feet and everything!"

More often than not, my help wasn't worth the trouble. The first time Mama told me to "stay right here in this line," she came back to find me standing on the very same spot while the line was busily moving past me. The next time she put me in line, her instructions were to "stay right behind this lady"; the lady walked off to another department after asking the person in front of her to hold her place, and I dutifully stayed — or rather waddled — right behind her. Mama had to go looking for me, and of course lost her spot in the line.

As I got older, I went with her more and more often. Soon I knew all the shops in our neighborhood and even those two or three trolley stops away. By the time I was fourteen or so, I was trusted to shop for certain kinds of food on my own. This usually meant going to six or seven stores before I could get everything on my very spartan shopping list: one dairy store had no milk or cream and the other had no butter or cheese; one grocery store had no sugar and the other no buckwheat, and so on. And so I would shuffle from store to store, using the time to recite poetry to myself or to compose in my mind a novel about a slave girl in ancient Rome and to daydream about the reviews it was going to get.

Our neighborhood's main shopping attraction, the Sokolniki supermarket and department store (*univermag*, alternately known as *universam*, for *universalny magazin*, "universal store"), was a fifteen-minute walk or two trolley stops away. It occupied the first and second floors of a very long, squat-looking, ten-story residential building. The department store, with rather nice interior decoration, was on the second floor. The supermarket on the first floor was noticeably more modern and less grubby than a typical food store. It also had self-service, something that only a few very advanced Soviet shops were beginning to adopt. Selecting your own purchases, putting them in a basket (in 1980 the Sokolniki supermarket went quite revolutionary and introduced *pushcarts*), and then paying for them at the cash register, standing in just one line instead of two — what dazzling efficiency.

Still, nothing was easy. As you approached the cheese and butter shelves, you never knew whether they would be stocked or quite empty. You might find nothing but salted butter and dried-up, stale-looking cheese. Once, just as I discovered that there was no butter, out came a saleswoman in the traditional white gown to make an announcement: a fresh batch of butter would be brought out of the packing/storage room in a few minutes. People clustered together at once, tensely waiting, their eyes on the heavy metal doors of the packing room. Finally the doors swung open and a saleswoman emerged, pushing a shopping cart filled with irregular blocks of butter wrapped in wax paper. *Now!* The crowd around me swooped down on the cart. I struggled to make my way through, ignoring the elbows painfully jabbing into my ribs. When I managed to break free, I was not unruffled, but not empty-handed either.

Then there were the pyramid-shaped cartons of milk, cream, and kefir (a plain yogurt drink, a staple of the Soviet diet). The cartons had an annoying tendency to leak at the edges. On some days you could find your way to the dairy section by following the trail of whitish liquid on the tile floor. Even if you succeeded in finding a carton that wasn't leaky, you couldn't really breathe a sigh of relief until you got home, because the carton might start leaking in your bag. Getting eggs home safely from the store was an even greater trial; I attempted it twice, and delivered a scrambled mess. As a rule, eggs were sold with no containers. In the stores they were kept in yellowish cartons stacked on top of one another on the counter. Each carton held three dozen eggs, and unless you were buying the whole carton, the saleswoman just took out the eggs one by one and loaded them into your bag. It was up to you to figure out how to transport the precious cargo. I held my arm very straight to keep the bag at some distance from my body, and prayed that no one would bump into me. It didn't work.

I could not be trusted to buy meat, either. Even in the event that I came upon chicken or beef in the Sokolniki supermarket, choosing a decent bird or a chunk of meat without too much fat and bone was definitely beyond my capabilities. Sometimes I would accompany Mama to a regular meat store. You had to stand in line at the counter, have a chunk of meat cut off and weighed for you, then stand in another line to pay the cashier and come back to pick up your purchase. Along with a cut of meat, every customer got some stringy, fibrous scraps the glum saleswoman threw on the scale for good measure. Some tried to protest, but the woman would snap, "Well, what are we supposed to do with this stuff? No one wants it any more than you do." What they were supposed to do with the stuff was write it off as damaged goods. And so they did, selling 100 kilos of meat by the books and 130 over (or under) the counter, keeping the difference. In the disputes that often flared up between customers and salespeople, the former would often yell, "You're all thieves and crooks!" and they weren't being all that unfair.

In 1978 or '79, long before the present orgy of open criticism in the Soviet press, a satirical novelette serialized in the weekly *Literaturnaya Gazeta* depicted a crooked provincial store manager and black marketeer who could do anything — obtain deficit goods, get a total bonehead into a top college. This hard-hitting realism was somewhat deflected by the author's clever plot, designed to show that such reprobates were the exception, not the rule. A decent man grievously wronged by this character seeks revenge; since he doesn't know the name of his tormentor or of the store, he sends identical telegrams ("You've been found out.

Get out of town.") to every store manager in the area. A hundred and fifty-odd honest managers shrug and throw the telegram in the wastebasket, while three, including the villain of the story, try to skip town but are speedily nabbed and brought to justice. In reality, even a reversed rate of a hundred and fifty-odd crooks to three honest managers would have been a tad too starry-eyed.

Not long before we applied to emigrate, my father told us, chuckling, that he had been talking to a man at work who made him a great offer for a career change: from sound engineer to meat cutter. The income on the side, the guy said, amounted to thirty rubles *a day* — more than many Soviet citizens earn in a week. You just had to know where and how to cut. And it was perfectly safe, too; all the government inspectors whose job it was to investigate such doings were paid off. So were the higher officials whose job it was to investigate graft among the inspectors.

Customers and salespeople, I quickly learned, were class adversaries — no term can describe it better. The class warfare was complicated by the fact that the customers were not a united front; on the contrary, their ranks were torn by constant and vicious infighting.

Imagine yourself in a Moscow vegetable store. You're buying beets, potatoes, carrots, or cabbage over the counter. You try to select them yourself, because you would like to minimize the time you will spend in your kitchen separating the good ones from the rotten ones or trying to salvage the edible part of a half-rotten vegetable. You humbly ask if you can have that potato instead of this one. The class enemy scowls at you: "Listen, you don't want it? Take a walk!" If people are in line behind you, they are anything but supportive. What you hear is, "Hey, you! Hurry up! How long you gonna take? You're holding up the line!" Somehow, it doesn't occur to them that showing more solidarity with a fellow customer could be to their advantage, since they will get to the head of the line before too long and have to deal with the same salesclerk.

Or suppose you are in a line for bananas sold from a vending stall in the street, and perhaps the weather is windy and chilly and the air bloated with rain. Everyone is frazzled, angry, nervous that no bananas will be left and all the time spent in line will be wasted. If there is no limit on how much one person can buy, those buying too much risk the wrath of everyone behind them. There will be cries of "Look at her! She wants everything for herself!" and, to the saleswoman, "Girl! Why are you giving so much into one pair of hands?" — the Soviet phrase for "per customer." ("Girl," in this case, is not a sign of rudeness. The Russian versions of "sir" and "madam" were abolished by the Revolution, and the population never willingly took to words like "comrade" and "citizen," which sound forbiddingly official. Therefore, anyone under sixty or so is addressed as "girl," *devushka*, or "young man," and anyone over that age as "grandma" or "grandpa." The words "man" and "woman" are sometimes used as well, but they are considered impolite.)

The only thing that sometimes proved stronger than the belligerence of the people waiting in line was, alas, sexist attitudes. Grandma once mentioned a former neighbor who always let a male customer go ahead of her in the belief that "it ain't dignified for a man to wait in line." Aghast, I repeated the story to Mama, who shrugged and said there was nothing unusual about this. Quite often, she said, a man would come up and brazenly cut in. Not all the women took this placidly; there would be cries of "Hey, you! Man! Where do you think you're going?" Other women would say, "Oh, let him go ahead. A man shouldn't be standing in line." And it would all turn into another squabble, with the feminist faction yelling, "Why should we give the bastards a break? All they ever do is loaf and get drunk and beat up their wives!"

Sometimes Mama would drag me to one of the better-stocked fruit and vegetable stores in the area, which were usually crowded beyond capacity. Her idea was to leave me in the line at the counter while she got in the line to pay at the register. And there I was, bugging her with my hang-ups: "What if it's my turn and you still haven't got the receipt?"

"Look, I'll make it in time! And if I don't, it's no big deal, just let one or two people behind you go ahead."

"But Mama, I can't, it's going to be so *awkward*," I would moan, and she would roll her eyes and mutter something about my extraordinary capacity for feeling awkward on all the wrong occasions. (That's what she still says, when I begin to feel awkward about ordering just a cup of coffee or about not buying an item I have asked a salesclerk to show me.)

My scruples kept getting in the way of developing shopping smarts. I even had problems with pretending that Mama and I were not together so that each of us could get the maximum of a half kilo of butter (in 1978 or '79, when butter shortages got bad) or four rolls of cotton allowed "into one pair of hands." To make it worse, Mama would suggest that we come back ten minutes later and get in line again for a second helping. No, I would moan, they might recognize us, and *it's going to be so awkward!* "Well, take off your cap and they won't recognize you," Mama would say, trying to be patient. "They can't remember every customer, and anyway they don't care, everybody does this."

The less fortunate ones who shopped alone would try to secure a spot in the line at the register and then madly dash over to the line at the counter, fervently hoping that other shoppers wouldn't notice the ruse. You could also try your luck by running to a nearby store for milk or kefir or sausages. But that was not without its risks: when you came back, the person you asked to hold your spot might brazenly look you in the eye and claim never to have seen you before ("You weren't standing here" is the eternal refrain of the Soviet shopping line). Done by the person behind you, this was understandable; to have one less competitor ahead of you is a matter of self-interest. Yet sometimes even the person ahead, with no discernible reason to wish to get rid of you, could do you in just the same.

Another ritual feature of shopping was someone trying to cut ahead of the line by asserting that she (or, on rare occasions, he) had a sick child/spouse/parent/sibling in the hospital and was buying something for this person. You might think that at least a quarter of the city was hospitalized, with another quarter buying treats for the sick. Sympathy was scarce among other shoppers, whose attitude was not unlike the cynicism of New Yorkers approached in a train station by a person who claims he has lost his wallet and needs money for a ticket home. How many times does one want to err on the side of charity? Before my own eyes, a girl in her twenties bought strawberries "for a sick little boy," and five minutes later I spotted her right outside the shop, nonchalantly popping the strawberries in her mouth and sharing them with a nattily dressed boy who didn't look sick and was definitely not little.

Only a few trolley stops away from us was a very different kind of shopping place: a farmers' market. It was a rather large area surrounded by a yellow stone wall. You walked through the gate to the long open-air stalls and the wooden structures like barracks occupied by indoor vendors. Behind the stalls were women and men, usually middle-aged, with drawn faces and gnarled hands; in winter they wore dark, heavy coats or quilted jackets, the men's heads covered with felt caps, the women's with knit shawls or kerchiefs. These were country people who worked their own plots of land and offered their produce at prices set at their own discretion. They sold potatoes, apples, cabbages, pickles, sauerkraut, carrots, homemade sour cream, meat — you name it. Summer brought luscious scarlet tomatoes, crimson cherries, strawberries bursting with ripeness, downy peaches, pears, plums . . . and more.

Besides the assortment and quality of food, there were no lines here; but very few could afford to shop at the market on a regular basis. It was where you went when you were expecting guests for dinner, or when you *really* were going to visit a sick family member. The prices were two to five times higher than those at the state stores. That is, the cherries you *couldn't* buy at a state store would have cost about one fourth what they cost at the market where you *could* buy them.

People grumbled, convinced that they were being ripped off. You might hear a young woman with bleached hair, wearing a stylish coat with a fur collar, arguing shrilly with a stooping old-timer holding up strings of dried mushrooms: "Six rubles a string! Why, Grandpa, you've got to be crazy! It's a rip-off! You didn't have to pay anything for them, did you?" "Grandpa" would strain his raspy voice trying to defend himself: "But don't you understand, citizen? I had to get up at four o'clock in the morning to pick these mushrooms, and it's an hour's walk from the train station to the woods!"

Here the balance of power between customers and sellers was tilted in favor of the customer much more than in the state stores. The seller, after all, was anxious to sell his product, and customers rarely failed to take full advantage of that. Many expected to get a little over the amount they were paying for. If the scales were even, they would snarl, "Hey! How about a little more? We're not in a store, you know!" The vendors often added a little extra on their own; ironically, the customer, seeing that the scales were tipped, sometimes automatically assumed that she or he was being cheated, and raised hell. Private market sellers even allowed customers — no, enticed them — to sample the product: a slice of apple or pickle, a few strands of sauerkraut, a couple of strawberries, a spoonful of sour cream. Mindful of unsanitary conditions, Mama would give me a warning tug on the sleeve every time a hospitable vendor began to coo, "Come on, just try a bit!" Other people, less squeamish than my mother, would go to the market for a free lunch, having a sample at this stall, a sample at that one, until they had a full stomach.

Unfortunately, my parents knew no one who worked in trade or in the food industry — a far less expensive way to get one's hands on endangered species of food. A school friend of mine once gave me as a birthday present a small box of delicious cream candy known as *pomadki*, which can be loosely translated as "creamlets." They had long since disappeared from the confectionery stores where you might have seen them once in a while, once upon a time — but my friend was blessed with a relative who worked for a candy factory.

My mother once spotted a snappily dressed lady striding briskly down the street with a salami sticking out of her bag, and asked her where she got it. The lady shot back, "Where I got it, they wouldn't give it to *you!*" This meant that she had either connections or privileges to shop at a special store.

Thanks to an enterprising colleague, Valery Geller, my father once got an unexpected chance to visit a store of that sort — as well as another chance to get into a scrape. It was a sunny day in spring, and my father and Valery both had a rather long break between recording sessions. They decided to go for a stroll, and ended up near the so-called Government House on Serafimovich Street — an apartment building inhabited by many midlevel members of the city and state government. As they were passing by, Papa spotted an exquisite little old church in the corner of a courtyard. "Let's go in there," Papa said to Valery. "I want to take a closer look." They went into the cobblestoned courtyard and stood for a few minutes looking at the little church, and then, just as they were about to leave, Papa noticed a small building from which people were emerging carrying tightly wrapped brown paper packages.

"Old man, you know what this is?" Valery said suddenly. "It's a special distribution center." A special distribution center is a store restricted for the use of special people — usually, but not necessarily, government or Party officials. "Ever seen one?" Valery asked. Father said no. "All right, then, come on."

My father, his curiosity stirring, followed Valery to the inconspicuous entrance. The elderly security guard was about to ask them for their identification, but Valery warded him off with a casual "I'm here to see Pavel Petrovich." He had no idea if a Pavel Petrovich really was on the staff. The security guard probably had no idea either, but names, if announced confidently and casually enough, tend to have an "open sesame" effect on low-ranking and perhaps even high-ranking service personnel in the Soviet Union. At least the guard at the special distribution center was susceptible, and my father and Valery found themselves in the middle of a beautiful clean shop with no lines, just a couple of well-dressed people at every counter. The shelves were a cornucopia of riches: out-of-season fruit that hadn't even appeared at the farmers' market yet, meat of all kinds, fish, caviar. And all of this, in a place catering to a clientele that was not exactly impoverished, was being sold at a fraction of the fixed state prices. (That, by the way, was a "second category" center.)

As my father took it all in, he thought of his little girl back home. He approached the fruit counter and asked the salesgirl for a kilo of cherries. "Your card, please," said the amiable young woman. "I'm sorry, but I don't have a card," Papa said stoically. The young woman's mouth fell open. "Whaaaa — ? Who are these guys? What's going on? Who let them in here?" she screeched, gasping for air. "Get them out of here this very minute!"

Papa and Valery quickly headed for the exit. As they ducked out, a woman emerged from the distribution center with her discreet brown paper packages in a net bag. My father lost whatever cool he had retained and yelled, "So it's for this that the workers and peasants died in 1917! It's for this that people fought in the trenches — so a fucking bitch like you can stuff her face at a store where the common people can't even go in!" The woman shuddered, pulled her head in like a startled turtle, and scurried away.

Geller got a tremendous kick out of the whole thing. He wasn't really risking his own hide, after all, and he enjoyed the vicarious thrill of watching someone else rail against the powers that be. He himself had a genius for talking his way out of almost any difficulty and into almost any place that seemed beyond the reach of mere mortals. Once he and Papa went on a business trip to the town of Ivanovo-Voznesensk, a center of the Soviet textile industry. At the train station ticket window, predictably, they were told that there were no tickets. Geller went to see the station manager and told him in a tone of great urgency that they were going as interpreters for a delegation of American congressmen or senators who were touring the textile factories of Ivanovo-Voznesensk. It was absolutely imperative, he said, for them to get tickets. The Americans had left by bus, but they, the interpreters, had to get there first so as to make hotel arrangements and so forth. Minutes later he was out of the station manager's office, tickets in hand.

Geller loved to brag about his exploits. On one occasion, a conductor on a bus approached him and asked for a ticket; he had none. Geller pulled out his Broadcasting House ID, which happened to be bound in red leather, just like the identification cards of government officials, KGB agents, and the like, and quietly said, "You will apologize immediately." The conductor apologized.

Valery Geller's mastery of this sort of game may have been rarely matched, but he was far from the only one to try his hand at it. Here is my father's favorite story on the subject. He and some friends went to a restaurant. The waiter's response to anything they tried to order from the menu was "We're out of that." One of Papa's buddies mysteriously beckoned the waiter to come close and then said in a low and ominous tone, "If we don't get some decent service at this place, I am going to have a very serious talk with Ivan Nikolayevich." The waiter blanched and at once became a model of courtesy. The party got the best meals they had ever had in a restaurant. They even got — wonder of wonders — cold beer. Of course, everyone was dying to know who Ivan Nikolayevich was. The man to whom they owed their pleasant experience grinned and said with a shrug, "Who the heck knows? I made him up."

I cannot say that the food shortages caused me much personal anguish. We always had a decent meal in the house, due more than anything else to Grandma's cooking skills and creativity.

Matters were complicated for a while when my parents were caught up in an imported fad that swept the educated circles in Moscow: health food diets and fasting. This fad generated a flood of new *samizdat*, the self-published underground literature that consisted of stacks of typewritten pages and often barely legible carbon copies. There was a volume by an American nutritionist, Dr. Bragg, that promised its readers lasting youth and happiness through fasting and eating the right diet, and a book on nutrition by another American, Dr. Herbert Shelton, and books on yoga and holistic medicine. Every day brought a new story of how so-and-so had had all but one foot in the grave and had brought himself back to life and vigor by following these precepts. It seemed certain that in enlightened America, whence the sacred scrolls had come, everyone but the dumbest of clods was now on a salt-free and sugar-free or macrobiotic diet, and that Dr. Bragg and Dr. Shelton were the biggest celebrities since Elvis Presley. Alas, the American authors of the nutrition *samizdat* had not been considerate enough to give any thought to the circumstances of their Soviet disciples: they kept writing about things like avocado and a dozen varieties of lettuce.

I was annoyed by my parents' conversion, not only because of gluttony but also because of my conservative attachment to habits that would have to be drastically disrupted if they really got serious about this stuff. Grandma was a skeptic too. As far back as she could remember, she explained with a shrug, there had been fad diets and experts saying that you shouldn't eat this or you shouldn't eat that, and then somebody else would come along and tell you the exact opposite. Her obstinacy exasperated my parents. Eventually, though, their zeal more or less fizzled out (Papa even began to make fun of people living on "dried grasshoppers"), though they were still health-conscious enough to not skimp on fruit and vegetables any more than they absolutely had to.

Thus I did not feel deprived. Despite my gourmet inclinations, it took no more than a bag of *soushki* — small, crunchy poppy-seed bagels — to munch on to keep me content. I was all the happier, too, on those occasions when something out of the ordinary was on the table: fruit juice, bananas, salami, strawberries . . .

What an adventure shopping was! As you started out, you never knew what was around the corner. You might have to make the rounds of five or six stores before you found the bare essentials, or you might come across something thrilling and unexpected. I went to the bakery one day to buy bread, only to find the confectionery section bustling with people. Goodness gracious — Stratosphere chocolates with a delicious soufflé filling! And me with just enough money for bread! Luckily, home was only a five-minute walk away, this time a three-minute sprint (what if they ran out of chocolates by the time I got the money from Grandma and sprinted back?). It turned out that to get the chocolates, you also had to buy a packet of some lousy lollipops; it was a fairly common practice to put such riders on hard-to-find goods. But that couldn't spoil the day.

Sometimes the adventure was not over even when you were home with your catch. The bananas you bought at a vending stall in the street after a couple of hours in line were usually green, and when you brought them home and put them on a shelf, there was still an element of suspense: would they eventually ripen, or would they rot without ever becoming edible?

My recollections of my teenage years in the Soviet Union are peppered with memories such as these: "Mama, remember when we had this huge chunk of ham in a metal box?" The ham Mama occasionally managed to get in a store had so much fat and reeked so badly that I couldn't eat it. But once Mama's cousin Vega got an opportunity at the music college where she worked to order a large metal box of ham imported from Yugoslavia. My mother now assures me that it wasn't too different from the cheapest kind of boiled ham sold at New Jersey supermarkets. All I know is that to me, it seemed fit for a king.

And there are other memories: a small brown bag of tomatoes brought to us in midspring by a generous guest; peaches, over-ripe and a bit squishy, at a fruit store in Zelenograd; tender seedless grapes at the fruit department of a town supermarket; baskets of only slightly squashed strawberries at a vendor's table in Kryukovo. Fairly often we came across watermelons, and even golden melons once in a while, in Zelenograd in the summer. Outside a fruit and vegetable store would be wooden crates, an oilcloth-covered table with a scale and weights, a saleswoman in a soiled white gown, and, naturally, a line. Sometimes the class enemy would amble off on her lunch break, and the people in the line could do nothing but wait. Here again, the advantage of shopping in a twosome was obvious: Mama would leave me in line for anywhere from half an hour to two and a half hours and go off to run other errands. Then the watermelons had to be lugged home, a forty-five-minute walk through the woods. Did all these things taste better for being so hard won?

A Soviet Jew is asked why he wants to emigrate. "Because there are too many things that make me happy," he says. The questioner is natu-

rally puzzled. "You see," the would-be émigré explains, "I snag a nice shirt and I'm happy. I snag a kilo of sausage and I'm happy. I snag some oranges and I'm happy. I'm getting fed up with being so happy all the time!"

I did not realize how lucky we were until I began to hear about the way so many other people lived. After all, my parents and I and our friends and acquaintances were all living in Moscow, in the metropolis, and not in, say, Gorky or Yaroslavl or Kaluga. The smaller the town, the more dismal the conditions.

About a year before we left the Soviet Union, my family made a trip to the town of Yaroslavl, a treasury of old Russian architecture with exquisite Byzantine churches. My parents had decided that we simply had to see them before we left the country for good. Other sights were no less impressive, in their own way. A peek into the first-floor window of a house revealed a room not unlike the pictures I have seen of turn-of-the-century tenements in the immigrant ghettoes of New York. Store shelves were nearly bare. Mama struck up a conversation with a local woman who bitterly remarked, "Meat? We don't even remember what it looks like." (We overheard someone saying, "All those tourists come here, that's why we got nothing to eat.")

Rumors proliferated about food rationing in this or that town, about people getting up at five o'clock in the morning to line up at the padlocked doors of a grocery store that opened at eight, only to find out that no provisions were to be brought to the store that day. When we were going through the emigration process and my father went to the Dutch embassy in Moscow (which represents Israeli interests in the USSR in the absence of diplomatic relations between those two countries), he shared the waiting room with a crowd of Jews from provincial towns. Of course the talk revolved mostly around emigration, and Papa heard the same question over and over: "Tell me, why do *you* want to leave? You people in Moscow, you've got it made! You have *everything* in the stores! Now we in Chernovtsy . . ."

Black humor on the subject mushroomed along with the rumors. *An old man is wandering the streets of Odessa, yelling at the top of his lungs: "How come there's no meat? How come there's no fish? How come there's no cream?" "You'd better shut up or you'll be arrested and shot," the passersby tell him. The old man, however, keeps shouting. Finally a policeman picks him up, takes him to the station, and asks the sergeant, "Well, what are we gonna do with this old codger?" The harried sergeant waves him away, saying, "Aw, who gives a damn — let him go!" Once out of the police station, the old man takes to the streets again and shouts, "How come there's no meat? How come there's no fish? How come there's no cream? And I'll tell you something else — they're even out of bullets!"*

Another one was *What's long and green and smells of sausage? A local train going out of Moscow.* Local trains were indeed painted green, and "smelled of sausage" because they carried out-of-towners who flocked to Moscow for meat products and other food they couldn't buy at home. Around 1977, most food stores started closing on Sundays; it was tacitly assumed that this policy was meant primarily to reduce the flow of out-of-town buyers, most of whom were employed full-time and could only come to the city on weekends.

There was no love lost between the Muscovites, who believed they were being robbed by the out-of-towners, and the out-of-towners, who believed that the reason they had nothing at home was that all the goodies were going to the Muscovites. Once when my mother was in a grocery store, a withered little old woman, obviously from the country, was buying a few kilos of *soushki*, those crunchy poppy-seed bagels, and a few cans of *sgush-chonka*, condensed milk with sugar, a nutritious meal that is very popular in Russia. Neither were in short supply, yet people in the line began to pelt her with rebukes. "Oh, you see," the old woman began to explain in a soft, shaky voice, "I'm taking this to my grandchildren in the village! The kids are going hungry — you don't even know how much joy it's going to be for them when I bring some *soushki* and *sgushchonka!*"

Much as my mother loathed getting involved in shopping brawls, she tried to come to the old woman's aid: "You ought to be ashamed of yourselves! Instead of helping a grandmother carry her bags, you're all jumping on her!" But this reproach did not make the other customers shed tears of shame and penitence; they did not warmly embrace the old lady and fight one another for the privilege of carrying her bags. "Well, why don't *you* carry her bags if you're so generous!" someone snarled. Another chipped in, "She must be from out of town herself! Sticking up for one another, eh?"

Even pets were the innocent targets of resentment over the shortages. You couldn't walk a dog, especially a large one, without having to put up with comments along the lines of "Look at 'em — they've got these dogs eating up all the meat when there's not enough for people!"

In the winter of 1977, Moscow suddenly was abuzz with rumors of a price hike on bread, meat, and dairy products. Prices, we heard, would double as of March 1. The stores were even more jammed than usual as people rushed to buy up everything that could be hoarded. As usual, Mama put off everything until the last moment, and on February 28 we were pushing through the crowd in our local bakery to buy breadsticks and *soushki*. The saleswoman was grumbling that people had gone crazy.

Then came March 1. A spokesman for the city government made a statement on television: the recent rumors of a price increase were totally false, nothing but the work of panic-mongers and subversives. Everyone breathed a sigh of relief.

The rumors proved hard to kill, however. People said that a price increase actually had been scheduled — supposedly, food store employees had even seen the new price tags — and then the whole thing had been called off at the last moment. Explanations differed as to why. Some people said that the City Party Committee and the City Executive Committee had been flooded with letters threatening riots and terrorist acts in the event of a price hike. Others swore that Brezhnev had personally vetoed the measure and said that this was not going to happen during his tenure.

A while later there were some price hikes after all; taxicab fares doubled, and the price of coffee went up from about 4.50 to 20 rubles a kilo. Coffee jokes were not far behind: *A Russian boy gets a letter from a pen pal in Africa saying, "Dear friend: I live in Africa. I'm black. My parents are black too. We drink a lot of black coffee and don't wear many clothes." The Russian boy writes back: "Dear friend: I live in Russia. I'm white. My parents are white too. And if we drank a lot of black coffee, we wouldn't be wearing a lot of clothes either."*

Once when my mother and I were in a store, the radio blared: *"A new victory for the Party and the people! A historic reduction of prices on consumer goods!"*

"Just listen to that," Mama said, shaking her head. "And they've been talking about a price hike for weeks. God, the way people will wag their tongues when they don't know what they're talking about."

Meanwhile, the jubilant radio announcer went on to list all the items on which prices were being reduced: Soviet-made shoes with rubber soles, regular silk stockings (not the pantyhose women now hungered for), Soviet-made cotton dresses, and other things that cluttered the shelves of department stores and that no one wanted to buy. At the very end of this list, the announcer casually added that prices on a few items were being raised. Everyone pricked up their ears. Furs, crystal glassware, imported footwear and clothing . . .

It was not in the lines for food and household necessities, but in the lines for what one might call luxury items — clothes, leather goods, furniture, cosmetics — that shopping frenzy ran at its highest. Remember the Cabbage Patch Kids craze? A few years ago Coleco vastly underestimated the success of its own advertising and produced a relatively modest number of the cute-faced dolls for the Christmas season. There were mob scenes in department stores — scuffles, hysterical fits, customers snatching dolls from one another. Those who recall the frenzy should not have a hard time imagining what goes on in Soviet stores day after day.

It's not that you can't get a handbag or a sweater without putting yourself through this inferno. Some Soviet-made goods are widely available, though the quality is usually abysmal and the choice of styles and colors is extremely limited. If you need something specific — say, a white shirt, or black socks — the search might take months. If you comb the stores very persistently, you will come across some Soviet clothes of about the same quality that you find here in five-and-dime stores. Yet sometimes it is not even quality but simply *imported* things — a status symbol — that people are after. If the drabbest shoes and dresses from Woolworth's were shipped to a Soviet store with their American labels, hundreds would line up to buy them. In contrast, if decent Soviet-made coats appear in a department store, they will sell out in no time — but people do not grab them with the same kind of maniacal passion they have for foreign goods.

I accompanied Mama to clothing and cosmetics stores rarely and with little enthusiasm (and she went to such stores almost as rarely and with almost as little enthusiasm). I could spend some time lovingly gazing at a peignoir with ruffles and lace frills, conjuring up visions of languid countesses in boudoirs. But such items were expensive (about thirty rubles, a quarter of Mama's monthly salary), and my mother had no intention of spending that kind of money. Mostly I got bored, and silently marveled at the girls in my class who habitually loitered around department stores as spectators.

Once or twice Mama took me along to the world-famous GUM. My memories of this up-scale shopping center, the Bloomingdale's of Moscow, are not pleasant. In the handbag department on the second floor, there was pandemonium over imported leather handbags of one design but in two colors, blue and brown. There was a limit of one of each color to a customer, and the line was quadruple or even quintuple file, stretching over the entire floor — hundreds of people, most of them female, most of them overwrought. As we tried to elbow our way through to the exit, one woman went over the edge; the floor manager was trying to reason with her, and the result was something like a small riot. In a shrill, hysterical voice, the woman was demanding that only one handbag be issued to a customer.

"They'll sell out!" she screamed, her face crimson and blotchy. "I've been waiting for hours and I'll end up walking away empty-handed! You can't do this!"

"Look, citizen," the manager was saying in a startlingly gentle, almost apologetic tone, "that's the policy we have — one article into one pair of hands. The colors are different, so it's really two different articles, and we have to allow two per person. There's nothing we can do."

"Then change your policy! It's not fair!"

"I can't change it," the floor manager replied, politely but firmly.

"Well, you're going to regret this!" the woman ranted. "You don't know just *who* I am! But you'll find out! You don't know *what* kind of people I know! They're going to investigate you all, you'll see! I'm going to get you all fired!"

That most likely was a bluff. Usually people who wield enough clout to get a GUM floor manager fired do not have to get their imported handbags the hard way. Nevertheless, the manager was obviously nervous, which was almost certainly the reason she was being so conciliatory. After all, a good number of these handbags had no doubt been stashed away for the sales-girls, the managers, their relatives, and perhaps their friends — and maybe for sale "on the left" as well. So the mere mention of an investigation could make the manager squirm.

I do not know how the conflict was resolved or whether the woman got her handbag, because Mama and I were finally able to jostle our way out of this sea of humanity and flee. A while later I began to talk about this horrible scene with some of my parents' friends who were over for dinner, but they shook their heads and chortled indulgently: I must have been born yester-day, to get so excited over an ordinary shopping squabble!

Happily, I wasn't around when my mother witnessed some-thing far more traumatic in the Passage (pronounced "pass-AZH," in the French style), another posh department store in the center of Moscow.

The Passage is structured like an American shopping mall, with a long aisle with small stores on both sides, except that in this case they aren't really stores but departments — shoes, umbrellas, stationery, fabrics, and so on (there are actually two aisles and three rows of departments). The aisle was jammed when Mama went in — there was clearly a line for something. She had to go to a department at the far end and began to make her way through. From snippets of conversation around her, she realized that the store was selling (or "giving," as the Soviet expression goes) some sweaters or blouses or something. Whatever it was, the entrance to that department was barricaded with a steel barrier and guarded by two uniformed cops. The shoppers in the line were being let inside ten or fifteen at a time.

As Mama made her way through, she started getting jittery. There were so many people crowding and shoving her on all sides. They were not just standing in line; there was a constant flurry of frenetic activity, with everyone on the alert against any attempts to cut in. And since the line was not single file but a human wall four to six people wide (and God knows how many people long), arguments flared up every now and then as to who was behind whom. It was a whirlpool of nervous tension.

When Mama was already on the sidelines, the barrier was moved aside to let ten more people in. Those behind the lucky ten must have charged forward, for the guards were almost swept off their feet. In the commotion there were wild, bloodcurdling female screams.

When Mama came home, exhausted and frazzled, she was wondering whether someone had been trampled to death for a mohair sweater. She had heard of such things happening. One summer while we were staying in Latvia, a new department store opened in a nearby town. The opening-day sale turned into a riot that left at least one person dead, many people injured, and plate-glass windows smashed. (Sale, in this case, means not that goods were being sold at reduced prices — there is no such practice in Soviet retail trade — but simply that the goods were *there*.)

As for myself, it was only from hearsay that I knew about the crazy things people did when seized by shopping frenzy. My parents once saw hundreds of people lined up in GUM to buy some Western pop music records. A saleswoman was walking along the line announcing, "There are no more records, comrades. All the records are sold out. Get moving, please. There are no more records." Yet not one person in the line moved; they just kept standing there as if hoping — for what? That the records would miraculously appear?

People would get in line before they knew what was being "given" — as reflected, of course, in a joke: *A woman standing next in line to a man asks him if he knows what they are standing in line for. "For Shakespeare," he replies. "Oh," she says. "Is that better than taffeta?" "I don't know," he answers. "I haven't tried drinking it yet."* And a real-life parallel: my father approached a long line that had just formed at the doors of a bookstore, and inquired of a matronly woman what writer's books were for sale. "Some fella named Harpoe" was her reply. As it turned out, what she had heard and was trying to repeat was "Edgar Poe." What was she doing standing in line to buy a book by Edgar Allan Poe? That was the kind of question you didn't bother to ask in Moscow.

Lines for some coveted items — furniture, a suede coat, or a ticket to a hit show — would turn into waiting lists. People lined up when the object of desire was not yet available but was to materialize in a day, in three days, in a week. Sometimes they huddled overnight outside locked stores in the bitter cold, making small fires to keep themselves warm. The line, swelling to hundreds, would become a complex social entity with its own leaders. Here there was no choice but to band together and cooperate; no one could stand in a line continuously for three or four days in a row.

Invariably, activists would emerge and start organizing. To begin with, everyone in the line was assigned a number, which was written down on the person's palm with a ballpoint pen. (Often people would try to cheat by altering the number to move closer to the head of the line — say, from 92 to 32.) People were delegated to take turns standing guard at the doors of the store round the clock, to prevent someone else, some upstart with a lot of nerve, from organizing another line. If the waiting took days, everyone had to come in for a roll call at the store's closing time, and if someone didn't show up, the activists would strike him from the list with gladness in their hearts. Cooperation was fine, but only as long as it wasn't to someone's advantage to stab someone else in the back.

It was only natural for people to get a little worked up under such circumstances. Take the sister of my mother's music professor, who got on a list for a German cupboard. She waited and waited and waited, and showed up at the store again and again. First, when a batch of cupboards finally arrived, she was too far down the list to get one. Then the salespeople told her several times that cupboards would be in, but these proved to be false alarms. Finally, one day she came to the store and was told that a cupboard was hers. The lady, who was in her fifties, collapsed on the floor with a heart attack. Lovers of macabre endings will be disappointed to learn that she made a full recovery and became the proud owner of that German cupboard.

Not long after the redecoration in our apartment was essentially completed, Mama's cousin Vega called us with exciting news: she had just found out that this one furniture store, all the way across the city, was going to have bookshelves — home-assembly walnut bookshelves with sliding glass panels, imported from Czechoslovakia, just what we were looking for, as was she. Father already had his wall-to-wall bookcase/home entertainment center, but that was not enough for even half of my parents' ever-growing library. The bookcases we did have were old and shabby, an eyesore in our newly furnished apartment; and even with them, we were running out of space for books.

Aunt Vega managed to sign us up on the list to get the bookshelves. According to the rules, she and my mother had to show up for roll call every day: Aunt Vega couldn't answer for Mama, or vice versa. Some people tried to hold spots for friends, but exposure meant immediate cries of cheating ("Oh, you think you're smarter than everybody else!"). I suppose the underlying attitude was the "equal sharing of miseries" that Winston Churchill defined as the cornerstone of socialism. Anyway, the waiting went on for several days, then one night Vega called to say that there had been word the shelves would arrive from the warehouse the next morning.

By a lucky coincidence, I was on vacation from school and could go with Mama — not so much to help carry the shelves as to help her get more of them, because of the usual limit on how much could be given into one pair of hands. We arrived — Mama, Aunt Vega, her husband, Zinovy, and I — about an hour before opening time, which for nonfood stores in Moscow was eleven o'clock. And then, as the store was about to open, a rumor ran through the crowd. The shelves were not going to arrive — they had just been taken from the warehouse to *another* furniture store.

Being by nature something of a quitter, I was quick to suggest that we all go home, almost glad to have avoided a hassle. My relief was premature. No one had any intention of going home. Some enterprising person managed to find out which store the shelves had been taken to, although the salesclerks were by no means eager to release this information. The other store was not too far away, and everyone in the line rushed frantically to hail cabs or to get a ride in private cars. We managed to get a cab, squeezed in, and were at the other store in no time.

When the throng of consumers swooped down on the second store, the first question that arose was, Should the order of the original line be preserved or should those who got to *this* store first have priority? In addition, a comrade who hadn't even *been* in the original line showed up, claiming that he should have preference as a handicapped person. He was a husky fellow, though, his energy dampened by no apparent handicaps. He yelled that he had an ID certifying that he was indeed on disability, but he would not deign to produce it for the sake of such an ill-mannered rabble.

Preoccupied with the fighting in its ranks, the star-crossed shopping line almost let itself get bushwacked by the class enemy. The bookshelves were at the store, the cartons stacked on the floor, but the salesgirl coolly announced that no shelves were for sale.

"And what about these?"

"Oh, these? They've been sold."

"Sold? To whom?"

"To people. They already paid for them. They just went off to get some transportation and they're going to come back and pick them up."

"Show us the sales slips!" roared a chorus of angry voices.

Hearing this racket, the store manager showed up. She too said that the shelves had been sold, or at least were being held for earlier customers.

And when were these elusive early-bird customers going to come back for the shelves?

"Oh . . . they said in about a half-hour or so."

The manager was obviously wavering under the onslaught of so many stubborn people. She even muttered something about other bookshelves still being available in the back room. The handicapped line-crasher suddenly turned into a most aggressive activist for consumer rights. Though he had suffered much less than anyone else, he yelled louder, calling the manager and the salesclerks no-good thieves.

"All right," said Aunt Vega, "let's stay here and wait for those customers to come back." By the rules in place in all Soviet stores, no merchandise can be held for a customer for more than an hour unless the customer gets special permission to have it held for three. I don't remember how long we waited, but finally there could be no more doubt that no earlier customers would show up, because none existed. The whole thing was clear as day: the store personnel had simply decided to keep the shelves and sell them "on the left" at twice the state-fixed price. The bookshelves were ours.

There is a widespread opinion in the West among social commentators, political scientists, and just plain folks that the Soviet state, whatever else one can say about it, provides for the basic material needs of its citizens, while in America people have to fend for themselves and struggle to get things. This wisdom is such a commonplace that it has even rubbed off on some Soviet émigrés, who ought to know better. I recall a middle-aged woman describing to me how her family had moved from a communal apartment they shared with anti-Semitic louts to a modestly comfortable co-op apartment for which they had to pay loads of money. The housing exchange involved such complex, multitiered machinations — including a divorce and a remarriage — that I still didn't get it even after she had explained the entire process in detail two or three times, even drawing diagrams. If the energy and ingenuity that went into these schemes were applied on Wall Street, they might well create a multimillion-dollar profit.

And yet the conventional wisdom persists, voiced with praise by those who have a soft spot for socialism ("Soviet people don't have to face daily uncertainty or look out for number one or scramble for the good things in life") and with scorn by free-market advocates ("Soviet citizens are infantilized by a baby-sitter state that takes away their capacity for individual initiative and enterprise"). I have our bookshelves to remind me why I am inclined to think something is wrong with both these assessments.

8

Mothers and Warriors

WHEN I WAS EIGHT or nine years old, I decided that I wanted to be a boy. For about a month I insisted on wearing pants, which I normally disliked, and on being called Anton instead of Katya. I was of a mind to inscribe one of my school notebooks "Anton Jung," but my mother drew the line at that. Was this a rebellion against the established female role, or just another one of my make-believe games (which included such disparate identities as an eighteenth-century countess and a child in a Stone Age tribe)? I don't remember exactly what went on in my head, so I can afford to hope that I did not really believe I was going to turn into a boy. Eventually I settled for becoming a feminist.

I was about fifteen when I first came across the word "feminism," in a prerevolutionary edition of a history of ancient Rome by an Italian named Ferrare or Ferrari. He viewed the decline of the Roman Empire as the result largely of the fact that Roman men gave up "the most reliable instrument of masculine dominance, the stick" (I was so struck by the phrase I remembered it verbatim). He deplored the weakening of male authority and the rise of feminism, which he defined as the abandonment by women of the traditional submissive roles so dear to his heart, and the adoption of male ways, habits, and occupations. *Hmm*, I said to myself, *that suits me*.

I dimly recall that one of the reasons I wanted to be a boy was that our grade school teacher, Lyudmila Alexandrovna, said girls weren't supposed to fight. Not that I was very eager to fight — it just wasn't fair, as a matter of principle. My other gripe was a far more serious one: it wasn't fair that at least nine tenths of the books in my parents' library, as I discovered upon scrutiny of the authors' names, had been written by men.

The assaults on my budding feminist sensibilities grew worse as time went on. At school, no opportunity was missed to remind us that boys were boys and girls were girls. The so-called labor classes seemed designed especially for that purpose. The boys had two hours a week of shop (wood- and metalwork) taught by Yevgeny Nikolayevich, a tall, wiry, fortyish fellow with a crew-cut who doubled as gym teacher and whose thin red face and purplish nose indicated that he possessed at least one essential characteristic to be a role model of Soviet manhood. Girls spent the same periods studying something that approximated home economics: cooking, sewing, cleaning, and so forth. Years later in America, where many schools no longer segregate such classes by sex, I picked up either *Pravda* or *Izvestia* at the college library and saw a front-page picture of two smiling little girls and their smiling teacher (the obligatory feel-good photo that dominates the front page of virtually every edition of the leading Soviet newspapers), with a caption explaining that the girls were learning not only a useful trade but also housekeeping skills, "and after all, that's so important for girls!" I could just imagine the flood of irate mail such a caption would have elicited in, say, the *New York Times*.

I wonder what would have happened if a girl in my class had all of a sudden declared that she wanted to take shop with the boys instead of home ec with her own sex, or if a boy had expressed a desire to learn baking and sewing alongside us. At the time I did not think about such what-if's. Katya Vorontzova did complain once, as we were sitting at our sewing machines in the labor class: why couldn't the guys learn some practical skills that could be of use around the house later, like fixing the sink or something, she asked, instead of wasting their time making use-less wooden or metal objects? Not a very feminist proposal, but perhaps a small step for womankind. The height of injustice was

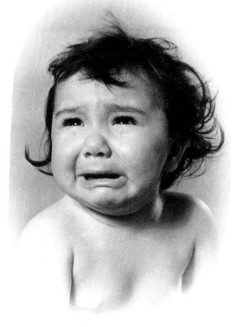

When I was fourteen months old, Mama took me to a photography studio. After taking a few pictures of me with toys and picture books, the photographer suddenly removed my dress and slapped me on the face — not very hard, but hard enough to produce the effect she wanted for the picture to the left. "For diversity," she casually explained to Mama.

A happy father . . .

. . . and a proud mother.

Grandma: as the plucky young woman who confronted Siberian
wilderness . . . and as the grandmother I knew.

The dacha where we spent our summers.

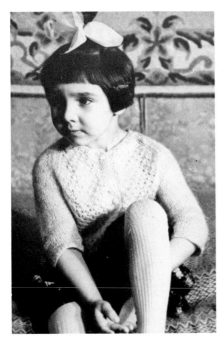

My parents had no camera, so most of my pictures were taken by Grandma's brother, Victor, and sister, Anna, who were amateur photographers — either when we visited them in Leningrad or when they came to our dacha in the summer. This one was taken in their Leningrad apartment.

My snowflake costume for the New Year's party at school in first grade.

This photograph was taken moments after we became Pioneers at the Kalinin Museum, when Lyuda-the-Pioneer-master tied the red ties around our necks. I am second from left; to my right is Rita Kuznetzova. Sixth from the left is my future friend Alla Makarova, the diplomat's daughter.

I was in fourth grade when another photographer came to our school and took individual portraits. The Pioneer badge, with Lenin's profile in the center of a red star surrounded by an orange flame, is visible on my black pinafore.

This picture of my class — then group 4B — was taken on a day when I was not in school, in the classroom of mathematics teacher Nina Ivanovna. On the back wall is a display of illustrated math problems under the heading THINK AND SOLVE, and on the bulletin board to the right is "The Class Corner of Komsomol Group 10B," of which Nina Ivanovna was the class guide. In the bottom righthand corner is Mark Kozlovsky, object of my puppy love somewhat later. Behind him is Rita. In the center row, supersensitive little Ella Shimanskaya is in the second seat from the front. In the same row, my short-term friend Nina Yanovskaya (the one with the interesting career ambitions) is in the next to the last desk; behind her, slumped over his desk, is the unruly Borya Fedoseyev.

On the last day of class in ninth grade, our class, group 9B, posed on the front steps of the school building. Rita and I are in the first row. Ella Shimanskaya has turned around to hand a bouquet to Katya Vorontzova; between them is Natasha Gamaley, the acid-tongued girl who always invited herself to my birthday parties. In the second row, second from right is Alla Makarova, with Olya Sukhova to her left. In the third row, on the far left, is the ultra-hip Alyosha Vasilyev. And in the very back, toward the center, Pasha Litvinov with a joyful grin on his face, sticking up two fingers like horns on Natasha Timina's head . . .

When we were getting ready to apply for permission to emigrate, we thought that I would apply as a minor; in that case,
I had to be on a joint application with my mother. However,
by the time we applied, I had turned sixteen and had to get an
individual picture taken . . . and this is how I appeared on my
exit visa.

New York, 1988 (Photo by Ellen
Jaffe).

that on the days we cooked (with our own ingredients, brought from home), we were often told to invite the boys to share with us the chops and fried potatoes or the tea and cookies. We had to clean up the dishes after them, too. What had they ever done for us, those beastly boys who would ambush us in the schoolyard after classes to pelt us with snowballs or stuff snow under our collars?

Beginning in the eighth grade, labor classes were replaced by one day a week of UPK, the Russian acronym for "educational-industrial complex" — something akin to vocational training, and still a feminist's nightmare. Boys could choose from courses in welding, auto mechanics, and cabinetmaking. Girls were offered training as hairdressers, typists, or garment factory workers. These courses (then a very recent innovation in the Soviet educational system) were taught not in our school building but at a vocational school a fifteen-minute bus ride away, and were also attended by students from other schools in the district.

The welcoming speech we got from the vocational school principal on our first day of UPK left me quite perturbed. He spoke, with rather stunning frankness, about the Soviet Union's economic woes (he even mentioned the fact that we were buying wheat from Canada) and ascribed them all to the sappy liberal practice of allowing young people to choose their own professions regardless of the country's needs. Soon, he predicted with glee, this policy would be discarded; the state would tell you what to do, and you would do exactly that. (No more easy street for you, you spoiled brats.) The picture he painted was so vivid that I returned home dejected, taking his prediction more seriously than it warranted. All in all, though, UPK did fairly well by me. The course I chose was typing. My friend Rita opted for garment-making, which meant training at an actual factory, where, she told me, the air was thick with profanity.

I tried to sort out the dilemmas of the Woman Question and ended up getting more and more confused. On the one hand, our textbooks were constantly hammering into us the idea that the revolutionary Soviet state had been the first and perhaps really the only society to lift women up to full equality with men. This assertion was backed by statistics on how many of the deputies in the Supreme Soviet were female and, invariably, on the numbers of women doctors in the Soviet Union — 70 percent of all doctors. (This fact impresses many feminists in the West, until they learn — if they ever do — that the medical profession is one of the lowest paid in the Soviet Union, and that those posts that do pay well in money and prestige are held mostly by men.) In our history textbooks, the paragraphs on the status of women in czarist Russia were positively bursting with outrage at the constraints on higher education and professional achievement for women, the dependent legal status of married women, the low wages of female factory workers. The Napoleonic code was exposed and castigated as a bastion of the values of the "bourgeois family" ("A husband's duty is to protect his wife. A wife's duty is to obey her husband and follow him wherever he goes"). There were many bombastic words about the trampled human dignity of woman, a state from which she was rescued by the Great October Socialist Revolution.

On the other hand, an article in the *Literaturnaya Gazeta* on the importance of teaching the right values to teenagers said that although the October Revolution had liberated women and opened all avenues of life to them, we mustn't forget that this blessing of equality should by no means overshadow the primacy of woman's role as Wife and Mother (yes, capitalized in the original). To be fair, the article also urged men to get more involved in child care, but the author's argument for male involvement made me cringe: we live, he said, in an age when early exposure to science and technology is of great importance, and who would dispute the fact that men are the technological sex?

Even in the little I read of Soviet newspapers and magazines, it wasn't hard to notice that articles, essays, humorous sketches, and reviews of books, plays, and films teemed with casual references to "the weaker sex," "feminine meekness," "womanly self-abnegation," "feminine coyness." These attributes of womanhood — along with "masculine pride" and "male bravery" — clearly were taken for granted by the writers. The occasional jabs at men who refused to lend a helping hand with housework could not begin to compete in numbers with articles by female journalists that berated women for not being graceful and pliant enough to smooth over family differences, for wanting to be too strong and independent, for making their men feel inadequate. Women, they pronounced, should be weak and tender. I could just imagine them melting in the beauty of their own sentiment.

The tidings from the Soviet Union of *glasnost* and open discussion are still contradictory. Gorbachev's pronouncements on women's issues are a bizarre combination of hackneyed rhetoric about the marvelous equality that women have won in all walks of life as a result of the Revolution, and phrases that Phyllis Schlafly couldn't quarrel with, about the need to recapture the time-honored role of woman as keeper of the home and "the person who brings up the children." In the press, one finds both assertions that women long to go back to weak, tender femininity and criticism of the inadequate representation of women in the top ranks of political leadership, management, and the professions. In a recent article, sociologist Larisa Kuznetzova complains that womanly family virtues have been used to hold women back in their careers, but at the same time she seems hardly to question the traditional insistence that family virtues are *womanly* ones. (The same author, however, was the first to raise the issue of the need for a women's movement in the Soviet Union.)

Back in my day, with the glorification of sexual equality and front-page pictures of beaming women welders or engineers on the one hand and the paeans to the sweetness of femininity and the holiness of motherhood on the other, the official message to Soviet womanhood was simply quite confusing. I suppose the only thing that has saved millions of Soviet women from going crazy trying to sort it all out is the long-developed salutary habit of paying no attention to any official messages whatsoever. Perhaps it boiled down to something like this: you can have education, you can have jobs, you can sit on the Supreme Soviet, as long as you remember to stay in your place — a pace or two behind the men.

Nor could I, in my teenage years, expect much relief from the enlightened, more or less secretly liberal intelligentsia. Who would care to espouse a cause like the equality of women, a bromide of the daily press? If anything, dissenting or semidissenting intellectuals were, I found out, likely to believe that Soviet women suffered from too much equality (after all, wasn't equality what they had now?). I tried to share my feminist worries with my parents; they weren't too responsive. When I carried on about Nora in *A Doll's House* or Chekhov's heroines in such stories as "The Bride" (in which a young woman from a good family breaks off an advantageous engagement, choosing to become a teacher and live on her own), Mama would shrug and reply that battles over things like jobs and education for women had long been won, and these issues no longer had any relevance in our day and age. It was of much more immediate concern to women, she said, to be a little less burdened by responsibilities outside the home.

I got into furious debates with my father (I was the furious one) when we went for walks together, around the blocks of our Sokolniki neighborhood in the city or along the country road strewn with chips of hard coal in Kryukovo. Papa, who did not consider it beneath his masculine dignity to do the dishes and had spoonfed me scrambled eggs when I was a toddler, emerged as a great believer in feminine gentleness and the high calling of mothers. For once in his life, he even quoted Karl Marx *with approval:* "You know, Marx's daughter once gave everyone in the household a questionnaire on various subjects, including 'What is woman's greatest strength?' And you know what Karl Marx answered to that? 'Her weakness.' " Well, Marx wasn't much of an authority for me; Papa himself had taken care of that. He and Mama also cited the words of Serov, a notable turn-of-the-century Russian artist, about his charming little niece, who served as the model for his painting *A Girl with Peaches*, very famous in Russia. Though only eight years old, he marveled, she was already all woman: gentle, affectionate, and eager to please (or something along these lines). I listened sourly, showing little gentleness and even less eagerness to please.

Things got no better when I decided, around the age of thirteen, to change my future vocation from poet to novelist. My father, always so supportive, devoting so much of his time and his attention to my intellectual development, responded with the prevailing view among the educated reading public in Russia: generally, women did not make great novelists. They simply didn't possess the intellectual stamina to keep going for the length of something as formidable as a novel, or the breadth of vision or the objectivity to handle it. Poetry, which was subjective and dealt with the inner life, emotions, and things on a smaller scale, was much more suitable to feminine talents; just think of Anna Akhmatova and Marina Tsvetayeva, two of the five greatest Russian poets of the twentieth century. Papa conceded there was one novel by a woman that deserved a place among the great books: Harper Lee's *To Kill a Mockingbird*. But on the whole, if I wanted to be a novelist, the odds were against me. Of course, he added on a sobering note, there wasn't much of a chance that I would turn out to be a poet of the same caliber as Akhmatova or Tsvetayeva, but my chances of becoming a first-rank novelist were even slimmer.

Funny, isn't it, that exactly the opposite view of female abilities used to dominate the literary tradition of English-speaking countries, which boasts few first-rate women poets but quite a constellation of women novelists. (In Russia, where Dickens and Thackeray are widely read, Jane Austen and George Eliot enjoy about as little popularity as Akhmatova and Tsvetayeva do in the English-speaking world; the novels of the Brontë sisters, somewhat better known, are dismissed as reading for teenage girls.) Here, too, there was a handy argument: the novel dealt with social relations, a proper feminine sphere, whereas the poet's calling required an unwomanly intensity of personal vision and strength to affirm one's individuality.

I remember a *Literaturnaya Gazeta* tribute to the best-known woman poet in the Soviet Union today, Bella Akhmadulina, which I read right in the middle of one of the winters of my feminist discontent. The author of the tribute, the respected poet and literary critic Pavel Antokolsky, found no higher compliment than to say that Akhmadulina was not a poetess but a *poet*.

This meant, as far as I could gather, that her style was clear, precise, not at all maudlin — *like a man's*, you know.

I also remember the reflections of Yevgeny Yevtushenko, the celebrity poet whose rather special status combined all the security of belonging to officially recognized literature with all the titillation of toying with dissent. Yevtushenko lamented in one of his poems that "men have become effeminate these days, / And women have turned into something mannish," and all because "woman has been debased / To a level of equality with man."

I looked all around me in vain for evidence of such debasement. What I could see was that virtually all women were in fact "debased" to the level of either working or going to college. In a bow to tradition, I learned eventually, married women were legally allowed not to hold a job — the only category of able-bodied adults so privileged. However, very few took advantage of this legislative magnanimity. When I was little, my mother once took me for a stroll in the park on a weekday afternoon, which she could do because she worked only three days a week, and struck up a conversation with another young woman out for a walk with her small daughter. After a while the young woman hopefully inquired why Mama was not at work in the daytime — could it be that she too was a stay-at-home mother? She seemed disappointed when Mama told her that she was not; she had hoped to find a kindred soul. The young mother explained that she was an engineer by profession, and had decided to stay home until her daughter went to school. Her family was having a very hard time surviving on the salary of her husband (also a rank-and-file engineer, which meant living on a pittance). Even worse, she found herself nearly shunned by former friends, who treated her as if she were a freak. These women were not militant feminists who believed that a woman without a career was worthless or that a woman who quit her job to raise a baby was a traitor to the movement. Such things were not done, that was all. Apparently this woman's friends were also shocked by her willingness to lower her living standards so she could take care of her child.

By the age of seventeen (that is to say, in all the years of my Soviet life), I knew only two Soviet women who did not work. One was the wife of a more or less prominent writer, Kamil Ikramov. The other was Masha Fedorova, our country neighbor across the road, whose son, though a few years my junior, was a frequent playmate of mine. Masha's husband held a top engineering job at some airplane factory. A giant with a shiny bald pate, a square jaw, and beady eyes, he was an absolute and unabashed domestic tyrant. Masha was no pushover in dealing with salespeople, neighbors, government officials — anyone to whom she was not joined in matrimony. But my observations of life *chez* Fedorov when I went there to play or watch TV strongly suggested to me that being a housewife was not so different from being a slave.

Grandma told me that Fedorov had divorced his first wife because she had borne him only daughters, in whom he seemed to show no interest whatsoever. (He also appalled me by casually remarking that war isn't such a bad thing because "it spurs technological progress.") Masha once delivered a discourse, as I tagged along on a shopping trip to Zelenograd — a walk through the woods that lay just outside our dacha — on the misfortune of having only female children. "Now, your papa, for instance, doesn't have any sons," she said sententiously, the way she always spoke, "so there won't be anyone to carry on the family name." I was rather stunned to have my filial deficiency so flatly pointed out to me.

When I opened the World Literature Library volume of ancient Eastern literature that I took from my father's shelf, lines such as "A daughter is a source of sorrow, a man-child the radiance of the sun in high heaven" leaped from the page to slap me in the face. That was India around 1000 B.C.; in the Soviet Union around A.D. 1975 there were no such high-minded paeans to men-children but plenty of jokes casually reflecting the preference for boys. One that I remember actually made fun not so much of this preference as of the all-pervasive practice of having all sorts of favors, from a restaurant reservation to college admission for one's offspring, arranged by a telephone call from an influential acquaintance: *A man comes to a maternity ward where his wife has just given birth, and asks the nurse if it's a boy. "No, it's a girl," says the nurse. "What do you mean, it's a girl? Hasn't there been a call from the Central Committee?"* Fortunately, neither Hindu texts nor Soviet jokes carried enough weight to give me the idea that I might be an unwanted child; even if my father thought that my gender would get in the way of my becoming a first-rate novelist, he showed no signs of loving me any less.

All the women in turn-of-the-century short stories by Chekhov seemed cheerfully to assume that employment and education were synonymous with liberation and equality. I was beginning to suspect that there was something they didn't know: in the promised land of education and/or employment, "getting settled," for a woman, still meant getting married. Security was a good match. A daughter or a sister still had to be "married off." Parents of sons who stayed single too long might not be very happy, but it wasn't the same thing as the disaster of a girl not married by the age of twenty-three.

I pestered Grandma (the family member most often available for pestering) with questions like "Why is it considered wrong for a girl to ask a boy out?" and, by extension, for a woman to propose marriage to a man? My grandmother — she who had braved the wilderness of Siberia on horseback as a land surveyor, who had gotten her reluctant male companions to accept her on equal terms — gave me the most hopelessly retrograde answers. It is considered that when a man marries a woman, she explained, he is going to take care of her and support her. And since man is the breadwinner, for a woman to ask a man to marry her is like asking him to accept a liability. Grandma did not necessarily believe this was right. She was, after all, an independent woman — had been one throughout her life. But she was also a realist: those were the facts of life, like it or not.

This, I later came to realize, is perhaps the key paradox of gender roles in Soviet society: near-universal female employment goes hand in hand with a powerful man-the-provider mystique. The view of man as breadwinner is not without its basis in reality; male salaries are indeed, on the average, higher than those of women, and jobs with prestige usually accrue to men as well. Husbands and wives may pool their earnings, but my parents knew quite a few men — mostly among those who were making a lot of money by Soviet standards — who turned over only a portion of their biweekly pay to the little woman for the household and kept the rest to spend as they saw fit. Some wives, too, kept a secret nest egg, often garnished from the money received "for the household" from the husband's pay.

Grandma never gave much thought to the effect her sociological forays would have on my self-esteem. What it all boiled down to, as far as I could see, was that a man did a woman a tremendous favor by marrying her. (When I complained to Natasha, a girl a year older than myself who lived in another Kryukovo dacha, how horribly unfair it was that it was all right for a man to be a bachelor but shameful for a woman to be an old maid, her reply was beautifully logical: "But don't you see? When a man is not married, everyone knows it's because he doesn't want to get married. When a woman is not married, everyone knows it's because no one will take her.") The woman, being a beneficiary of such largesse, was the one who had to worry about keeping the marriage together, because there were plenty of younger and prettier girls out to steal him, even if he was in his midforties with a receding hairline and a lumpy nose. All of this, except for the pretty young girls lying in wait for respectable married men, sounded suspiciously like Chekhov's stories. But that was in the old days, *before* the emancipation of women! And now . . . ?

With college creeping up on me, I was also learning that girls had less of a chance of passing the dreaded college entrance exam. Admissions committees had full discretion to accept or reject anyone, almost regardless of grades or test scores, and I heard time and time again that boys who did worse on the exams were routinely admitted over girls who did better. Girls were also reputedly asked tougher questions. (There was perhaps one acceptable rationale for such treatment: a girl who failed could reapply the next year, whereas a boy would fall into the clutches of the armed forces for the next four years.) I would have been in double jeopardy as a girl and a Jew, if not in triple jeopardy as the Jewish daughter of parents with no connections to speak of. Some colleges, they said, were virtually impossible for a girl to get into. The very prestigious, not to say awe-inspiring, Moscow Institute of Foreign Relations (MIMO), which trained future diplomats and members of the government, was one of them. The bastions of manhood — non-Jewish manhood, with all but a handful of exceptions — also included all the top physics, mathematics, and engineering colleges in the country. None of these institutions had the remotest connection to my plans for the future, but even if I was personally unaffected, principle was principle.

Grandma told me that at the civil engineering college where my late grandfather had taught, the predominant attitude was that a less capable boy would in the end be a more valuable asset than a bright girl. A girl was going to have boys and makeup on her mind more than her studies, and once she got married and had kids — no, she wouldn't quit, she'd stay on the job, but she would be of little use, her energy consumed by home and hearth.

Apparently this view of the relative merits of the sexes prevailed in music colleges as well. I was present when my mother discussed it, very matter-of-factly, with a graduating student of hers named Nadya. The antifemale bias was not something to challenge, not even something to get angry about — just something a girl had to put in an extra effort to overcome. I checked the urge to cut in on their conversation, but my distress must have been visible, because Mama had to explain, in the tone of someone apologizing for a hopelessly naive idealist, "Katya here thinks that it's a terrible injustice." Nadya murmured with a sheepish smile, "Well, Katya, it really isn't such an unfair assumption — you know, it is true by and large that boys are more goal-oriented and girls have their heads filled with all sorts of silly stuff . . ." And this wasn't some Soviet sister of the Total Woman, whose only pursuit was to capture a man, but a thinking person, passionate about her work. *That* was the kind of thing that hurt and puzzled me most.

Lying ahead of me in America was the discovery of *The Second*

Sex, The Feminine Mystique, and such expressions as "sexual ste-
reotypes." As I got used to women's lib (and even, to a degree,
succeeded in converting my parents), the traditionalism of gender relations in my former homeland became more glaring and
more laughable than ever. I was amused, but not at all surprised,
to read about an utterly nonideological cultural barrier that
popped up on a joint wilderness hike by Soviet and American
youths. The Soviet boys kept offering to carry the American
girls' backpacks for them, expecting them to be flattered by such
chivalry. Instead the girls got upset at such male chauvinism,
which baffled and hurt the Russian boys. "American girls," one
of them complained, "are very independent."

One thing that we ladies did have was our own holiday: March
8, International Women's Day, for which all working people and
students got not one but two days off. Otherwise, it was celebrated much like Mother's Day, except that gifts, cards, and
flowers were given not just to mothers but to all female friends
and family members. There was no official Men's Day, but by a
custom that was probably long established, the male equivalent
of March 8, the day when women of all ages were to give gifts to
their menfolk, was February 23, Soviet Army Day. (However,
that holiday was not a day off.) Comments on what this says
about Soviet perceptions of male roles would be superfluous.

In the 1940s and early 1950s, primary and secondary school
education in the Soviet Union was sex-segregated, the rationale
being that boys and girls had to be trained for different roles:
boys to be warriors, girls to be mothers (of future warriors,
presumably). Despite two decades of coeducation, many vestiges
of this attitude (which Stalin apparently shared with Napoleon,
the champion of the bourgeois family) survived into the years of
my girlhood. Images of the glorious Soviet warrior were all over
the place, and needless to say, the warrior was male.

In primary school, the warlike heroes the textbooks offered us
were mostly of a kind kids were supposed to relate to easily:
other children. In second grade, one of our extracurricular readings was a short story entitled "Word of Honor," in which a

watchman in a park sees a small boy standing still on one spot for several hours. It's getting late, the park is about to close for the night, so the watchman asks the boy what's wrong. Holding back tears, the boy explains his predicament. Some older kids invited him to play a war game and put him on guard duty. Then they just ran away and left him alone, and now he can't leave, because a guard isn't supposed to leave his post until relieved by a commanding officer. The watchman tries to persuade the boy to go home, but in vain. He goes to fetch a policeman, who offers to relieve the boy, but the little hero stubbornly insists that only a military officer can do that. In despair, the watchman and the cop go to look for a military officer, and lo and behold, they see a man in uniform getting off a bus. (Nothing implausible about the coincidence — military personnel in uniform are a common sight in any Soviet city.) Told of the boy's plight, the officer agrees to help. First the boy is careful to inquire whether his rescuer's rank is high enough to relieve a guard of his duty. Assured that it is, he reports to the major with a military salute, gets his leave to go, and can finally run home.

I read this moving tale to Grandma, expecting her to share my admiration for the little boy; instead, she found the story quite offensive. There was nothing heroic, she said, about staying in a park after dark for the sake of some meaningless principle like strict obedience to "duty," when it was of no use to anyone. It was just plain stupid. Besides, what about the boy's parents — weren't they going out of their minds with anxiety while their son was doing his so-called duty?

We also had World War II stories — many of them true, or at least partially based in fact — about boys aged from twelve to fifteen who distinguished themselves in partisan groups living in the woods and fighting the Nazis. Every little bit helped in the fight against "the German-fascist invaders." In one probably fictional story from our third-grade reader, which popped up again in an English translation in our sixth-grade English textbook, the hero, a twelve-year-old on a farm taken over by the Germans, distracts the Nazis' attention by bringing them a helping of fine sour cream and then cleverly puts some sand in the barrel of their huge tank. As a detachment of Soviet troops approaches, the Nazis try to fire from the tank, and its barrel blows up.

War heroes who were girls would turn up occasionally. There was Zoya Kosmodemyanskaya, a Komsomol girl of eighteen (almost middle age to me then) who went into an occupied village as a partisan scout, fell into the hands of the Nazis, and was tortured and hanged. (My father told me that according to some unofficial sources, she was actually captured by pro-Nazi villagers.) And in seventh grade we read Alexander Fadeyev's fact-based novel *The Young Guard*, about Komsomol members — boys *and* girls this time — who formed an underground resistance to fight the Nazis in the occupied Ukrainian city of Krasnodon and were eventually caught and executed. (As I learned years later, there is at least a hypothesis that these teenagers were not Komsomol patriots but a group of Ukrainian nationalists who opposed both the Communist power and the Nazi invaders. What I found out from Papa back then was this curious bit of gossip: after the first printing of the novel, Fadeyev was taken to task by the authorities for "distorting the facts" of the events he described. His account of the Soviet troops' retreat along the Ukrainian frontlines showed a panic-filled, chaotic flight; he was told to rewrite it as a strategically planned, well-organized retreat. He did. He was also told that the original version did not reflect the true role of Communist Party leadership. He added a fictitious character, an older Party member who supposedly directed the Young Guard's activities. In the second printing, Fadeyev got everything right.)

To be sure, we also read about the horrors of the war and the Nazi atrocities. We were reminded of the twenty million Soviets who were killed in World War II; but strange to say, these twenty million became almost a source of pride as well as grief. (Even in the number of our war dead, we were ahead of everybody else!) The hair-raising actions of the Germans were overshadowed by the valor of our soldiers and partisans. As a topic in our readers and our textbooks, the Great Patriotic War (which is how the Soviet front of World War II is known in the Soviet Union) took second place only to the Great October Socialist Revolution and Lenin; sometimes it seemed to get equal time.

The war had its saints and its holy relics. In a story we read in seventh or eighth grade, a boy is about to throw into the sea (at the insistence of his mother) an old rifle he has found in the attic. On the beach he runs into a rugged-looking retired seaman, who asks him where he's taking the rifle. Hearing the answer, he erupts with anger. "Look at this," he says, his voice cracking with emotion. "There are six marks on the butt of this rifle. That means the man who had it killed six Nazi enemies with this gun. It must be treated as a sacred thing. It is a symbol of our readiness to defend the Motherland against all enemies. And you were going to throw it away!" (I am paraphrasing, but that was the gist of it.) Thus properly shamed, the boy takes the rifle home, reverently pressing to his soon-to-be-manly breast the sacred symbol of national defense.

Our modern hero, the peacetime defender of the Motherland, was the border guard, another mythical figure that looms large in the Soviet pantheon. He patrols the borders in the snow, dressed in white, his faithful German shepherd at his side. The role of this heroic creature was slightly misrepresented to us: from the textbooks, the stories, and the songs, one infers that the border patrol's principal function is to stop spies and saboteurs from villainously sneaking into Soviet territory, not to prevent people from sneaking in the opposite direction.

May 9 is V Day, a celebration of Soviet victory over the Germans, for which working people as well as students get a bonanza of two days off (which makes May a great month: two days off for May Day, May 1 and 2, and two days off for V Day, May 9 and 10). May 8 was always a festive day at school. We were told to wear our holiday uniforms, the blue skirts or pants and white tops for Pioneers, frilly white aprons for the older Komsomol girls, and white shirts for the boys. There were school concerts sometimes, or a student body meeting with speeches and songs and ceremonies like saluting the flag; and there was always "a lesson in valor," which meant a lecture by a Great Patriotic War veteran. The Russian word for valor, *muzhestvo*, literally means "manliness"; however, this word is also used, without apparent contradiction, to characterize valiant women. In fact, one of the veterans who gave us a lesson in manliness was a tired-looking woman with numerous awards and medals pinned to her jacket; she had been an army nurse during the war. Few, if any, of the students listened to these people, who seemed unable to speak even of their most moving experiences in anything but the dreariest of clichés. Today, looking back with a slightly less cynical eye, I am a little ashamed of the flippant, somewhat mocking attitude toward these veterans that I shared with my classmates. After all, many of them probably had done truly heroic things and lived through genuinely horrifying experiences. On the part of those of us from good families, I suspect, there was also quite a bit of elitist contempt for these cloddish, unsophisticated, middle-aged men and women in drab clothes.

The pompous praises sung to valor and military glory were always flavored with insistence that the horrors of the war, the millions of deaths, the grief of mothers and wives and sisters, must never again be repeated. We do not want war! Peace to the world! *But* — every Soviet citizen, every male Soviet citizen in particular, must be prepared to answer the call of his sacred duty to defend the Motherland. It was not for nothing that our Pioneer ceremonies centered on the Pioneer master's ritual question, "Ready for labor and for defense of the Soviet Union?" and our ritual answer, with a military salute, "Always ready!"

A Frenchwoman I met at the age of fourteen (she worked for the French embassy in Moscow and married a friend of my father's, and I sometimes practiced French with her) was utterly horrified by the militarism in our schools and the all-pervasive war themes in our reading materials. "Even in your math textbooks," she said with incredulous disgust, "there are all those problems like 'If tank A leaves point X at the speed of so many kilometers per hour and tank B leaves point Y at the speed of so many kilometers per hour . . .' "

As early as fourth grade we had some "defense training," which consisted almost entirely of learning how to put on a gas mask and prancing around the gym hall, single file, wearing these masks, which we thought were hilarious, since they made us look like elephants or invaders from outer space. Later, as we sat in the math classroom, we would occasionally hear a strange noise out in the hallway. It sounded like a series of loud, abrupt barks: BOW-BOW-BOW-BOW-BOW! It always made us giggle, and I used to wonder what it was. In seventh grade I found out. Our math classroom happened to be right around the corner from the military instruction classroom. Before the beginning of the lesson, the class had to line up in the hallway outside and greet the military instructor with the words "Good day, comrade military instructor!" in a fast, crisp staccato that made every word sound like a monosyllabic BOW. After that the students filed into the classroom, which had on its walls a gallery of portraits of Soviet top military brass, civil defense posters, and posters detailing the duties of a soldier on watch duty.

Beginning in seventh grade, we had military instruction classes twice a week — providentially, nearly always in the last (seventh) period. Sneaking out was a cinch, especially in spring, when you didn't have to pick up your coat and get past our Cerberus of a cloakroom attendant. That is why I can't recall much of what was taught in these classes.

Our military instructor (*voyenny rukovoditel*, or *voyenruk* for short) was probably an officer on a pension. A scraggy little fellow with a thin sallow face, small cunning eyes, shiny, short black hair parted in the middle, and an oily smile, he looked far more like a meticulous office clerk than a valiant defender of the Motherland. Twice a week for four years (having left the country, I missed out completely on the last four months or so), he drilled us in military discipline and armed forces regulations: the stripes and epaulettes and various marks of distinction, the ranks and the hierarchy of subordination, who has to salute whom and in what manner, rules for all occasions in a soldier's life, and so on. We also saw slide shows on civil defense against a nuclear attack, shelters, evacuation stations. There were slide shows about first aid in the event of bombings, fires, and other wartime hazards, for different degrees of burns (with sickening photos of horribly burned people), and for heavy bleeding. Still others were used as visual aids to accompany lectures on injuries inflicted by various kinds of chemical and biological weapons, on symptoms of fatal and nonfatal poisoning (skin lesions, fatigue, nausea). I remember that the name of the chemical weapon yperite for some reason filled me with an almost mystical horror, perhaps because it bore (especially in its Russian pronunciation) a sinister resemblance to the word "afrit," an evil spirit in Arabic folklore that I often encountered in my bowdlerized children's edition of *The Arabian Nights*.

Military instruction was more than just talk and slide shows. Early on, both boys and girls learned not only to identify all the parts of the Kalashnikov submachine gun and their functions but also to take apart and reassemble the weapon. Every one of us actually had to get up in front of the class and demonstrate this newly acquired skill. I was nervous, fumbled miserably with the damned gun as some of my classmates, the boys in particular, began to snigger, and almost got my index finger jammed in a lock under the *voyenruk*'s mocking but patient stare.

We also learned how to fire the standard Soviet army rifle. This offered a precious opportunity to leave the gray brick walls of our school on class time; the *voyenruk* walked us all to a nearby shooting range. We had to lie down in order to fire, and that was a problem: the brown uniform dresses of most girls were as close to miniskirt lengths — just then, in the late 1970s, in vogue in the Soviet Union — as we could get without raising the eyebrows of our teachers *too* high. We had to worry not just about hitting the target but, perhaps more important, about stretching out on the floor in a seemly fashion, without revealing our panties to the eyes of the boys hovering nearby, waiting for their turn to shoot. As for the actual shooting, some of the girls could hold a candle to the best of the boys. A few times the boys were taken out of regular classes for target practice while we were left behind to get a taste of an all-girl school.

A teacher once gave us a homily on ideological purity, stressing in particular the perils of hobnobbing with foreigners and the need to be on guard even with those who came to our school as officially invited guests. She came up with a particularly shocking example that was to show the full extent of Western perfidy: "This delegation of Americans came to our school and they had cameras with them, wanted to take some pictures. Well, just at that time a class was doing some military instruction exercises out in the schoolyard. So these foreigners raced downstairs, took some snapshots, and then printed them in some foreign newspaper with the caption '*The Soviets are training their children for war!*' "

"And isn't that what they're doing?" I breathed into Rita's ear, wishing dearly that I could raise my hand and repeat the question aloud but never for a moment seriously considering such self-immolation.

9

Sex and the Soviet Teenager

IN NINTH GRADE, Natasha Timina came up to me during a break and said in an insinuating voice, "You know, there's going to be a lecture for tenth-graders in the performance hall — 'a talk on sexual hygiene for the ears of a young woman.' " "Sexual hygiene for the ears?" I asked, puzzled, and nearly died of embarrassment when the enormity of my gaffe dawned on me right away. Since my family left the Soviet Union in the middle of the next year, I never got to hear the riveting lecture. Whatever it was they told girls about sexual hygiene, that was virtually the entire extent of the sex education we got at school.

When I was first told, at the age of eleven (by a neighbor in Kryukovo, a girl my own age named Inga), about the process of baby-making, my immediate and probably typical reaction was *I can't believe my parents could have done something so filthy.* However, faced with the hard fact of my own existence, I had to conclude that they must have, and for years after that I often looked at them, wondering: *Do they know that I know?* My next preoccupation was with whether *I* would have to do something so filthy and almost certainly painful. Inga, way ahead of me in these matters, was nevertheless not flawless as a sex educator, and her description of the act increased my anxiety. According to her, it lasted for an hour on the average, and if the couple did it for two hours, they had twins. (The implications for the parents of quintuplets are rather formidable.)

Later that year, back at school, I had a short-lived friendship with a fallen woman. Nina Yanovskaya was a girl on the buxom side, with puffy half-open lips, a languid walk, and grades that placed her near the very bottom of the class. In the spring, when the wearing of lighter blouses and skirts was condoned if not officially allowed, Nina came to school in a see-through lacy blouse and a miniskirt that concealed so little I couldn't understand why boys took the trouble to chase her around the hallways trying to lift it. Rita, who was chummy with her, once whispered to me with little bursts of laughter that Nina wanted to be a prostitute when she grew up.

I occasionally helped out the aspiring prostitute with her English homework. (Our friendship eventually crumbled — to the vast relief of my family — after I failed to prompt Nina while she was answering a history question; returning to her seat with a fresh 2, she murmured, "You bitch.") One day, over at her place, I worked up the nerve to ask the question that worried me so much: if I wanted to have a baby, would I really have to do *that?* "You dummy," Nina said, her moist, heiferlike eyes beaming a benign contempt at me. "Everyone does it. It feels very good, you know." I was not convinced, though the girl sounded as if she knew what she was talking about. Could she, at twelve years of age? She did hang around with a crowd of tough, disreputable-looking older boys from her building. Before we had our falling-out, she offered to fix me up with one of them; I awkwardly refused.

By the time I was fourteen, some of the girls regarded *me* as well-informed on sex. I was the expert called upon to settle the argument between Ella Shimanskaya and Natasha Gamaley on whether intercourse invariably results in conception. My expert opinion (no) was double-checked with a kindly middle-aged English teacher, and Ella said proudly though shyly, "See, I told you — I know that some married couples actually, you know, do it once in a while just for pleasure . . ."

Being teenagers, we had a wild curiosity about sex and entirely inadequate means of satisfying that curiosity. Our educators' approach to the subject would have immensely pleased the Moral

Majority. The only formal mention of the biological aspects of sexuality in our ten years of school occurred at the end of eighth grade. That year we had a course in human anatomy, and the very last section of the textbook was entitled "Reproduction." It contained such titillating words as "impregnation," "ovum," and "spermatozoa," accompanied by pictures of the latter, with wiggly little tails. The textbook explained how the sperm fertilized the egg but said not a word about how the sperm got in there in the first place. Perhaps the authors assumed that we would already know about it from dirty jokes (which, however imprecisely, we did). To the best of my memory, the course discreetly omitted any reference to the genitals or to menstruation, let alone sexual intercourse. (If such words had made the briefest appearance, I doubt that I could have forgotten it.) The authors of the textbook quickly skipped over the biological part and added several bombastic paragraphs about human sexual relations being inseparable from emotional and spiritual intimacy. They concluded by duly noting that the Soviet family, the basic unit of socialist society, was the highest form of union between man and woman, founded upon shared views and the common goal of building communism.

For lack of anything better, even that seemed sexy to us — sexy enough for bashful grins and whispers and subdued giggles. We were all on the edge of our seats, everyone afraid he or she would be called to answer the day's lesson. To tell off-color jokes to other fourteen-year-olds was one thing, but to answer smutty questions at the teacher's desk. . . . This lot befell Pavel Litvinov, normally a sassy young man but now tongue-tied and blushing like an altar boy. Saying "sperm" and "ovum" out loud in such stressful circumstances proved too much for poor Litvinov. Turning a deeper shade of crimson by the second, he scowled and would not answer, and went back to his seat with a 2. The teacher had the mercy and the good sense not to call on anyone else.

Our real sex education went on in the hallways during the breaks, or just before the start of class, as we sat waiting for the teacher to come in. Our working-class tough, Borya Fedoseyev, who sat behind me and Rita in the chemistry class, described to us in a hot whisper, leering lecherously and smacking his fat lips, how he saw a girl and a guy in a back yard and the guy unzipped his pants and the girl got down on her knees and — "Ugh," Rita and I said, grimacing and finding it hard to believe that people could do something *that* gross. We also learned a lot in the girls' changing room before and after gym — the scene of conversations such as "Do you think sex is dirty?" (Anya Petrosyan to me) "No, I don't think it's dirty. Not unless it's perverted or something." (Me, shaking my head firmly) "Yeah, that's what I think. Perversions and stuff — that's really disgusting. But when it's normal, there's nothing wrong with it." (Anya, solemnly)

One day before a class meeting, a group of girls huddled around Alla Makarova, who had access to foreign things because her father was a diplomat. She had brought a copy of *Vogue* to school. Turning the pages like a group of historians examining a rare manuscript, we came across a glossy full-page ad for sanitary napkins. As we gaped, our class guide, Ksenia Stepanovna (who had set aside just enough of her propriety to join us), mournfully shook her head at this blatant display of Western decadence: "Oh — *that's* what it is. They would actually put a thing like that in a magazine!" (It would have been nice to see "a thing like that" on the shelves of a store, instead of having to use shapeless, bulky chunks of cotton wrapped in strips of gauze. It wasn't every day that you could find cotton or gauze in a pharmacy, either. I would rather not think about how women managed in the small towns and villages, where, Mother told me, most people hardly knew what cotton or gauze looked like.)

Some of the books we read in our literature classes, beginning in eighth or ninth grade, did more or less openly refer to sexual matters. Of course our wanton minds were also prone to discern sexual references and double-entendres where none were intended. The words "Pushkin was living with his old nanny," spoken in seventh grade by some unfortunate who had been asked to retell the poet's biography, were enough to make the class come alive with guffaws. Before eighth grade, we used either abridged versions of books in our readers or special school editions. Then we became adult enough for the unexpurgated texts. In ninth grade we read Dostoyevsky's *Crime and Punishment*, complete with Sonya, the prostitute, and the scene in which Raskolnikov's sister, Dunya, is nearly raped by her rejected suitor, Svidrigailov. Mark Kozlovsky, a big, dark-haired fellow with an engaging smile, object of the puppy love of several girls, including myself, did an oral report on an early episode in which Raskolnikov sees a very drunk, disheveled young girl stumbling along a boulevard. "Evidently," Mark carried on airily, "someone got this girl drunk, lured her to a deserted place, and then" — I could swear he paused for effect — "raped her." He looked up, as if daring us all, the class and Lydia Davydovna, to show some embarrassment.

It was also Mark who volunteered (to the great relief of many in the class) to recite a poem we had to learn in tenth grade — a poem with a dirty word in it. An early piece by Vladimir Mayakovsky, the celebrated poet of the Revolution, it concluded with the declaration that the poet, asked to conform to the stifling social norms of the bourgeoisie, "would rather be serving pineapple drinks / To sluts in a bar." The word *blyad*, "slut," was generally considered unprintable, but here it appeared in full and not as "b——," perhaps out of respect for the wishes of the great revolutionary poet. Here was a word, hitherto a part of the illicit universe of dirty jokes and drunken rantings one might happen to overhear when passing a liquor store, printed in a text officially approved for the school curriculum — mind-boggling! Never, I suspect, had the class listened with such attention to a student reciting a homework assignment. And Mark delivered the lines with gusto, flinging the unprintable word into the air, tense with anticipation:

> "I'd rather be serving pineapple drinks
> To SLUTS in a bar!"

And the sky didn't fall. Even the ceiling didn't collapse.

The bard of the Revolution provided us with another bit of risqué entertainment, this time quite unintentionally. The poem in question was "Verses on the Soviet Passport," an inspired account of an episode on board a Western ocean liner. A border official is inspecting passports, handling the documents of the British and American passengers with deference, those of Swedes or Norwegians with indifference, and so on, until he gets to Mayakovsky and his "red-skinned hulk of a passport." Horror-stricken at the sight of a Soviet passport, the fatuous official picks it up as if it were a bomb or a rattlesnake. The poet thunderously concludes:

> I take it out
> > of my baggy pants,
> Of all my possessions,
> > > the most precious
> > > > > by far.
> Read it
> > and envy:
> > > I am a citizen
> Of the USSR!

Those first two lines broke us up, each and every one of us. To giggle or otherwise show irreverence for so hallowed a poem was unthinkable; all we could do was silently bite our lips in little convulsions of levity.

Our curriculum also included *The Schoolmaster*, by modern Soviet writer Chingiz Aitmatov. The story takes place in the early years of the Sovietization of the Muslim nations of Central Asia. The heroine, fifteen-year-old Altynai, who has found a sense of freedom and dignity at the village school started by a young Komsomol member, Duishen, is sold by her family as a second wife to a loathsome red-faced brute. Before Duishen manages to rescue her, she is brutally raped by the groom in his tent.

The Schoolmaster had been made into a movie (by Andrei Konchalovsky, who has since moved to Hollywood and directed *Maria's Lovers* and *Runaway Train*), and Lydia Davydovna arranged for us to see it in the nearby movie theater/youth center Orlyonok ("Young Eagle"). "Ooh, this is gonna be something," said Rita, who had seen the film. "They show, you know, the guy ripping her dress at the front and then you see her lying there all

naked." However, for the purposes of showing the film to ninth-
graders in a literature course, the scene had been cut. We saw
the girl backing off in terror as her husband advanced toward
her, then there was a fadeout and a cut to a broken, already
dressed Altynai sitting listlessly in the tent. I regret to say I was
a bit disappointed, and forgot for a moment that this was a
beastly violation of a girl my own age — but there were many
others in the class who were no more sensitive.

There was little we could learn about sex from the silver
screen. Even our "adult" films ("children under 16 not admitted")
were tame ones. (Franco Zeffirelli's *Romeo and Juliet* was among
them.) The rating often had to do with subject matter rather than
visual explicitness. The adult film *My One and Only* (which I went
to see at the age of fifteen, accompanied by my ten-year-old
cousin Sasha) told the story of a young woman driven to adultery
by the need for warmth and intimacy, and her husband's eventual postdivorce realization that she loved him after all and that
she was the only woman he had ever loved. The adultery was
strictly off-screen, except for some hugging and kissing — no
skin except for a shot of the errant wife sitting on the bed naked,
her back to the camera, facing the husband. In the late seventies,
though, motion picture standards were relaxed enough to allow
a little frontal nudity, usually in an innocent context: the aristocratic heroine of an eighteenth-century costume drama being
bathed by her maidservants, her lithe young body — the shape
of the breasts faintly visible — glowing in a dim golden light. (A
couple of older ladies behind me gasped, "Look, look!")

It used to be — as I knew from my parents — that relations
between the sexes, no matter how tamely implied, were pretty
much a no-no in Soviet cinema, and in Soviet literature as well.
The public above the personal, you know. Love could be present
but always had to be subordinated to love for one's country, love
for the Party, and meeting the industrial plan. No on-screen
kissing or any such immorality. When my father was a teenager,
he went several times to see a Soviet stage version of Theodore
Dreiser's *An American Tragedy* solely because it dealt with the
risqué topic of love between man and woman, including some

physical displays of affection and even references to sexual intimacy. The plot underwent some modification. In Dreiser's
novel, an upper-class young man gets a factory girl pregnant,
kills her in a faked boating accident to prevent her from disrupt-
ing his engagement to a rich heiress, and ends up going to the
electric chair. The Soviet producers apparently decided that
Dreiser's social criticism was not strong enough, so they added a
factory worker who is hopelessly in love with the girl, is framed
for her murder by the upper-class young man's rich uncle, and
is executed. The young people who flocked to see the play didn't
care much about social criticism, Dreiser style or Soviet style.

By the seventies, the personal had wormed its way back into
the movies. Among the biggest hits of those years were the romantic comedies of the writer-director team of Eldar Braginsky
and Eduard Ryazanov. They were delightful films indeed, combining sparkle and warmth with relatively innocuous but nevertheless enjoyable digs at orthodox values, such as a highly
satirical portrait of a woman so involved in "public activism" at
her office that she doesn't even remember what her real job is. In
The Office Romance, the nerdy, mild-mannered hero begins, at the
instigation of a caddish buddy of his, to romance his ugly-as-sin,
unsmiling female boss in the hope of winning a promotion.
Needless to say, true love blossoms as the boss turns out to be
not only a person hiding a deep need for warmth and companion-
ship underneath her dry career-woman exterior, but also — once
she has put on a little makeup and traded her military haircut
and shapeless dark brown business suit for a permanent wave
and a more feminine dress — a very attractive woman. In another film, the title of which I've forgotten, a prim and proper
middle-aged matron whose job is to perform civil marriage ceremonies suddenly learns that her husband is leaving her for a
bimbo with frizzy red hair. She has to ask him for help when
their spirited eighteen-year-old daughter gets involved with a
boy; together they go to visit the boy's parents in the country,
and since, in the heroine's words, "nothing must cast a shadow
on the pure character of the future bride," they do not mention

the impending divorce. Guess what: Daddy ends up seeing the error of his ways, leaves the redhead, and comes back to Mama.

A movie with no ideological content, focusing only on the personal lives and feelings of characters who could have just as easily been members of a non-Soviet, nonsocialist society, was in itself daring. As a matter of fact, some Soviet filmmakers were cautiously beginning to tackle the inner lives and the problems of young people, including love and even sex. The movie *Surviving Till Monday*, which was embraced as a revelation by the educated public because it painted a shatteringly frank, even bleak picture of a Soviet high school, explicitly took issue with the taboo on the personal. In this film a senior class is given an essay assignment on the topic "What is happiness?" and a shy, intense girl writes that her idea of happiness is to marry a man she loves and bear him six children. The teacher who gave the assignment, typically prim and preachy, gulps and sputters in rage and disbelief, and wants to take up the matter with the principal. Feminism is not the issue; she is simply shocked, utterly shocked, that a student would write about such intimate matters. "It's like a striptease of some kind!" she declares to the sad, bewildered hero, a caring teacher with unorthodox ideas.

Another movie about high schoolers had a subplot in which a girl finds herself pregnant and deserted by the boy who fathered the child. All of this is handled very discreetly: a male character runs into the girl as she comes out of a pregnancy consultation center or something like that and naively asks her what she's doing there; her embarrassed smile leaves no doubt. In a later scene, the boy visits her in the maternity ward. Obviously, this was no *Fast Times at Ridgemont High*, but the nonjudgmental treatment of the girl was quite unusual.

My classmate Tanya Tumasian talked about having been on a tour of a major film studio in Moscow where they told visitors about a new movie about to be released. The plot as she recounted it was one long cliché: two high-school seniors become involved in a sexual relationship; the girl gets pregnant; the boy meanwhile is seduced by a predatory, heartless siren and abandons his loving girlfriend, who either kills herself or suffers some other lamentable fate. The girls clustered around Tanya in the hallway and drank in every word. Not only was the movie straightforward in handling the issue of teenage sex, she said, but it also contained some unprecedentedly explicit scenes. For greater authenticity, the filmmakers had decided to use young boys and girls still in acting school, not grown-up professional actors. "So, can you imagine, they bring this boy to the studio and tell him he's going to act in a movie — and the first thing he knows, they make him take all his clothes off and put him in bed with a naked girl!"

Shortly afterward, I left the Soviet Union; I never heard of the release of any movie with a plot remotely similar to Tanya's story, even though such a movie would have been unusual enough to be noticed by the Russian émigré press. Perhaps Tanya had made it all up, including the movie studio tour. Perhaps such a movie *was* made and was put on the shelf because it defied convention a bit too boldly. (These days, *glasnost* means more sexual as well as political openness: some recent Soviet films show men and women in various degrees of undress and in the tamer stages of sexual contact.)

For a decidedly un-Soviet, lighthearted treatment of sex, there were always foreign movies, mostly West European — French, German, Italian — and occasionally American. The posters for these movies usually bore the warning "children under 16 not admitted," but the rule was fairly easy to get around. I don't remember if Rita and I were underage or not when we went to see the Italian movie *Signor Robinson*, a delightful send-up of *Robinson Crusoe* in which the twentieth-century hero finds himself marooned on a desert island with a *girl* Friday. The ironic twist is that Signor Robinson, the civilized man, proves much less intelligent and much less capable than the "savage" girl, and at the end of the film, return to civilization is hardly salutary as the crew of a rescue ship drags the hapless hero away from lovely Friday and back to his vile-tempered Italian wife. Friday, being a child of nature, naturally wears an extremely skimpy costume: a grass skirt and a grass top that barely conceals the charms underneath it. If one really tried — and I'm sure the better part of the audience did — one could even get a glimpse of her pointed nipples. Who in my class would miss such a treat? A few weeks into the run of the movie, Lena Kashcheyeva was telling a cluster of girls lounging about in the school hallway how her mother woke her up by unsuspectingly cooing, "Ding-dong!" in imitation of an alarm clock. The peals of laughter left no doubt that everyone had gotten it: in the language of Friday's tribe, man's favorite sport was known as "making ding-dong."

So we went to foreign movies longing to catch a glimpse of a nipple or some other naughty body part, or at least to hear some sexual banter and innuendo. A great deal of the allure and glamour of the semi-real West had a sexual aura: the West was associated with lack of inhibitions, with images ranging from the titillating to the arousing to the shockingly obscene. At Ella Shimanskaya's birthday party, four or five of us were sitting around the bedroom in the mellow glow of a small lamp, and someone slyly inquired, "Now, with whom would you like to be in such a setting?" (Ella, dreamily and gravely: "With a husband"; I, intent on being wicked: "With a lover.") Then somehow the conversation drifted from these romantic musings to hard-core porn. "I've heard," said Lena Karpukhina, a diplomat's daughter who had been seen reading an American paperback of *Jaws* at school, "they have magazines abroad where they actually show *it* in close-up — you know, with blood and all." (Ellochka, with a troubled look on her little face, shook her head and muttered with a desperate sincerity, "You know, I just don't think I could ever do *that* with a man I loved. . . . I really couldn't respect him after *that*.") The blood meant, presumably, close-ups of intercourse with a female virgin. The girls winced and snorted. Mentally depraved as I thought myself to be, I had never heard that any bleeding was involved, and inwardly I shuddered.

In fifth grade, Borya Fedoseyev got in trouble for bringing Western pornographic pictures to school. It didn't come as a total shock to me; I sat next to Fedoseyev in our English class, and he had once tried to charge me ten kopecks for viewing a small black-and-white snapshot of his older sister, naked from the waist up and opulently endowed. If rumors were true, that was chicken feed compared to the pictures he was caught carrying this time.

I have the impression that one of the first things most Soviet émigrés (at least most of the males) do upon finding themselves in the free world is go to see an X-rated film. So do the lucky few who travel abroad. I knew that even in some Eastern-bloc countries — "fraternal countries" or "people's democracies," as they are known in Soviet parlance — one could walk into a movie theater and see things that would have never been allowed to pollute a chaste Russian screen. (*Sex Swedish style is a bunch of Swedish guys and gals getting together and having an orgy. Sex Polish style is a bunch of guys and gals getting together and watching a film of the Swedish orgy. Sex Soviet style is a bunch of Soviet guys and gals getting together with the Polish guys and gals, who tell them what they saw in the Swedish film.*)

Our guys and gals had to content themselves with watching usually edited versions of R-rated foreign films. Sometimes there were crushing disappointments. You had heard the girls say, "Oh you just wouldn't *believe* the stuff they show in this new West German movie"; you went to see the movie, and lo and behold . . . or, to be exact, there was little to behold — the juicy scene had been cut. Perhaps the censors who had approved the movie for release had gotten a bit lax, and then someone in a position of authority had gotten upset about it and demanded stricter standards of protection for public morals.

One of the not-so-bad consequences of film censorship was that many teenagers turned to books, including classics, as the only available repository of smutty material. (Much of my knowledge of the mechanics of sexual activity came from Boccaccio's *Decameron*.) For some reason, Guy de Maupassant, the nineteenth-century French writer welcomed by official Soviet criticism as a ruthless realist who stripped away the hypocritical covers of bourgeois society, was regarded by Soviet teenagers as their favorite pornographer. Poor Maupassant: among a large portion of the Soviet public, his very name was synonymous with salaciousness. People who had never laid eyes on any of his books would remark, after hearing a raunchy story, "Wow! That sounds like something straight out of Maupassant!" I had quite a shock when I picked up, with great trepidation, a Maupassant volume from the Library of World Literature series (a sort of Soviet Everyman's Library) and discovered that many of his stories had no sex in them at all. Nevertheless, I sought out the right passages and then, the next time Rita came over, opened the book with a conspiratorial air and pointed to a spot on the page: "From here, from 'Having locked the door . . .' " And Rita would read the steamy scene of the seduction of a virtuous wife and mother from *Bel Ami:*

> Having locked the door, he fell upon her like a beast attacking its prey. She resisted, struggled, whispered, "My God! My God!"
>
> He was passionately kissing her neck, her eyes, her lips, so that she was not swift enough to avoid his wild caresses: as she pushed him back and tried to escape his kisses, her lips brushed against him involuntarily.
>
> All of a sudden she stopped fighting, and, exhausted and submissive, allowed him to undress her. With skilled hands, like a chambermaid's, he quickly and deftly removed pieces of her clothing one by one.
>
> She grabbed her corsage from him and hid her face in it; now she stood all white, her clothes lying in a heap at her feet.
>
> When she had nothing left on but her shoes, he carried her to the bed . . .

Rita and I used to pool our resources, digging up such scenes for each other. By and large, Russian literature was no gold mine for these pursuits. Yet it was a turn-of-the-century Russian novel, *The Pit,* by the well-known writer Alexander Kuprin, that enjoyed a cult classic status with teenagers. Soviet critics routinely condemned the novel for its naturalism and "biological determinism," but Kuprin was a recognized master of Russian literature and his complete works had to include the full text of the novel. Maupassant read like a Sunday school textbook by comparison. The subject of *The Pit* was day-to-day life in a Moscow brothel, described in often nauseating detail, including the prostitutes' discussions of the strange sexual tastes of some clients. Girls in my class and girls from the nice families of Kryukovo dacha owners would inquire with naughty smiles and winks, "Have you read *The Pit?*" Eventually, I did, and I could hardly think of a worse choice for an introduction to sex, with the exception of the Marquis de Sade. Sex in *The Pit* was a beastly form of degradation inflicted by slobbering males on suffering females.

Soviet literary criticism and biography, in contrast, were securely bound by the rules of propriety. It took me a slight acquaintance with a less prudish kind of writing to realize how strict these rules were. I once picked up a biography of Beaumarchais, the author of *The Marriage of Figaro*. Beaumarchais's prolific sex life received candid treatment here, and his incredibly bawdy letters to one of his mistresses were quoted at some length. I read on, puzzled. Something was wrong, different from all other biographies of famous people I had read. Perplexed, I looked at the title page: "Translated from the French by . . ." Oh. That explained it.

A Soviet biographer would have decorously sidestepped his subject's sexual foibles. Great men and women, like Caesar's wife, must be beyond reproach, sexual reproach in particular. One of my teenage passions was Lord Byron, and as I hunted down everything about him that could be found in Soviet editions, I was convinced that all the stories about the poet's incestuous relationship with his half-sister Augusta were slanders concocted by starchy reactionaries from upper-class British society. It was not until I stumbled on a biography of Byron by the French writer André Maurois (which turned up at a library in Moscow with an unusually large collection of foreign books) that I realized the stories were in all likelihood true.

No kind of sexual behavior was shunned as completely as homosexuality. At the time of this writing, with the new openness blossoming in Gorbachev's Russia, there seems to be a little more candor on this subject as well. In the fall of 1987, reading an article on AIDS in the *Literaturnaya Gazeta*, I was shocked to see the word "homosexual"; it had been hard for me to imagine the letters of Soviet newsprint combining to form that word. A recent article on AIDS in the mold-breaking *Ogonyok* magazine went so far as to call for more tolerant attitudes toward homosexual AIDS victims, castigating the mentality of "they got what they deserved."

When homosexuality was mentioned at all in my time, writers usually resorted to Victorian euphemisms like "deviancy." The terse article on homosexuality in the *Medical Encyclopaedia* informed me that male homosexuality was a felony punishable by imprisonment — five years, as I found out by furtively looking it up in one of the weighty volumes of the Soviet penal code, under the heading "sex crimes." On paper, the antisodomy statutes in the southern American states may look even more draconian; the difference, however, is that people in the Soviet Union actually do go to jail for homosexual activity. (This is not to say that the law is enforced very strictly. An émigré friend who once worked for a venereal disease clinic in the Soviet Union told me that people who worked there were supposed to report all cases evidently involving homosexual contacts to the police, but they hardly ever did. In a couple of cases when an overzealous staffer did file a report, the guilty patients were never bothered anyway.)

Decorum was such that a film biography of the composer Tchaikovsky, whose homosexuality was an open secret among the sophisticated, supplied him with wholly fictitious heterosexual love interests. In the part of our Russian history course dealing with the culture of the nineteenth century, our history teacher, Henrietta Sergeyevna, propriety incarnate, gave us a brief summary of Tchaikovsky's life, including his short-lived marriage. The composer's wife, she explained, was a narrow-minded, hysterical woman who could not understand her genius of a husband (those women!) and pestered him with unreasonable demands (such as making love to her and not to young men?).

In an even more remarkable contortionist stunt, the biographical sketch of Oscar Wilde in the volume of his works in the Library of World Literature managed to avoid any mention of you-know-what. One could logically ask why; after all, Oscar

Wilde was not a Communist, not a Marxist hero, not even a Russian national treasure like Tchaikovsky. Why, then, the concern for his reputation? Perhaps the editorial board of the LWL simply decided that a writer whose works appeared in the series had to have a character that was at least acceptable, if it couldn't be impeccable. The charge on which Wilde was tried and imprisoned was referred to as "moral depravity." Needless to say, Wilde, like Byron, was simply a victim of persecution by starchy upper-class British society. The fact that his crime was also a crime in our most progressive society in the world was somehow omitted.

As I read this Orwellian gem, it began to dawn on me (I was fourteen at the time) that something was amiss. I finally asked my father what it was that Oscar Wilde had gone to jail for. Papa, with his usual candor, explained to me that Wilde was a homosexual, which meant that he loved men. It was then that I looked up the word *gomoseksualism* in the *Great Medical Encyclopaedia* and hurried to share this discovery with the girls at school. It was news to most of them (Ella Shimanskaya whimpered, with tears in her eyes, "Oh, *why* did you have to tell me about something so sick!"). My reputation as an expert on sex received a boost.

The mothers of my male classmates, whom Mama saw at the parents' meetings at school, endlessly kvetched about how their sons were chased by brazen females who called them all the time on the telephone — not to ask them out or anything like that, just to talk. Still, the mothers fretted and complained and could already see their precious men-children caught in the trap of an early marriage. In this day and age, they kept repeating, the girls have gotten so impudent, the mother of a boy just can't be too careful. If nothing worse, the boys were spending too much time yakking away with chatty females and not enough time studying and preparing for the serious business of life. (They felt free to discuss all this in front of my mother because I, though a girl, apparently wasn't considered a threat; I was either too homely or too nice: "Oh dear, I hope you don't think I'm talking about

Katya! Katya is such a sweet little girl!") Still, I don't suppose it ever crossed their minds to worry that their fourteen- or fifteen-year-olds might actually be having sex — an entirely justified complacency, if only because there was no place to go.

Things were considerably looser among the proletariat, in the mass schools. My neighbors Raya, the concierge's daughter, and her cousin, Olya, spent most of their time in the company of boys from the age of fourteen or so, and I doubt that these relationships were platonic. Some of the kids in my class were acquainted and even hung out with teens from the local mass schools, and the debauchery that went on within the walls of mass schools was the stuff of legends. Petya Mogilevsky, a freck-led red-haired boy with shameless bulging eyes and a lascivious smile (he was known to take liberties with girls, going so far as to try to pinch breasts and fondle knees), gathered around himself in the school lobby an audience of boys and girls alike, saying *sotto voce*, "You know how it is in School X? Bobrov was telling me . . . they're all sitting in class, and in the back of the class-room you hear 'em going *ooooh . . . aaaah*. . . . The teacher calls on a guy in the back of the class, and he gets up like this." Mogilevsky demonstrated the act of slightly raising himself off the seat so as to remain hidden by the desk from the waist down. "In fact," he continued, the lewd smirk growing wider and wider on his face, "you can even *smell* it." Some of the girls in his audience groaned and pursed their lips in an exaggerated expression of disgust. I shuddered, for all my sophistication. Smell? No one had ever told me it *smelled* . . .

For the girls I knew, chuckling over naughty words and naughty subjects seemed mostly a way of letting off steam. Take my friend Rita, who pored indiscriminately over good and bad books in search of wedding nights, seductions, and rapes, and who shocked the other girls in our class by her rather too frequent and too gratuitous references to sexual activity. (I remember her bursting into the changing room one day, giggling and breathless, shouting, "Oh, my! Oganian has just raped me!" by which she meant that Vadik Oganian, a swarthy Armenian boy from group A, had coerced her into accepting some public ser-

vice assignment. Just to make sure everyone had heard, she repeated her cry.) And yet Rita, a prime candidate for having her
mouth washed out with soap if such a practice had existed in
Russia, was in fact as much — well, perhaps *nearly* as much —
of a sexual conservative as any Victorian matron. How censo-
rious she sounded, at the age of sixteen, when she let me in on
some shocking information about a classmate of ours! Liza, who
had beautiful long legs and chestnut hair and a slender face,
apparently had confided in some girls that an older boy she was
going out with had asked her to have sex with him. Her story
was that she had rebuffed him, yet Rita shook her silver-blond
head in dismay. "Can you believe it? She's still seeing the guy!
And she's not even embarrassed to tell people!"

It was around the same time, in the spring after I turned
sixteen, that I had a very brief crush on a second cousin of mine.
He was a translator of poetry (a glamorous profession to me), in
his late twenties, and handsome, with jet-black hair and a curly
beard. Perhaps the main attraction was his fabulously super-
cilious, conceited behavior when I met him at a gathering of my
father's relatives. We argued about the death penalty; I was for
it, and cited Stendhal in support of my viewpoint. "I think," my
cousin pronounced haughtily, "that Jesus Christ is a higher authority than Stendhal." I fell in love with him for about a month,
and ventured to share my daydreams with Rita. "You know," I
said, "I'd sleep with him if he asked me to." What I got from my
friend was an incredulous look of condemnation and a sharp
"How stupid of you." She probably wrote it off as just another
eccentricity of a crazy poet, which was what she considered me
to be.

There was at least one girl in our class who was more than all
talk — and did she talk! She happened to be the daughter of
Lilia Andreyevna, our onetime literature teacher and teaching
staff superintendent. These two were a study in contrasts, the
short and pudgy mother an upright guardian of ideological and
of course moral purity, and tall, stringy Lena with the filthiest
mouth of any girl at school. She went out with a rather good-
looking, curly-haired boy of proletarian stock, and entertained

us with salacious stories about him (such as one about an embarrassing physical condition that occurred when he had to strip
before an army recruiting committee). In ninth grade I had a
chance to observe Lena in Slavik's company when my new friend
Alla Makarova invited me to her country house for a weekend,
and on the second day these lovebirds showed up too. Most of
the time, Lena was sitting in Slavik's lap and they were fondling
one another. But despite the filthy mind I thought I had, I never
suspected a thing until I got word from Rita, some time after my
emigration, that Lena had dropped out of school in the middle of
tenth grade after becoming pregnant. I can't say I was too surprised; I just wished I could have seen Lilia Andreyevna's face.

With Alla (of whom more anon), I had quite a few discussions
about love and sex. She told me tales from an English-language
library book about history's famous lovers. I told her about Ma-
dame Roland, famous victim of the French Revolution, and her
platonic romance with Buzot, a young member of her political
circle. "See," Alla mused, "that's why he loved her to the end —
because she wouldn't let him have his way with her! Men are
like that: they get what they want and then they don't care any
more." Alla, a glamorous creature, was one of the few girls in
our class known to have boyfriends, and I now wonder whether
she was speaking from experience or merely from books and
films. Anyhow, we piously agreed that only women were capable of true love, whereas men were capable only of lust.

Alla often bemoaned the passing of chivalry, real men, and
true love. Some time after learning that I was going to emigrate,
she said, only half facetiously, "You know, if you find true love
over there, you should send me a telegram. Just something like
'I found it' — I'll know what you mean." I laughed and promised
I would; but even if she were to remember, how could I be sure
that Alla's notion of true love was the same as mine?

10

Are We Having Fun Yet?

EVEN THOUGH NO ONE in my family had been blessed with the predatory skills required to shop for quality clothes, I was not dressed shabbily. That was mainly due to the fact that Mama made most of my outfits. When she started on a new dress or skirt or blouse, she never knew whether it would be a hit or a flop; but when she was good, she was very, very good. I was wearing her handiwork — a red silk dress with black stripes and dots — when I struck up a conversation with a bunch of extremely elegant French tourists in Leningrad's Hermitage Museum. They complimented me on my dress. And they weren't just any foreign tourists, either — they were *French*.

Unfortunately, there were some things even Mama at her best could not do. I didn't pine too much for blue jeans, because I knew I had no hope of getting a pair. Needless to say, the blue denims Mama had bought me, made in mundane India, without the rugged stone-washed look and without the all-important designer label, did not count. Well — I didn't like pants anyway.

My one source of anguish was winter boots. Mine were of black felt, scarcely more than ankle-high and generally of the shape and appearance of those worn, as I angrily claimed in arguments with Mama, only by old ladies. To this Mama retorted that, number one, they were perfectly good boots, and number two, she wasn't going to shop herself to death to get me high-heeled leather or at least imitation leather boots imported

from Czechoslovakia or more tantalizing places — the kind other
girls had. They occasionally twitted me about my "granny"
boots, which did little to lift my spirits.

One day Mama and I were approaching the Sokolniki supermarket and department store when we began to run into people
carrying shoeboxes. There were the inevitable what-are-they-
giving questions, and it turned out that high-heeled Czech boots
were on sale. "Well, Katya?" Mama turned to me. "You've been
asking for nice boots. Of course we'll have to stand in line, but
— you want to give it a shot?" I took up the challenge, at first
raring to go, but a peek inside the department store was enough
to take the wind out of my sails. The line's turbulent human coils
were wrapped several times around the entire second floor, a
space hardly smaller than your average Sears. I was truly astounded, which goes to show what an ingénue I was. Mama gave
me a nervous glance, hoping I wouldn't have the heart to insist,
and said, "I don't think it makes any sense to get in — we won't
even be close when they run out of boots." I quickly agreed and
we slipped out. Even if it hadn't been hopeless, I doubt that all
the self-consciousness of a mousy fifteen-year-old could have
made me go through *that*.

All in all, my dumpy boots cast only a very light shadow over
my adolescence. I wouldn't have traded places with Olya Sukhova, who once washed a new pair of designer jeans to shrink
them, hung them out to dry for the night on her third-floor
balcony, and woke up to heartbreak the following morning:
someone had had the ingenuity and the agility to swipe them,
apparently with the help of a long pole.

The reason Olya had a new pair of designer jeans to agonize
over was that she belonged to the select group of ultracool young
people in our school whose fathers were in the diplomatic profession. She had actually been to Austria, though only for a short
time; the aforementioned Alla Makarova had spent three years in
New Zealand with her parents. They were the rare birds who
had boyfriends. The secret of their popularity was probably less
in their looks (Olya, a well-groomed, languid blonde with a
round, bland, milky-white face, wasn't even that pretty) than in

the reflected glory of foreign lands, blue jeans, sparkling boots, and tanned sheepskin coats known as *dublyonkas*.

They were, in a word, hip — a word preserved nearly intact in the modish Russian youth slang as *hippovy* (which also came to mean simply "swell" or "cool"). There was also the word *hippar* (pronounced "hip-PAR"), which could mean either "hippie" — a species that I later was astonished to learn existed somewhere on the outskirts of Soviet society but definitely beyond my reach — or something much more akin to "hipster," a far more familiar figure. Of course, using slang made up mostly of such butchered American words was in itself a hallmark of being hip.

For a portrait of a (male) hipster, one has only to look at the photo of our class taken after our secondary school graduation at the end of ninth grade. There, on the extreme left in the second row from the top, stands Alyosha Vasilyev: chic bell-bottom pants, longish hair, coat flying open, hands in pockets, mean scowl. To be a hipster was to wear the coveted blue jeans with designer labels, to carry on with a slight swagger and a studied hint of boorishness, and to chew gum, prominently displaying the wrappers with magical-sounding American names like Wrigley's, and listen to Western music. Alyosha even boasted among his possessions a portable cassette player, an object of intense envy.

Being hip also meant braving battles with teachers and school administrators, who did not cotton to fashion-conscious behavior among their flock. The relentlessness of a Gennady Nikolaye-vich, who sheared the longish hair of Petya Mogilevsky with his own hands, was not often matched, but my mother recalls that when one of her music students let his hair grow a bit longer than decorum dictated, quite a few fellow teachers remonstrated with her for being so lax. One suggested that she arm herself with scissors and nip off a strand of his hair, leaving him no choice but to cut the rest to the same length.

On another occasion, Mama was waylaid by a colleague who accusingly told her that a tenth-grade student of hers wore a tinge of eye shadow. "But if she does, it's so slight you almost can't see it," Mama said. "How can I reprimand her for wearing makeup if I'm not sure she does?" The woman was very helpful. "Well, I'll tell you what you can do. Sprinkle some water on a handkerchief and tell her to rub her eyelids with it. Then you'll know for sure. That's what I do with *my* girls."

Our assistant principal, Vera Nikolayevna, a woman with a rodent's face and a rotund figure always enclosed in the same blue suit, constantly combed the hallways and raided the bathrooms on the lookout for transgressors. The bathrooms were where the older girls — beginning in seventh or eighth grade — went to put on lipstick and eye shadow, or even earrings, undeterred by the raids and the summonses to the principal's office. (I never dared — or wanted, for that matter — anything more than a dab of Mama's powder on my cheeks.) By the middle of ninth grade, the girls also began to flout the uniform code. Many of the teachers more or less looked the other way; almost anything brown, even dark purple or dark blue, could pass for the required dress, and forget the white cuffs and collars. These dresses could not by any stretch of the imagination be called modish, but at least they were a relief from monotony. I stretched the authorities' tolerance a bit too far by showing up in a checkered brown-and-green skirt (Vera Nikolayevna: "You consider *this* a uniform?"). I ought to add that this is another instance where I think we could use a happy medium between Soviet and American ways, and find a balance between the ferocity of teachers seeking out scarcely visible makeup on students' eyelids and the spectacle of twelve-year-old schoolgirls more concerned with looking like fashion models than with their studies.

In ninth grade, quite suddenly, I became friends with the hip Alla Makarova, after we walked home together a few times. A bit on the plump side but athletic, with short reddish-brown hair and a glowing, winsome face, Alla was bubbly and dynamic and snappily dressed. She won me over by fretting that she was *soooo* fed up with girls talking about nothing but boys and rags, and by her penchant for politically risqué chatter and humor, which was especially disarming in view of the fact that her own papa was entrusted with the mission of representing our socialist fatherland in various citadels of imperialism and was undoubtedly a Party member. *Oh good*, I thought, *now we're going to have intellectual conversations.*

When we made a trip together to one of Moscow's two foreign-language bookstores and I discovered that my new friend was much more enthralled by *Vogue* than by the Penguin Classics, I shunted my disappointment into some remote corner of my mind. Our conversations often turned, you will recall, to men, and love, and sex. At a library with a large selection of foreign books where Alla and I went a few times, she once picked up a dog-eared copy of a Harlequin-type romance novel that had (God knows how) found its way there and coyly pointed out to me, not unlike unsophisticated Rita, the phrase "we made love" on a page. She also enjoyed my recitation of some of my favorite misty, melancholy poems by Alexander Blok. I would entertain her on our walks home from school with stories from the lives of famous Russian poets, drawn from a collection of biographical essays by the émigré poet Vladislav Khodasevich which I had read in a Western edition. Yes, it was a banned book, though not a terribly hazardous one; from the authorities' point of view, it would have been the literary equivalent of marijuana, if we consider Solzhenitsyn analogous to crack. Perhaps it wasn't very wise to let my tongue run away with me, but Alla didn't mind and didn't turn me in.

I cannot resist giving myself a light pat on the back for the utter lack of so-called feminine envy in my attachment to foxy, poised, popular Alla. She in turn deserves credit for treating me pretty much as an equal from the height of her social status and of her Levis- and sheepskin-clad elegance.

At least I did not have to worry about dating. I never had a single date in all my years of high school; but then, that wasn't at all unusual. This is probably one of the biggest differences between the Soviet and American teen subcultures: dating as a social institution just doesn't exist in Soviet high schools. Of course we girls had crushes on boys, but there was no ritual of going out for the evening with a member of the opposite sex (although boys and girls did go out together occasionally). In ninth and tenth grade (ages fifteen and sixteen) some of my classmates had steady boyfriends and girlfriends. They were mostly the same hip kids who wore foreign boots and tight jeans with American labels and sheepskin coats. Having a boyfriend or a girlfriend added to their sparkle and made them the envy of many less lucky souls. For a girl, to have a boyfriend a couple of years older was especially hip. But the dateless were not outcasts, since they were the majority, if not a particularly glamorous one. There was no pressure to date, no anxiety over finding a companion for Saturday night. I am rather inclined, in this instance, to chalk one up for Soviet ways — perhaps because I know in my heart of hearts that if dating had been a social custom in my high school, I would have been the one stuck without a date on Saturday nights.

Socializing, whether in single-sex or mixed company, was fraught with other difficulties, though. For one, we didn't have much money. For high school students to work was virtually unheard of. When Katya Vorontzova and Masha Lyakhovskaya took summer jobs as bakery salesgirls after ninth grade, everyone gaped at them in envious wonder — that was even rarer than having a boyfriend. There are probably many reasons. The service sector that employs millions of teenagers in the West as salespeople, waiters, and so on is kept to a bare minimum in the Soviet Union; to the extent that it exists at all, it is a highly lucrative source of shadow income and is therefore tightly controlled by a mafia that allocates profitable jobs on the basis of connections and bribes.

Whether as a psychological adaptation to this paucity of jobs for teenagers or independent of it, a sort of snobbery about work exists among both adolescents and parents, at least among the educated middle class — "What, me work?" "What, my children work?" There may be something in common here with the attitude of the traditional American male who sees his wife's employment as an affront to his manhood, which he equates with his ability to take care of his woman. It is the parents' pride and joy to provide their offspring with all the comforts of a carefree life. In summertime, the little darlings must be resting — out of town if at all possible, enjoying the trees and the fresh air, not slaving away at a job! I have spoken before of the somewhat disapproving bewilderment of Russian vacationers at the fact that the daughter of our Latvian landlady, home on a break from college, spent her few free days working like a mule around the house and the garden instead of sunning herself in a hammock.

Maybe it was, in the typical case, more of an adaptation after all, and not a reflection of deep-seated attitudes. I have heard that today, when some private and cooperative enterprise in the service sector is being tolerated, it has become much more common for young people to seek part-time work. The Soviet press has even begun to discuss the desirability of jobs for high school and college students as an alternative to idleness, boredom, and alcohol and drug abuse, and to deplore the present-day obstacles to such employment. And those same doting Russian Jewish parents who pamper their sons and daughters rarely have any scruples about their children bringing home a paycheck after the family has emigrated.

The allowances most of my classmates had were usually just enough for transportation and school lunches. To set aside some money for anything else, you had to either go hungry or steal service on a bus, trolley, or tram — although the latter wasn't much of a money saver, public transportation being very cheap. Five bus fares could buy you a cup of coffee and a roll. One of Mama's students decided to buy her father a birthday present — a quality fountain pen that was quite expensive by Soviet standards, perhaps about twelve rubles, or ten dollars — and had to skip lunch day after day to save up the money for it. (I remember the story well because the example of this devoted daughter was cited to me many times.)

Many kids in my class painstakingly saved whatever change they had left from their allowances or from trips to the bakery, using glass jars for piggy banks and adding to their savings lavish birthday gifts of ten or even twenty rubles. Even I got it into my head that I wanted to save money. Not that I needed it — my easygoing parents couldn't have been more liberal with cash —

but it was the thing to do, and besides, it would be *my* money. However, the novelty soon wore off, and so did the thrill.

Most of us got money from our parents for the movies (relatively cheap) and for modest treats like ice cream and bagels, sold at street stands. Going out to eat was something that even adults hardly ever did, except on special occasions. Restaurants and cafés that served a half-decent meal weren't something the average or even fairly affluent person could afford on a regular basis; besides, they were so scarce that no matter how seldom people dined out, they were always packed, with discouraging waiting lines at the doors. Looking for a snack one day in Leningrad, I wandered from monstrous lines to empty counters, and finally settled for three scoops of ice cream and a cup of coffee in a jam-packed ice cream parlor where the waiting took only ten minutes out of my life. I could count on the fingers of one hand all the times my parents and I ever ate out.

There were a few affordable places where teenagers could go — meat-pie parlors, *blinniye* or pancake parlors — but they too were mostly jam-packed, and you often had to eat standing up or crouched on a stool at the counter. Even buying a drink in the summer was problematic. One could get in line for a mug of dark, foamy *kvas*, a nonalcoholic malted drink dispensed from a barrel, which, my mother asserted, contained a generous helping of dead flies and worms at the bottom. But you couldn't always count on finding *kvas*, and the only option was a soda machine, Soviet style. This featured two varieties of soft drinks: plain seltzer water and a yellow fruit-flavored soda — orange, apple, or pear, all tasting exactly alike and smelling of hair spray. The soda was dispensed into a glass that successive customers took turns using, rinsing it over a rather puny jet of water.

Some supermarkets and some fruit and vegetable stores had a fruit-juices-and-drinks counter, with huge cone-shaped glass containers of usually watery apple, grape, or cherry juice. You still had to drink from collective glasses, and to gulp down your juice right there at the counter while quite a few people waited in line behind you, particularly in summertime. Mama, who cringed at the idea of sharing a perfunctorily rinsed glass with God knows how many and what kinds of people, couldn't talk me out of getting these drinks, especially a milk cocktail I still fondly remember, which was basically a milkshake with a touch of syrup. For some reason, stores in Zelenograd were the ones that most often offered delicious milk cocktails. In Moscow there were a couple of places where you could find the drink, but it was too foamy and thin, not thick and creamy like the ones in Zelenograd. They made shopping worthwhile, and I could gulp down as many as three on an especially gluttonous day.

When Rita and I got together, we would meet at her place or mine, go to the movies or the library together, or go for a stroll in Sokolniki Park. The park, no more than a fifteen-minute walk from my home, was a favorite teenage hangout. That was where the lucky few who had dates went with their boyfriends or girl-friends; that was where, on a fine spring day after completing eighth grade and learning that we had passed the important exams, a bunch of us, six or seven girls, went to celebrate and even to make a foray into the meat-pie parlor. Perhaps three times the size of Central Park in New York, Sokolniki Park had long pine alleys going off in all directions, and ponds and vast groves, and an amusement park with a Ferris wheel and a merry-go-round, and roller-coaster contraptions that I never had the guts to try. Sokolniki Park also had a stage for summer concerts and a dancing ground, and a few bagel and ice cream stands and a *shashlychnaya*, a shish-kebab café. In spring and summer, on Sundays and especially on holidays when the weather was fine, the park would turn festive and bright, with more ice cream and cold drinks and souvenirs, and sounds of the accordion bursting forth from clusters of revelers in their best finery. I suspect that these revels would seem drab and colorless to me now; knowing better is such a fun-spoiler.

Perhaps the day I anticipated the most eagerly every year was the Saturday after February 10, the day my school friends would come over for my birthday party. My friends' birthday parties (I got to attend four to six a year) came in a close second. I don't recall anyone ever giving a party for a party's sake, without a special occasion; but nearly everyone — with a few exceptions, one of whom was Rita — gave a birthday party. To be exact, your parents threw it for you, and you invited ten to fifteen people.

Mama and Grandma fussed and labored over the dinner, an only slightly scaled-down version of the customary sumptuous banquet of Russian hospitality: a plethora of hot and cold dishes, desserts, and juices, and (when we were mature ladies and gentlemen in our teens) a fruit drink ever so lightly and alluringly spiked with wine. And then the doorbell would start ringing and my guests would show up one by one, coming in from the frosty air, their cheeks glowing, cold, and fresh as we hugged and kissed with exclamations of greetings. The girls and boys would shove gifts into my hands for me to unwrap at once. Then we would sit around the table for the meal, just like the adults did at their parties, and talk, and play party games.

In a game known as "I went to a ball and ate sweets there too," you left the room while the others each made a statement about you. When everyone had chipped in, a designated spokesperson called you back into the room and rattled off the formula "I went to a ball and ate sweets there too, and here is the gossip I heard about you: that you are 'a slob.' " "Aha!" you would say. "I bet Gamaley said that." "Wrong . . . I also heard that you are 'the eighth wonder of the world' " — and so it went on until you got it right, and the "gossip" whose identity you uncovered was the next to leave the room. If all your guesses were wrong, out you went for a second round. The comments were mostly facetious, sometimes sincerely complimentary — and sometimes, perhaps, sincerely malicious.

My grandmother, always busy inventing some new twist on entertainment, came up with the idea of distributing little gifts to the guests — not just giving them out, but wrapping them up in paper and having my guests pick them out of a large sack. With an added twist of wit, she would sometimes hide the least desirable trifles and mock gifts (an eraser) in many elaborate layers of paper, to entrap the greedy, and make the best ones (an inexpensive but attractive little ring) look utterly nondescript on the outside. The gifts couldn't be wrapped in anything more elegant than newspaper (the only kind of gift wrap that was sometimes available, used in some department stores to wrap purchases, was rough brown paper with an ornamental print on it), but that detracted very little from the fun of it: the thrill of rummaging in the bag and knitting your brow as you made your choice; the suspense of peeling off the wraps — which you weren't allowed to do until all the prizes, three or four to a guest, had been picked — and the titters and spurts of mirth as you pulled out a much-chewed-on stub of pencil . . .

There was also the great Soviet national pastime for all ages: sitting around and swapping jokes. The humor ranged from politics to sex to vast subspecies like "crazy jokes": *This guy walks around dragging a shoe on a string and calling it Zhuchka* (the Russian equivalent of "Rover"). *So they lock him up in a booby hatch, and every time the doctor examines him, he keeps insisting it's a dog. Then one day the doctor asks him, "What's that you've got there?" and he says, "Oh, just an old shoe." The doctor says, "Oh good, now we can let you go." So the guy walks out into the street and turns around and says to the shoe, "Well, Zhuchka, we sure fooled them, didn't we!"*

Or else we would go on a binge of black-humor limericks, a less universal form of folklore but extremely popular with teenagers. These limericks, somewhat resembling the wicked verses of Edward Gorey, had a common thread running through them: children getting killed in the most horrendous ways imaginable, described in graphic and gross detail. Once I went with my parents for a picnic on the outskirts of Moscow with a student of Mama's and his mother; the feisty eleven-year-old took it into his head to regale us all with some of that lovely poetry, greatly relishing his genteel mother's dismay:

> The granddaughter due back from school any minute,
> Grandma heated some soup and put cyanide in it.
> Grandpa, however, worked faster than Grandma:
> He nailed the kid to the fence with a hammer.

Or:

A little girl found a grenade in the grass.
"Uncle, what is it?" she curiously asked.
"Pull at this pin," said Uncle, "right there."
. . . In the wind floats the ribbon that she wore in her hair.

It is curious to note that most often, the perpetrators of these very creative acts of violence against children were adult family members. Without getting too deeply psychological, one might well see these limericks as a bitterly sarcastic expression of youngsters' perception of themselves as victims of indifferent, callous, even outright sadistic grown-ups:

"Mommy, give me some candy," the little girl cried.
"Stick your hand in this socket," Mommy replied.
Over the charred bones rose the black smoke.
The dinner guests had a good laugh at the joke.

By eighth or ninth grade, my guests wanted more adult entertainment. For the last two birthdays I celebrated in Moscow, my fifteenth and then my sixteenth, our living room (my parents' bedroom in everyday life) was cleared for me and my guests to dance in. Natasha Gamaley, an acid-tongued little dynamo who year after year cornered me into inviting her to my parties and invited me to only one of hers, tried to bully me into asking some boys she liked; I didn't have enough boys, she said. Being bullied into inviting her was bad enough, but faced with the prospect of having her dictate my guest list, I at last reared up and said no. "Well," Natasha said with a sniff, "all the worse for you. It's you and your Ritochka Kuznetzova who are going to be stuck without boys and sit there while the others dance, because no one's going to ask you." One had to be a consummate doormat to not withdraw the invitation to the party — which, apparently, I was. Unfortunately, I don't remember how the dancing turned out and who, if anyone, got stuck without a boy.

And my guests wanted music. Records by the Swedish band Abba and other Western rock groups, whatever people could get their hands on, were standard fare at hipper birthday parties than mine. At the party for my sixteenth birthday, a long and on the whole disappointing search of my parents' record cabinet eventually yielded a Soviet-released record of some of the Beatles' tunes (without words) under the title "Dancing On and On."

In addition to Western rock, we had homegrown pop-music idols, from the traditional and officially sanctioned ones who crooned corny tunes about love (of the highly moral sort, to be sure), motherhood, and of course patriotism, to daring, semi-underground rock groups. I probably got my most extensive exposure to Soviet pop music by living next to the Pioneer camp in summer, unless you count an eight-hour train ride from Moscow to Leningrad during which a group of kids entertained themselves by loudly and raucously recycling a repertoire of five or six popular songs. The hottest song of the moment was Alla Pugachova's "The Magician," a humorous complaint of an incompetent sorcerer. I must have heard that one at least four times on the train ride to Leningrad, and then again performed by my cousin Alyona, an ardent Pugachova fan.

The lot of an avid fan of a celebrity in the Soviet Union is not an easy one — no *People* magazine, no posters, no late-night talk shows. Nevertheless, Alyona had an entire corner in her room covered with large, small, color, and black-and-white photos of the flamboyant singer. A slightly toned down version of Madonna, Pugachova was at the peak of her popularity. Adored by young people, she hovered in a sort of limbo between official tolerance or even approval and disfavor. Her very un-Soviet, let-it-all-hang-out style and image, onstage and off, obviously held a great appeal for the young. What she offered was neither gung-ho patriotic stuff nor mushy love songs imbued with all the conventional virtues, but songs with sassy lyrics such as these:

> Kings can do anything,
> Kings can do anything,
> The fates of millions they
> May rule from high above;
> But whatever you say,

No king ever may,
No king ever may marry for love!

By Soviet notions, Pugachova lived a life of dazzling, unthinkable luxury. At the same time, the establishment press aimed a volley at her once in a while. She was cited, sometimes as a nameless "popular female singer," as an example of a decline in tastes and manners, and taken to task for lack of restraint in her singing as well as her behavior. Everybody knew that when the very influential *Literaturnaya Gazeta* took such jabs at someone famous, it wasn't just one writer's or even just one editorial board's peeve but a signal "from above." (Perhaps, this once, they had a point.)

I saw Pugachova a couple of times on television, decked out in garish spangled gowns, bantering with other guests, swaggering about as she sang. She adorned such infrequent TV gala events as the much-loved annual New Year's Night program *Goluboy Ogonyok* ("The Little Blue Light"), which featured stars of Soviet pop culture — actors, musicians, standup comics (and such obligatory elevating fare as appearances by especially distinguished though inarticulate welders or tractor drivers, or a "heroine mother," the official title bestowed on mothers of ten).

With both my peers and my parents, I shared one musical passion: Vladimir Vysotsky. It was to his song "The Horses" that Mikhail Baryshnikov danced so dramatically in the film *White Nights.* A stage and film actor as well as a bard (a word that in modern Russian parlance means someone who writes songs — music, lyrics, and all — and sings them himself, strumming along on a guitar), he had a cult following comparable to John Lennon's, and died only a month before Lennon, of a heart attack. Few of his songs, except for some relatively harmless ones about love, were ever performed or recorded openly. He gave private concerts where tapes were made. These were sometimes abysmal in sound quality; Vysotsky had a hoarse, throaty voice, and with the background noises you really had to strain your ears to make out anything at all. And the lyrics in Vysotsky's songs were very important.

In contrast to those Russian pop idols who defied the establishment by imitating their Western counterparts, everything about Vysotsky was frankly Russian. The protagonists of his songs and ballads were mostly common folk — factory workers, drunks, soldiers, even bums and thieves. His style combined an aggressive toughness with heartbreaking warmth and emotion. The spirit of his songs ranged from rage and anguish ("Nothing is right, boys, nothing is right!" goes the refrain of one) to bitter, tortured satire (a devastating picture of the drunkenness, violence, and degradation of rural life in "A Village Wedding") to a good-natured but on occasion politically risqué humor. The typical hero of Vysotsky's "serious" songs is ferociously independent, daring and reckless, brash and desperate, a striver, often a loser but a loser who affirms his freedom and dignity in the face of defeat and even death. This hero might be an outlaw, a tightrope walker, even an anthropomorphized animal: a hunted wolf turning on his pursuers, a racehorse rebelling against the jockey.

I suppose the boys and girls of my age to whom the raspy tapes of Vysotsky songs were not only chic but genuinely beloved missed out on much of the tragic side, the searing pain and the yearning for faith, understood by the adults. Teenagers were excited by the defiance and moved by the rough tenderness (Rita never referred to Vysotsky except by the affectionate diminutive "Volodenka"), and they laughed at the comical misadventures of drunks and bums, often seeing only a side-splitting joke where Vysotsky meant an angry reflection on the miseries and follies of Soviet life. I too used to think "A Village Wedding" was only a barrel of laughs, until I heard my father call the song "nightmarish" and saw how true that was:

> And in the midst of all this revelry
> I whispered something in the bridegroom's ear,
> And he was gone at once without a trace:
> There's now the bride upstairs, all sniffs 'n' tears.

. . . And then at last they caught the groom
And beat him long and hard;
And then they danced around all night,
And with no malice had a fight,
And snuffed out every spark of light
Still left within their hearts.

At parents' meetings, my mother (or Grandma, when she was
the one to go) heard both parents and teachers complain time and
time again that the kids were spending far too much time in front
of the TV. I have no statistics at hand to compare the viewing
habits of Soviet and American teenagers, so I cannot tell whether
their notion of "too much" would have seemed that way to a
concerned American adult. I do know that some parents would
roll their eyes and lament, "What am I supposed to do? From the
moment she comes home from school, the television's on all
day!" I can only wonder what those kids were watching — doc-
umentaries on the production of steel, interviews with model
workers, reports on the achievements of Soviet agriculture?
(They say Soviet TV has gotten somewhat more interesting,
with some bold investigative reporting and more youth-oriented
programming, but I can only talk about Soviet TV the way it
was in the 1970s.) With just four channels, one of them educational and another a sports channel, there wasn't much opportunity for channel-hopping, and entertainment programming,
although available, certainly wasn't enough to fill up major portions of the day. Moscow TV usually went off the air around
midnight; sometimes a late-night film, teleplay, or special went
on longer, and I had a few bitter arguments with the grown-ups
about staying up for these.

If only because of the dearth of popular entertainment, it is
probably true that Soviet teenagers read more and better books
than their American counterparts do. Some girls in my class
(including Rita) who read Dickens quite possibly would have
been reading Harlequin romances if they had been born in
American families of a similar social and cultural background.

The important question is whether these girls got much more out of Dickens, intellectually speaking, than they would have gotten out of the romances. I have often wondered about that.

Probably the most popular writer among Russian teenagers is Alexandre Dumas, the nineteenth-century French author of *The Three Musketeers* and *The Count of Monte Cristo*. For some reason I didn't get around to reading *The Three Musketeers* until I was about fifteen, a fact I tried my best to conceal so as not to be "out of it." When another girl casually referred to a scene from the novel, I hastily pretended to recognize it. In my social milieu, D'Artagnan, Atos, Portos, Aramis, and the wicked Milady Winter were veritable cultural icons. Several foreign film versions of *The Three Musketeers* played in the Soviet Union, and in 1979 Soviet TV came out with a miniseries, starring the tall, dark, and handsome Mikhail Boyarsky (Rita adored him and detested all his female co-stars). The miniseries wasn't very good, but for months afterward everyone, including me, kept humming its theme song.

TV miniseries were extremely popular. They tended to be quite lengthy; the record was probably set by *The Road to Calvary*, based on the novel by Alexei Tolstoy, which had, I think, twenty-seven episodes. It was a story of an educated middle-class Russian family — two sisters and their husbands — coping with the Bolshevik Revolution, which one of the couples eagerly embraces at once and the other comes to accept after many trials and tribulations. The miniseries often got unbearably slow and tedious (a character would brood for two minutes, with mood music in the background), and viewers grumbled — but with nothing more exciting to watch, most people stayed glued to it anyway.

There was also the twenty-two-part miniseries *Seventeen Moments of Spring*, based on the real-life story of a Soviet agent who infiltrated the Third Reich and became an SS colonel. This one, too, suffered from incredibly boring stretches, but it had gripping sequences of action and suspense, and some very good acting. It also broke ground by portraying the Nazis as more than cardboard morons or devils — they were sometimes very smart and even personable. The series was such a hit that it was rebroadcast twice in the same year, and each time my classmates breathlessly followed the twists and turns of the plot. During the breaks between classes they animatedly went over the details of last night's episode, the boys often re-enacting a scene in which the hero comes up behind one of the bad guys and knocks him out with an empty bottle.

And so the Video Age took its toll. My upstairs neighbor Tanya, who was always pestering me to do her German homework — although my German was, to put it mildly, limited — once brought me yet another piece of writing to translate. Her assignment had been to write about a favorite book, and Tanya had chosen *The Shadows Fade Away at Noon*, a Russian civil war novel that had been made into a TV movie. The essay contained a puzzling sentence: "I really admired the actors who fought for Soviet power." I went upstairs and asked Tanya what she meant by "actors." "Well," she fumbled, "what do you call them? You know, the people who appear in the book?"

Entertainment, official style, did not amount to much. There was little organized recreation at school (and no scholastic sports except for gym). Occasionally our school sponsored trips to the theater, offering tickets at a discount — mostly to the Young Spectator's Theater, with fare geared to the authorities' idea of what children and teenagers should see. I bought these tickets a few times, once for what turned out to be a highly revisionist version of *Snow White and the Seven Dwarfs*. The prince was made out to be a rather droll sort of people's prince who has led an uprising against the wicked queen, has been captured, and is secretly kept in chains in a dungeon. If I remember correctly (although my memory of this remarkable play is somewhat hazy), the queen decides to have Snow White liquidated not only out of feminine rivalry but because Snow White accidentally discovers that the prince is incarcerated in the dungeon and falls in love with him. From then on, the story sticks to the original tale, with a modified ending. The prince breaks out of his prison, a kiss liberates Snow White from her deathlike stupor, and together they lead a revolution. The queen is overthrown; Snow

White, the prince, and of course the people live happily ever after.

If innocent Snow White could be turned into a revolutionary, what is there to say of plays like *The Aristocrats*, another show to which we were offered tickets at school? This one glorified the salutary effect of socially useful work on criminals at the construction of the Belomor Canal, which was built in the 1930s entirely by convicts, mostly political prisoners, tens of thousands of whom starved or were worked to death.

Most of the theater tickets were quite worthless to me, which was too bad for a slightly stage-struck adolescent. At fourteen or fifteen, I even gave little one-person performances at home, with my father as my only audience and with a sofa as my stage. I remember sighing enviously as I read in some American or British book about high school productions of plays. Once in all my years of school — I was in eighth grade then — some tenth-graders, under the direction of the eccentric teacher Cheburashkin, staged Shakespeare's *Much Ado About Nothing*, in English, with rather minimal sets but a good approximation of period costumes, in an abridged version of less than an hour's duration. When it got to the moment in the last scene when Benedick says to Beatrice, "Peace! I will stop thy mouth" and kisses her, I was waiting breathlessly to see if a boy was really going to kiss a girl on the lips on stage in our school. But nothing so scandalous was allowed to happen. Benedick spoke his line and advanced toward the comely Beatrice, at which time the duke stepped in between them, exclaiming in jocular dismay, "What! In public?"

Once, during my stint as member of the council of the *druzhina*, I got a chance to go to one of Moscow's several Pioneer Palaces, centers that offer various extracurricular activities shared, according to official Soviet mythology, by millions of Pioneers. My fellow council members and I were chaperoned by Lyuda-the-Pioneer-master. There were some inspirational ideological remarks for an introduction, then a sing-along (though, to be fair, we sang mostly popular songs with few ideological overtones and with lyrics like "A river is born from a blue little brook / And a friendship is born from a smile"). Then the gathering was broken up into three groups, each of which was given twenty minutes to improvise a miniplay on the basis of several words, like "merchant, trip, shipwreck, desert island, miracle." My part in that skit — which we ingeniously ended with the words "And then a *miracle* happened" — was to hold an umbrella over the Queen of the Sea, whose handmaiden I humbly represented. Another group, given words that included "princess, kidnap, bandits, rescue, knight" (not the kind of subject matter one would expect at a Communist youth center program), decided to spice up the skit by having a guy in very tame drag — a shawl draped over his shoulders — play the princess. It broke up the audience, but it seems that the adults in charge were not amused. A steely-voiced Lyuda, her lips tight with displeasure, admonished the kids who came up with the idea not to let their imaginations run *too* wild.

Before New Year's or some other major holiday (usually no more than once a year), students put on a variety show in the performance hall. Many of the numbers were to some degree ideological or political in content. For the thirtieth anniversary of the victory over Nazi Germany, we had a student concert devoted entirely to World War II songs, and one group prepared a striking rendition of the well-known Soviet song commemorating Nazi victims, "The Bells of Buchenwald." The choir sang before a huge charcoal drawing of a mother holding a baby behind barbed wire, and two of the singers lifted on their shoulders an earnest-looking small girl in a flimsy white dress, three stems of red carnations clutched in her little hands.

There were some apolitical songs and poems as well; some classical music in very amateurish performances by children who took music lessons; some dancing in ethnic costumes; and even comedy skits. From what Mama told me, the school where she taught had much livelier student variety shows, with skits lampooning the personal quirks of recognizable teachers. Whether because of a more restrictive atmosphere or because we had less creative minds, my schoolmates' comic imagination never went further than a mildly amusing skit about a boy floundering in a history class. "What did the Nazi invaders leave in their wake?" asks the teacher, expecting to hear something like "charred ruins and thousands of victims," and the boy stammers, "Well, I guess empty cans and beer bottles and other trash." The student audience laughed and clapped, but our history teacher, the austere Henrietta Sergeyevna, looked most somber. ("She was so upset," I heard some girls saying during the intermission. "The sacred memory of the war made into a joke . . .")

And we had school dances, with music that was up-to-the-minute modern, official disapproval of rock notwithstanding. Not only were rock records played, but our school had a student rock band. The dances were given once or twice a year — just before the end of the school year, sort of like a prom night, and sometimes before New Year's Eve — in the performance hall or the gym. These events were restricted to eighth-, ninth-, and tenth-graders; the price of admission nearly always was a mandatory brainwashing session before the dancing could start, including speeches on international affairs, reports on the heroic labor of the Komsomol, patriotic songs and poetry. Our formidable cloakroom attendant, Nadezhda Konstantinovna, a huge, heavyset female in her sixties, sat at the front desk like Cerberus to see that no freeloader sneaked in for the dance without having attended the meeting first — probably one of the *very* few times she had to be on guard against people trying to sneak *into* the school.

There were no snacks or drinks of any kind, but the dimmed lights in the dance hall flickered mysteriously, and the music made the floors, walls, and windows of the building vibrate slightly. As my schoolmates stomped and whirled around the dance floor, it would have been hard to tell them from their American counterparts, except for a more conservative dress style. Some of the girls wore jeans; others came in flowered skirts or fifties-style (*American* fifties, that is) dresses. No bare shoulders, of course, and no low-cut blouses; but at least on these occasions we could wear makeup without fear.

I joined in the stomping and whirling around and probably did no worse than the rest, but I soon got exhausted and retreated to the sidelines. When the music was slow, couples danced together, swaying gently, most of them holding each other quite chastely by modern standards, the girl's hands resting lightly on the boy's shoulders and the boy's hands on the girl's waist. (I was among the wallflowers, though I believe a boy asked me to dance at least once. And then there was the giddy moment of dancing with Mark Kozlovsky, on whom I had a crush: I worked up the nerve to ask him for the "White Waltz," an opportunity for the girls to take the initiative.) A few boys and girls dared to imitate the couples they had seen dancing in Western movies, locked tightly in each other's arms. The more timid dancers looked at this decidedly non-Soviet decadence with a mixture of excited admiration, envy, and shock.

Even at parties for the senior classes, many girls danced with each other; interestingly, it wasn't considered shocking for boys to dance with each other either. Not because taboos against anything that could smack of homosexuality were less severe than they are in America — quite the contrary. Homoeroticism was so far beyond the pale of the thinkable that it would never have occurred to anyone, teachers or teenagers, that dancing with a person of the same sex could have such connotations.

I don't think I ever missed a school dance, since I hoped every time that I was finally going to have *real* fun and wantonly abandon myself to the excitement of mindless pleasure; but somehow the fun remained elusive, and I never quite managed to turn myself into a social animal. My head and ears would ache from all that ultrahip music, and I didn't see any point in having a party where you couldn't talk because you couldn't hear a word. By the time of the next dance, though, I somehow had forgotten the lesson I should have learned and would go back looking for fun.

I must admit I was an intellectual snob. I was sincerely convinced that the greatest disaster that could befall one in life was being nonintellectual, and I even toyed with my own modest proposal for social improvement: all people who did not read books and had no interest in culture were to be stripped of their parental rights, and their children were to be raised in institutions where love of books and knowledge would presumably be inculcated in them. And I believed, deep or perhaps not so deep down, that the poems I scribbled, the number of books I read, my command of English, the fact that Lydia Davydovna so often read my essays as a model for the rest of the literature class, made me a superior person.

At the same time, I thought — or should I say I *knew* — that I was something of a nerd. I felt left out of the things that interested most of my peers, and much as I believed that those things were silly and unimportant, I still had periodic urges to fit in and do the "in" things, such as saving money in a piggy bank. When the whole class was reliving a TV movie the next day during recess, I would pretend to have watched it. I would listen to discussions of one of the biggest pop events in the Soviet Union, the annual singing competition held in Sopot, a town in Poland, with Soviet and Eastern-bloc singers participating. Then, the summer I was fifteen, I went to Rita's dacha for a few days and we stayed up late one night watching the competition on TV. (Rita, lucky girl, had a small TV at her dacha.) Most of the singing, to my mind, was nothing much — I vaguely remember a woman doing a rendition of "I Could Have Danced All Night" from *My Fair Lady* in a Russian translation — but I felt the thrill of partaking of something that bound my peer group together, a kind of community spirit. When I came home, I proudly announced to my parents that I had seen the Sopot competition. My parents said, "Why do you want to waste your time watching such garbage?"

A couple of years earlier, I had tried my hand at keeping an album, which was quite a fad among girls. (Boys, as far as I know, did not do such things.) Rita had one, and so did my neighbors Raya and Tanya, the ones who went to mass schools and were always after me to do their homework. An album, also known as a songbook (*pesennik*, from *pesnya*, "song"), was a thick notebook into which a girl would copy the lyrics of her favorite songs and paste glamorous pictures: photographs of movie stars, stills from movies, and cutouts from fashion magazines, none of which are easy to come by in the Soviet Union.

On a rare lucky day, Mama would manage to snag an issue of a Polish beauty magazine at a nearby foreign-press newsstand, which carried some Eastern European periodicals and several newspapers of the more pro-Soviet Western Communist parties, like the American *Daily World*, the British *Morning Star*, and the French *Humanité*. Raya, then about fifteen, once begged to borrow a few copies of the magazine and returned them a couple of weeks later in a dismal state, with a lot of the pictures cut out. She had used the pictures, she explained with a shrug of innocence when questioned, to paste into her songbook.

That must have been what gave me the idea of starting a songbook of my own. I borrowed Raya's to copy song lyrics and dug up a few pictures to paste into my would-be album — with no help from Mama, who didn't think too much of my new endeavor and would not let any more of her fashion magazines be mutilated. And then . . . most of the lyrics turned out to be so schmaltzy and primitive that for all my eagerness to fit in, I couldn't bring myself to waste my time copying them. Two pages into my songbook, I succumbed to the temptation of writing some verses by Pushkin in it. Four pages into my songbook, I was bored with the whole idea.

In ninth grade, I unexpectedly came into possession of a hot property: a recording of *Jesus Christ Superstar*, not a tape or even a cassette but a real *album*, borrowed by my parents from a friend who had brought it back from a trip abroad. We kept it, or rather, *I* kept it, for about two months. Music by Abba and the other Western rock bands my classmates liked left me cold, but I instantly fell for *Jesus Christ Superstar* and listened to it over and over again, until I'm sure my parents were sorry they had ever gotten it. What a social success I could have been in my class, at least for the little while that I had the album! But instead of marketing my resources properly, I invited only Rita and one other girl to listen — and then I played it myself until I knew all the lyrics by heart and walked around all day humming "I Don't Know How to Love Him" and "Everything's Alright Yes" and other tunes. I suppose I just didn't know how to be cool.

11

Who Controls the Past . . .

Two or three days every week between the ages of sixteen and seventeen, I knowingly and unrepentantly committed an illegal act: fraudulent presence in a library.

About a year earlier I had read, in some inspirational book for teenagers on the importance of good manners and culture, about the Lenin Library, where you could locate virtually any book you wanted, provided it wasn't banned (this wasn't mentioned, but it went without saying). My two hobbyhorses then were the life of Lord Byron and the history of the French Revolution, and I yearned to get my hands on all those French and English and American books listed in bibliographies at the end of the Russian-language volumes I managed to find on these subjects. Every time I passed the Lenin Library, I would eye with longing its ornate columns and sculptures and latticework. I was most aggrieved to discover that only college graduates were allowed access to the colossal blue-and-white building. Yet hope rose from the ashes: the Foreign Languages Library, also remarkably well stocked, was open to anyone over sixteen.

A few days after my sixteenth birthday, I headed directly to it. With my newly issued passport, a certificate of coming-of-age, I marched peppily to the registration desk. A few more minutes, and Byron's diaries, complete and unabridged, would all be mine . . . Michelet's history of the French Revolution . . . biographies of the Girondists and of Charlotte Corday . . .

The blank-faced woman clerk took one glance at my passport and said, "You have to be over *eighteen* to use the reference reading room." In that moment, my world crumbled. I may even have tried to plead with the desk clerk, but if I did, my pleas naturally fell on deaf ears (what other kind do desk clerks have?). There were no exceptions to the policy. Those under eighteen could use the borrowing section, but a look at its shelves did not revive my flagging spirits. Even the foreign-language section of our local Youth Library offered a more alluring selection.

It occurred to Mama as she tried to soothe my distress that her former student Nadya Kozhevnikova looked quite a bit like me, only her face was thinner. Surely they couldn't tell the difference on a card-sized photo ID. Nadya, by then at least twenty, obligingly went to the library with her passport and the tiny photo for the library card, got the card, and turned it over to me.

At first I would break out in a cold sweat every time I showed the registration card at the front desk before going upstairs, and double-check every request slip to make sure I had signed it Kozhevnikova and not Jung. Eventually, though, my second signature became second nature to me (in fact, I had to watch myself to make sure I didn't sign my school journal Kozhevnikova), and I took in the fact that the desk clerk in the lobby wasn't going to study the picture on the ID card carefully to make sure it was me.

These trips to the library actually spanned a rather short period of my life — from the spring of 1979 to January 1980, when we received permission to emigrate. But they were the most cherished part of my daily life, and make up a disproportionate share of my teenage memories. Even in the summer months, when we lived in Kryukovo, I took the train to dusty, sweltering Moscow at least once a week. I reverently touched the eighteenth- and nineteenth-century volumes: golden lettering on the spines, papyrus-shielded engravings, the one-of-a-kind, intoxicating, pungent smell of the crisp yellowing paper. The library had no photocopiers; I had no idea that there existed on this earth a machine that could instantly reproduce a page. So I went armed with thick notebook and two pens, just in case one should run out of ink.

I would get my books, sit down at a desk, and patiently, painstakingly copy whole passages, summarize, make notes. I would lose track of time, only occasionally glancing out the windows at the fading and then darkening sky. I could hunch over my notebooks for hours without eating, until I got dizzy and my hands started trembling with hunger. I took a sort of pride in my fortitude: what pains I stoically endured in the pursuit of Knowledge! What I didn't know for quite a while was that the library had a cafeteria on the premises. I wandered into it one day by sheer chance, probably while heading for the women's room, and realized that my martyrdom could have been so easily avoided.

My first introduction to the French Revolution, at the age of five or six, had come from my grandmother, and in a rather quirky form, too. I had been complaining about a girl in the back yard of our building who had been bullying all the other children. Bullies, Grandma told me, can intimidate everyone until just one person stands up to them, and then all the others, emboldened by the example, rise up and follow suit — a truism she decided to illustrate by this excursion into history: "At one time in France, they had this ruler named Robespierre, and he was always saying, 'Cut off this one's head' and 'Cut off that one's head,' and all his enemies were sent to the guillotine. And no one ever dared contradict him. And then one day, someone at a council of the government spoke up and said, 'Off with Robespierre's head!' And everyone else shouted, 'That's right, down with Robespierre!' and Robespierre was overthrown and guillotined."

I had no idea whether it all had happened fifty years ago or a thousand years ago — I didn't know that there had been any other revolution in history besides that of 1917 — but the story of Robespierre's downfall in Grandma's fanciful if simplified rendition left a lasting impression on me. I must have heard it from Grandma a few more times, probably at my request ("Remember the story you told me about this guy Robespierre who ruled

France and was cutting everybody's heads off?"). And then one day, in third or fourth grade, I was talking to Grandma about some story in our Russian reader and I said, "You know, it's just like what you told me about Robespierre, how everyone was scared of him and then just one man said, 'Off with Robespierre's head' and he was overthrown." To which Grandma remarked, "By the way, better not tell that story about Robespierre in school. Officially, he's considered a good guy." A good guy? For all my budding political awareness, I was nonplussed. I also made a note of the fact that truth about Robespierre was one of those things I wasn't supposed to bring up at school.

Later, in my library days, the human drama of the French Revolution and its larger-than-life characters — the sinister Robespierre, the boisterous sensualist Danton, the tender-hearted, vulnerable Camille Desmoulins and his poor Lucile, the martyred assassin Charlotte Corday, the nobly intellectual Girondists who died so stoically and the easygoing aristocrats who died so casually — crystallized itself into two issues, really two sides of one issue: the destruction of freedom in freedom's name, and the human capacity for cruelty.

I obsessively mulled this over as I walked to school or was jostled on the metro or shuffled my feet in a line at the Sokolniki supermarket, and before going to bed at night, I scribbled my reflections in a diary. Images of the September massacres of 1792 exerted a morbid fascination over me. I thought of the Parisian mobs storming the prisons and slaughtering the suspected counterrevolutionaries, the bloody affair eventually turning into a spectator sport, the infamous tumbrels taking self-possessed or pensive or dazed or hysterical victims to meet their fate as Parisians cheered or looked on indifferently.

I began to draw some conclusions. For one thing, in the standard Soviet interpretation of history, anyone who called for mercy and compassion, anyone who thought it was wrong for a revolutionary government to kill real or suspected political enemies, was automatically tagged as a reactionary defending the interests of the haute bourgeoisie. At best, such faint-hearted attitudes (if shown by people officially counted among the good guys, like Victor Hugo) constituted the sin of "abstract human-ism." Abstract humanism meant believing it was wrong to kill innocent people regardless of the sociopolitical situation and the dynamics of class. The right kind of humanism, *revolutionary* humanism (which reached its pinnacle in *proletarian* humanism), recognized that killing people whose continued existence might be bad for the revolution was a necessity, if a painful or mildly unpleasant one at times.

It was duly pointed out that Robespierre and the Jacobins were not and had never been Communists, no matter how much they railed against wealth and the wealthy. Such analogies, Soviet authors cautioned, were unscientific and lacking in a true and rigorous class-based perspective; the Jacobins were really spokes-men for the petty bourgeoisie and staunch defenders of private property. Still, you didn't need prodigious powers of perception for the unscientific analogies to leap out at you. People arrested for an ill-considered remark that was interpreted as counterrevo-lutionary, for having been too friendly with a disgraced and executed political leader, for a reckless joke, or simply for being unable to prove their reliability; people living in daily uncer-tainty, in the shadow of the guillotine, as it were . . .

Our eighth-grade modern history textbook talked about the 1793–94 Reign of Terror in language barely distinguishable from that of the ninth-grade textbook's circumspect paragraph about Stalinism: of course it was necessary to defend the conquests of the revolution, but there were some excesses as well. In the case of the Reign of Terror, our textbook gave one example in three or four lines of small print: after an insurgency in Nantes, the revolutionary representative Carrier had people indiscriminately rounded up, bound hand and foot, and loaded onto barges, which were then sunk. The small print did not fail to mention the heartening fact that Carrier was eventually recalled by the revolutionary government in Paris.

Leafing through *The History of the Girondists* by Alphonse de Lamartine, a nineteenth-century exercise in romantic history writing, I came across the author's speculation that if Robes-pierre and his cohorts had remained in power, they would eventually have stopped the Terror and reverted to a more liberal fashion of ruling the country. That night I had this to jot down in my diary: "If such rose-colored theorizing still had a right to exist in the 1830s, no one could in good conscience think so after seeing the end result of a revolutionary reign of terror allowed to run its course unimpeded by a Thermidor."

I must have been seven or eight years old when my parents, sorting through some old stuff in a closet, came across a black-and-white portrait, which Papa showed to me, asking, "Do you know who this is?" I examined the broad face with short dark hair and a flashy mustache, then hesitantly said, "Is this my grandfather?" Papa doubled over. The man in the picture was Joseph Stalin.

I eventually learned the story behind that faded picture. When my mother was a schoolgirl with braids and a Pioneer tie, she once came home with a portrait of Stalin, fully intending to hang it up on the wall. Grandma, who was certainly no anti-Soviet at that time but simply had a gut revulsion against all kinds of hype, including the frenzied adoration of Stalin, rebelled. "You know, Marina," she said, "I just don't like the whole idea of hanging up portraits of leaders. When I was a child we never had a portrait of the czar in the house, and I'd rather not have a portrait of Stalin, either." "What!" sputtered my future mother. "Do you realize what you're saying? How dare you, how *can* you compare *Stalin* to the *czar!*" (She had a point.) Fortunately, Mama's zeal for the Great Leader and Teacher did not push her so far as to report her mother's unwholesome attitudes to the authorities at school, or Grandma would have spent years hauling logs in Siberia.

Grandma often recalled those days when she and I were at home alone and she spun her tales to entertain me. She told me how one of her neighbors, a man named Pasteur, was arrested on charges of stockpiling gold and weapons in his apartment. My guileless grandmother at the time heatedly insisted she would never believe such a thing about Pasteur — he was just a nice ordinary guy, what was all this baloney about stockpiling weapons? Political protest was the last thing on her mind. Pasteur's arrest just didn't make any sense to her, and she said what she thought. So little did she understand the nature of what was happening all around her that she had not an inkling of the trouble she could get into for coming to the man's defense.

It seems that she hardly ever consciously questioned official dogma; she just instinctively trusted her own common sense, and could not force herself to believe that two plus two equaled five. The flagrant discrepancy between what she saw with her own eyes and heard with her own ears and what the state was telling her she had seen and heard did not so much make her angry as simply puzzle her. "It's funny how they're saying that Stalin was Lenin's right hand," she would say to her daughter the Stalin worshipper. "When I was young, we always used to hear about Lenin and Trotsky, never about Lenin and Stalin." That comment alone would have been enough to get Grandma twenty-five years of hard labor for Trotskyite propaganda, if any good soul had been near enough to hear it and report it or if Mama had been stupid enough to repeat it at school. All Mama did, however, was shout, "How can you say that! How can you say it's not true when it's written right here in the history textbook!"

After Pasteur's arrest, his wife looked away silently whenever Grandma said hello on the stairs or in the lobby. Finally, one day my perplexed grandmother stopped the woman and with some embarrassment asked whether she was angry at her for something — why wasn't she talking to her? "Oh, you see," the wife stammered, "I thought maybe you were taking me for someone else, because none of the neighbors say hello to me anymore. . . ."

Few seemed to doubt that those arrested were in fact "enemies of the people," or "pests," as they were also dubbed. And yet my grandfather, a Party member with an emotional allegiance to the Soviet régime, which he felt had given him opportunities he had been denied under czarism because he was Jewish, said to

Grandma more than once, "If I am arrested, please do not believe I am an enemy of the people." Did he then know that innocent people were at least sometimes arrested and sent off to the labor camps of the now-infamous gulag? He did and he didn't, or at any rate he didn't blame the government — mistakes happened occasionally, that was all. In 1952, when the "Jewish doctors' plot" to kill important government officials was "uncovered" and the press was in a froth of frenetic denunciations of "Zionists" and "rootless cosmopolitans," Grandpa, like many others, said he felt ashamed of being a Jew.

When Stalin died in 1953, even Grandma worried, saying, "What's going to happen to us now that Stalin's gone?" Throngs of people in the grip of unfeigned sorrow stampeded to the funeral. A neighbor was all set to go with her five-year-old son and tried to get Grandma to join her; Grandma did her best to talk the woman out of going, and she was right. Because of some obscure precautions, many of the streets in Moscow were sealed off, and things got ugly; a number of people, mostly women and children, were trampled to death in the commotion.

When I was fifteen, I got a few peeks into a copy of *The Gulag Archipelago* that my father brought home. I also heard excerpts from Solzhenitsyn's work on foreign broadcasts. But it was one thing to read and hear stories about strangers, men and women who might as well have been Martians, dying or surviving in hellish labor camps; it was something else when Papa suddenly told me, in response to a question about the mass arrests and jailings, "Why, your grandmother Polina, for instance, spent seven years in a camp."

The information was hard to digest. Grandmother Polina in a camp! Pudgy, buoyant, loquacious Granny Polina, perhaps a bit gushy, supremely and serenely confident that she knew what was right for herself and for everyone else — in a camp! Dignified, matronly Granny Polina pushed around by guards, led from a prison cell to a freight car in manacles — good God! And yet, no matter how implausible it may have been, Granny Polina and my paternal grandfather, Moisey, had both spent seven years in the labor camps. It was somewhat ironic that unlike most of the people arrested at that time as "enemies of the people," they had actually committed the crime they were charged with: namely, trying to leave the Soviet Union. In 1946 they made plans to escape to what was soon to become Israel. Four years later they were prosecuted on charges of treason and each sentenced to twenty-five years of hard labor.

Papa, then fourteen, was left with an older sister and a ten-year-old brother. When relatives or friends of the family ran into him, they would cross over to the other side of the street to avoid being seen talking to a person who had been compromised. When my mother began to date my father (they were in the same class at school), Grandma's friends were appalled: was she insane, letting her daughter get involved with a guy whose parents were in jail as enemies of the people? Grandma, however, refused to interfere, as did Grandpa, and my parents got married in 1955. Stalin's death spelled freedom for my father's parents ("What a creep that Jung is," the girls at my parents' school said in pious horror. "Stalin is dead and everyone is so grief-stricken, and look at him walking around with a smirk on his face"), but it took four years for the amnesty process to get to them.

Hard as I tried to incorporate this knowledge into the image of Granny Polina as I knew her, it remained somewhere in the realm of the not-quite-real. She never spoke of her experiences in the camps, not to me, at least. The only thing I remember hearing from her on the topic was the pathetic story of a fellow prisoner, a peasant woman whose misfortunes started when her cow wandered into a neighbor's yard and wiped out his vegetable patch. She and the neighbor began to quarrel, the neighbor threatened to complain to the authorities, and the woman yelled, "To hell with your authorities!" The remark was reported "to the right place," as the saying goes in Russia to this very day, and that was enough.

I was hearing more and more such stories — perhaps because I wanted to hear them, and because my parents wanted me to hear them or at least didn't mind. There was Grandma's old friend Aunt Katya, a hulking, tough-talking woman stodgily loyal to the Soviet régime. An aunt of hers had been arrested and jailed after she was reported for playing a funeral march on the piano on the day Marshal Tukhachevsky, a notorious "enemy of the people" (now restored to his good name), was shot. It was a fact orthodox Aunt Katya didn't particularly like to talk about; she bristled when someone else brought it up.

I learned that one of my father's best friends at work was born behind barbed wire, in the maternity ward of a labor camp where his pregnant mother had been brought after the execution of his father. He spent the first two years of his life in the camp, then was moved to an orphanage. His mother emerged from her ten-year ordeal with her faith in the Soviet régime and in the shining Communist future unscathed — which, I found out, wasn't unusual.

For the most part, people were not overeager to air such episodes in their own or their families' past. My mother and a colleague of hers, Tonya Svetlova, were good friends for a while before Tonya told Mama that her father had served years in a labor camp. A few days after the German invasion of Russia, he was in the kitchen of their communal apartment catching every word of Stalin's radio address, and worriedly remarked, "Stalin sounds really sad." These heretical words were promptly reported "to the right place." Presumably, Stalin was supposed to sound merry and nonchalant in the days when Hitler's troops were victoriously marching across hundreds of miles of Soviet territory. I suspect that Tonya's father's fate might not have been all that different if he had remarked that Stalin sounded really merry.

Somehow the subject came up again and again — one evening, for instance, when my mother's close friend Lena was over. As we were having tea and jam at the kitchen table, Lena began to talk about the horribly tragic life of her beloved Aunt Dora, whose only son had just died in a mountain-climbing accident. It suddenly came out (Mama had known about this, but I had not) that not only Aunt Dora but also her sister had been imprisoned for many years. One day after her arrest, during questioning, Aunt Dora was standing between a table and a red-hot stove, and at one point the investigator moved the table forward a little, pushing her right against the stove, and held it there for about a minute. "Aunt Dora is the kindest, the gentlest person in the world," Lena said, "and yet she used to tell me that if they gave her a gun and offered her a chance to shoot that investigator right between the eyes, she would do it without the slightest hesitation."

And it came up again while I was riding in the car of Kamil Ikramov, the father of an awkward girl who took private piano lessons from my mother and the only member of the Soviet élite (though not of the highest order) that I ever got to know personally. Ikramov was a writer, and in addition to the car had a typewriter, a three-room apartment that bespoke affluence, a poodle, and a stay-at-home wife. A tall, broad-shouldered, and rather portly man, balding but with a magnificent black beard and a jovial look, he was taking us to his place for dinner. Somehow the conversation drifted to his youth, and it turned out that he hadn't always been so fortunate. His parents had been high-ranking Communist Party activists in the Central Asian republic of Uzbekistan in the 1930s. High-ranking Party activists were especially vulnerable in those times, and when Kamil was about twelve, both his father and his mother were arrested and, after a speedy trial, executed by firing squad. Kamil was taken to an orphanage. When he turned sixteen, he was apparently deemed mature enough to become an enemy of the people like his late parents, and so he was transferred to a labor camp for juveniles. The rations there were so meager that the boys tried to supplement them by scavenging in garbage heaps. As a result, scores of them died of food poisoning. What saved Kamil was his fastidiousness, a holdover from the childhood days of growing up in an élite family and being used to clean, high-quality food. He simply couldn't bring himself to eat off garbage heaps. Eventually he became so weak and emaciated from constant malnutrition that he began to have fainting spells and was taken to the camp hospital. There a doctor took pity on him and had him stay at the hospital as a nurse's aide.

After a while it began to seem that everyone had such a tale to tell, that I couldn't find a single person in whose family there had been no arrests, no jailings, no post-Stalin — and sometimes posthumous — "certificates of exoneration." Just how many people, how large a part of the population, had been affected by it all? I asked Mama how many of her high school classmates had had a father or mother in prison or camp. My mother shrugged and said she had no idea: "The kids didn't talk about it. I remember that there were some students whose fathers were missing; they told everyone that their fathers had been killed in the war, but it's quite probable that some of them were actually in labor camps. There was one girl I know for sure — there was a time when she always came to school looking like she'd been crying, but nobody knew what was going on, we just thought there must have been some trouble in her family. And then eventually we found out that her father had been arrested — he came back from the camps and was exonerated a few years later. But we didn't know anything about it at the time."

When I went to Papa for a similar rough estimate, he said, "Well, it might have been as many as a third." He had yet another story for me. In 1954 he and my mother were at a party; one of the guests, a fellow student named Agamirov, announced that he and his mother had just received a letter telling them that his *disparecido* father had been executed but was now cleared of all charges. Agamirov was understandably rather angry about this, and his anger began getting out of control after he had had a few drinks. He began to shout that he was going to go to the Kremlin (only a few blocks away) that very minute and tell all those murderers on the Central Committee just what he thought about them. After the other guests talked him out of this plan, all he could do to get even was grab a small plaster bust of Stalin that stood on his host's bookshelf and throw it against the wall, chipping off the tip of the Leader and Teacher's nose. Although Stalin had been resting in the mausoleum for about a year, the host was horrified. (An interesting side note is that the host's father was also doing time in a labor camp — and still the family kept a plaster bust of Stalin on a bookshelf. I wondered what they did with that bust later. Papa said, "I'm sure they just took it off the bookshelf very late one night and very, very quietly carried it to the dumpster in the back yard.")

And the official approach to all this? Well, here is an example. The year 1978 saw the appearance of a collection — a slim one but the first of its kind — of verse by Osip Mandelshtam, one of the quartet of poetic geniuses in postrevolutionary Russia. For the Soviet intelligentsia, the publication of this book in the Poet's Library series was an electrifying event, not only because of Mandelshtam's poetic greatness, not only because of the excitement of rediscovery; there was the added stimulant of his fate. Mandelshtam died in Siberia, probably in 1938, sentenced to labor camp for the indiscretion of writing and showing some friends a bitter poem satirizing Stalin.

The power and beauty of Mandelshtam's poetry aside, some of the truly remarkable and revealing things in this edition, handsomely bound in blue with gilt lettering like all the volumes in the series, were actually to be found in the foreword. Father read aloud, in a voice heavy with irony: "From 1928 on, his poems were either published sporadically or existed only in manuscripts. Because of this, the poet's further spiritual evolution remained unclear and unknown to the reader." There was this: "The poet found himself in difficult circumstances. After a short stay in Cherdyn-on-Kama, he took up residence in Voronezh." My parents, who years before had read the world-famous memoirs of the poet's widow, Nadezhda Mandelshtam (an illegal book, of course), knew what this meant; I did not. For my benefit, my father explained that Mandelshtam had been exiled to Voronezh.

Then came the real gem: "In the hardships of daily life, his spirits were often low; he succumbed to despair and experienced nervous depression. . . . In 1937, Mandelshtam's creative work came to a halt. The poet died in early 1938." My father seemed all the more enraged because the writer of this introduction was a Jew, one A. L. Dymschitz; loyal Soviet Jews, extracautious and groveling, made Father's blood boil. "Succumbed to despair! Nervous depression!" he jeered. "And for no reason! Just bad moods, that's all! And then he just stopped writing and just died!" Actually, the mendacious introduction was in all likelihood the only way that the wretched Dymschitz could ever have gotten Mandelshtam's poems published; one might say he sacrificed his integrity to bring Osip Mandelshtam to the Soviet reader at last, in a legal and legible edition.

When my mother was a high school girl, her textbooks were filled with panegyrics to Stalin, the Great Leader and Teacher, the Father of the Peoples, the Greatest Genius of All Times. Her college history textbooks a while later made a single mention of Stalin: in the chapter on the conference at Yalta, along with Franklin D. Roosevelt and Winston Churchill. Otherwise, students might think that for a quarter of a century the Soviet Union had had no head of government. Our ninth-grade history textbook strove for the middle ground, covering Stalin's existence along with the "personality cult" in less than a page of bland text. All those things that were done to God knows how many people were mentioned in decorous terms that amounted to "mistakes were made."

The textbook authors must have been uneasy about the potentially negative impact this passage, no matter how brief, might have on impressionable youngsters. To be on the safe side, they concluded it with a rousing and confident affirmation that all these "flaws" and "shortcomings" notwithstanding, everything was basically all right and the country was moving forward, firmly and unswervingly, on the path of socialism. To this our teacher, Henrietta Sergeyevna, added that Stalin had been a man of extremely suspicious and authoritarian temperament, that indeed Lenin — the infallible Lenin — had warned about these dangerous aspects of the man's character in a letter to the Party leadership shortly before his death. Besides, she said, Stalin had suffered from the bad influence of "adventurers" he surrounded himself with, such as Yezhov and Beria — two safe targets, since both had been executed (the former at Stalin's orders, the latter after Stalin's demise) as "agents of international imperialism."

Other adjustments were made in our high-school history curriculum in response to the needs of the time. It turned out, for example, that the history of World War II, and of the Great Patriotic War in particular, had not been taught correctly. Some very crucial parts had been overlooked: namely, the role of the battle at Malaya Zemlya and of the person of Leonid Ilyich Brezhnev.

Leonid Ilyich had ambitions more sublime than just being a beloved statesman. In 1977 he came out with a wartime memoir entitled *Malaya Zemlya*, or "Little Land." Malaya Zemlya was a small patch of land where, during World War II, a young and peppy Colonel Brezhnev had served as a political instructor (*politruk*) with the Soviet troops. The glorious military history of that outpost consisted, I dimly recall, of a two-day standoff between the Soviet and German troops, and at most a minor skirmish.

Brezhnev's opus, a campaign book by a victorious and unopposed politician, became a priceless contribution not only to literature but to history as well. It turned out that the truly pivotal action in the Great Patriotic War — oh, granted, not the most spectacular but of the utmost strategic importance — took place at Malaya Zemlya. We hadn't known this yet when we took our fourth-grade course in Russian history. By the time we studied the Great Patriotic War in ninth grade, this unfortunate oversight had been corrected. There were brand-new historic maps of World War II showing the familiar arrows — black for the Nazi troops, red for the Soviet troops — going off in this and that direction around Malaya Zemlya. Indeed, the fact emerged that the events at Malaya Zemlya had really been the turning point in the course of the entire war, the point at which the Soviet troops successfully stopped the German offensive and regained military advantage. *Malaya Zemlya* itself became required reading on the history curriculum, although somehow I managed to steer clear of it.

It did not take long for some songwriter to come up with a tribute to the newly discovered great moment in Soviet war history. The song "Malaya Zemlya" was performed at one of our amateur variety show evenings at school by a chorus of girls in white shirts and blue skirts, with red ribbons and red carnations, crooning the schmaltzy refrain "Malaya Zemlya, Malaya Zemlya," with a great deal of feeling. Joke makers responded just as promptly: *A war veteran, when asked if he fought at Malaya Zemlya, replies, "No, I was having an easy time at Stalingrad."* Another quip suggested using a line from a Soviet pop song, "Things that I have never seen, I remember," as an epigraph to the general secretary's war memoirs.

It also turned out that *Malaya Zemlya* was only the first installment in a trilogy. The other two parts were *Virgin Land*, about the agricultural development of lands in parts of Central Asia — with no credit given to Khrushchev, the real author of the project, to which Brezhnev had some tenuous connection — and *Rebirth* (I have no idea what that one was about). Rumors were afloat that Brezhnev was going to be awarded the Lenin Prize for Literature, the highest in the land. I think someone first said it as a joke ("You'll see, he'll get the Lenin Prize too"), and then it didn't seem all that far-fetched any longer, and few were surprised when the award was announced. At the zenith of the general secretary's literary fame, the radio listings for a single week featured daily readings of excerpts from *Rebirth* and a play or something like that based on *Malaya Zemlya*, and the song of the same title haunted the airwaves as well.

At some official banquet or celebration my father glimpsed on TV, a veteran of the virgin lands project rose to pay homage to dear Leonid Ilyich for his unsurpassed contribution to the project, for being the heart and soul and brain of it — another historic discovery in the making, as it became evident that the virgin lands development would have never happened without Leonid Ilyich Brezhnev. "And what do you think?" my father said. "That old moron, who ought to know better than anybody else just how much he had to do with the virgin lands — he was *moved to tears!* There he was wiping his eyes! He *believed* it!"

People were saying that the posters with Brezhnev's portrait that were carried in the parades and demonstrations on the big Soviet holidays were now the same size as the posters of Lenin, and that that was an honor that only Stalin had enjoyed before. Little things mean a lot. The photo chosen to illustrate a newspaper profile of a little-known sculptor showed him standing next to a marble bust of Leonid Ilyich. There was a joke: *Is there a cult of personality under Brezhnev? There is a cult, but no personality.* A friend of Papa's spotted a remarkable moment on television: at some official event, a female representative of the working people said, in the middle of a panegyric to the general secretary, "Our dear Ilyich — " then blushed and stammered and quickly corrected herself, "Oh, I mean to say, our dear *Leonid Ilyich.*" The patronymic Ilyich is almost a ritual form of reference to Lenin, connoting warm, almost intimate affection and reverent filial piety; there seemed to be little doubt that the woman's flattering slip of the tongue had been carefully rehearsed under the coaching of some Party worker, complete with blush and stammer afterward.

Newspaper reports on meetings of the Politburo or sessions of the Supreme Soviet indicated "a storm of applause" every time the name Brezhnev was uttered, and transcripts of his speeches were peppered with asides in parentheses: "Applause," "Roaring, continuing applause," "Thundering applause gradually turning into an ovation. Everyone rises." These speeches and remarks even showed up in our curriculum; for the public studies class with Henrietta Sergeyevna, we were required to buy and read a thin pamphlet of the latest Communist Party program as presented in a speech "personally by L. I. Brezhnev," as they used to put it. *("You know, Brezhnev died." "You don't say!* PERSONALLY?")

On paper the words looked leaden and soporific, but one could breathe a spark of life into them by conjuring up a vision of Leonid Ilyich speaking. He was great fun to listen to, for about ten minutes of the hour or more of his oration. All right, it's not nice to make fun of an ailing old man who slurs his speech. But who could help snickering? Brezhnev said his *v*'s as *w*'s and stumbled over every word with more than three syllables ("im-perialistic," which in Russian is even worse, *imperialistichesky*, was the real killer) and made loud smacking sounds every few words, never for a moment taking his eyes off the sheets of paper and droning on in a level monotone, straining his voice to show feel-ing when he got to phrases like "Long live the fraternity of socialist peoples!" or "Onward, toward the victory of commu-nism!" Doing impressions of Brezhnev became a favorite form of entertainment at social get-togethers.

With his black bushy eyebrows, his pebbles-in-the-mouth mumbling, the rainbow of medals and awards on his chest, and the overall image of someone who wouldn't be able to put his pants on if left to his own devices, our dear Leonid Ilyich was a veritable gold mine for the anonymous wits who did so much to brighten up our lives. *Brezhnev is alone in his apartment. The doorbell rings. He goes to the door, puts on his glasses, pulls a piece of paper out of his pocket and reads, "Who . . . is . . . it?"* Or *Brezhnev says to an aide, "Look, I told you to write a fifteen-minute speech for me, and when I read it at the conference it went on for forty-five minutes!"* The aide replies, *"But Leonid Ilyich, I gave you three copies."*

In 1988, the pathetic old man who could be moved to tears listening to the accolades proffered by his loving subjects has become a target for blistering attacks in the Soviet press, a sym-bol of (and a scapegoat for) everything that was wrong with the Soviet system during the two decades of his rule. His name has been stripped from streets and squares, and the town of Brezh-nev (so named after the death of the "outstanding fighter for peace") has been given its old name back, as always "at the wish of the working people" — undoubtedly the same formula that accompanied the first name change. The dishonorable oblivion into which Leonid Ilyich Brezhnev is sinking so fast is unlikely to have taken many people in the Soviet Union by surprise. Rita, a good little Soviet girl at heart, told me a joke about a twenty-first-century man coming across the name of Brezhnev and look-ing it up in an encyclopedia, to find this entry: *"Brezhnev — minor Soviet politician in the age of Vysotsky"* (the famed actor and underground singer). I knew a much more pointed version of the same: *"minor politician in the age of Solzhenitsyn and Sakharov."*

I recall my father saying, only half facetiously, "It wouldn't be a bad idea to buy a copy of *Malaya Zemlya*. A little while after the old man croaks, it's going to become a curio — you won't find it in the stores anymore, that's for sure." Given Stalin's posthumous fall from grace and Khrushchev's postcoup ignominy, the fate of idols no longer in power didn't seem all that hard to predict.

Papa told me a delicious story: in the heyday of the Stalin "personality cult," a huge painting adorned the lobby of Forum, one of the biggest movie theaters in the center of Moscow. It showed Stalin surrounded by his henchmen, regally coming down the steps of the Palace of Congresses in the Kremlin. After Stalin's death in 1953, the henchmen one by one began to fall into disfavor. First Lavrenty Beria, the dreaded head of the secret police, was arrested and shot as a foreign agent. A few days later, my father went to the movie theater and suddenly noticed that Beria's figure on the canvas had been carefully painted over: there was no one in that spot now, just the marble steps. The "anti-Party clique" of Molotov, Malenkov, and Kaganovich was the next to go. The crowd around the Great Leader and Teacher kept getting thinner and thinner. Then came the Twentieth Party Congress, and Stalin himself was stripped of his halo. After that, the painting was taken down.

On a stroll through the countryside in Kryukovo, I told my summer pal Natasha Shereshevskaya this now-you-see-it-now-you-don't story. Natasha tittered and drawled, "Amazing! You know, when I hear about stuff like that, I just can't help thinking there are foreign saboteurs planted in our propaganda departments." My reaction to this comment was the slight shock and disappointment I always felt when people tried to get the Soviet establishment off the hook. Nevertheless, Natasha had a point — at least, if foreign saboteurs actually had been at work deep in the heart of the Soviet propaganda machine, they couldn't have done a better job of making their product look ridiculous to anyone with eyes to see. Put on trial, the Soviet system provided the most damning evidence against itself.

Take a volume I once picked up from my parents' bookshelves: *In the World of Wise Thoughts*, a Soviet version of Bartlett's dictionary of quotations, with a torch — the torch of knowledge — depicted on the cover. It had quotations from Homer, Shakespeare, Tolstoy, and others grouped under titles such as "On Man and Society," "On Work," "On Ideals," "On Marriage and the Family." There, prominently displayed side by side with the ancient Greeks and Romans, the *philosophes* of the Enlightenment, and the nineteenth-century German thinkers (even with Franklin and Jefferson), I found N. S. Khrushchev.

The book was published in 1962, three years before Khrushchev was stripped of his claims to wisdom. In it he was quoted as expressing wise thoughts such as this, in the section "On Courage and Heroism": "Our warmest greetings to the wonderful astronaut, the Soviet hero Yuri Alexeyevich Gagarin. He showed the highest moral qualities: courage, self-possession, and valor." And at the end of the section on artists: "In the conditions of Socialist society where the people are a truly free, real master of their fate and a creator of a new life, the artist who faithfully serves his people cannot be faced with the question of whether or not he has artistic freedom. For such an artist, the question of his approach to the phenomena of reality is clear, he does not need to adapt or to force himself, a truthful description of reality from the stand of Communist Party loyalty is an inner need of his soul."

These were apparently the wisest thoughts that could be picked from the then-growing heritage of Nikita Sergeyevich Khrushchev. Nearly every section of the book, whether it was about teachers, about science, or about human error, concluded with at least one Khrushchev aphorism, and sometimes several. Strangely enough, he had failed to comment on jealousy, poetry, love, childhood, or music. Perhaps if he had stayed in office a while longer . . .

The wise thoughts also included some quotations from the

latest program of the CPSU, the shortest of which was "Under Communism, all people will have an equal status in society, an equal relation to the means of production, equal conditions of work and distribution, and will actively participate in the government of social affairs." And Lenin was a mine of wisdom, represented more generously than any other author (with the possible exception of Tolstoy). Unlike Khrushchev, he even had a few things to say about love ("Lack of sexual restraint is bourgeois" and "I will not vouch for the reliability and fortitude in the struggle of those women who let their personal romance interfere with politics, or of men who will chase any skirt and let any pretty young thing lead them by the nose. No, no, that doesn't go with revolution" — truly a wise thought of universal and enduring human significance).

As for Khrushchev, his fate was best summed up in a limerick that made the rounds after he was ousted. Grandma once recited it to me, though in allegiance to old-fashioned decorum, she did lower her voice on the naughty word:

> What a mess! Oh, how disgraceful!
> How could this have come about?
> We have kissed an ass for ten years —
> But the wrong one, it turns out.

> Yet the people still march onward,
> There's no cause for great distress.
> There's one thing we know for certain:
> We will find another ass.

I didn't even know what Khrushchev looked like until I saw his photo — here in the United States. All I knew was that he was bald and round and somewhat porcine in appearance (there had been a joke about a picture of Khrushchev on a pig farm surrounded by pigs, with the caption "Khrushchev is third left in second row"), and that he banged his shoe on the rostrum at the United Nations.

One day at school, in seventh or eighth grade, we had a visitor from abroad: an American teacher named Mr. McDonald, a guest with some peace-and-friendship teachers' delegation. (In preparation for his arrival, we had painstakingly rehearsed in our singing class a country-and-western song, of which I remember a single line: "There's no place for blues out in the West." The teacher coaching us explained that "blues" meant sadness or depression, and for a moment I took that line to have a shockingly subversive meaning, but then I realized that it referred to a different kind of West.) A regular class — literature, I think — was pre-empted for the meeting with Mr. McDonald, who turned out to be a stocky, slightly bug-eyed, and rather engaging fellow. We sang our song and had some sort of a conversation with him, and then he entertained us with a guessing game. He would think of a famous person, then we would ask questions about the person that required a yes or no answer ("Is it a man?" "Is he or she alive?" "Is he an actor?") and try to guess who the person was.

The first one was Galina Ulanova, the celebrated Soviet prima ballerina; someone got that one rather quickly. In round two, we went through the following clues: a man . . . a statesman . . . dead . . . Russian . . . lived not long ago. . . . Hand after hand went up in the class; everyone or nearly everyone had a guess to offer. Yet the affable Mr. McDonald kept shaking his head — no, still wrong. Our principal, Nadezhda Pavlovna, who was present to keep a watchful eye on everything that went on, seemed to be getting pretty uncomfortable, and we were getting quite desperate. Finally the bell rang, mercifully announcing the end of the class and of our meeting with the American messenger of peace and friendship; as for the game, we had no choice but to give up. Well, then, who was it? "Khrushchev," said Mr. McDonald, looking somewhat baffled by our failure to guess something so simple. To make sure we knew who he was talking about, he added what must have been one of the few words he knew in Russian, *tolstyi* ("fat"), demonstrating wide girth with both hands.

A somber Nadezhda Pavlovna, the corners of her mouth turned lower than usual, must have been relieved that the bell had rung, and the class was far more interested in getting out as soon as possible than in whatever Mr. McDonald had to say. Mr. McDonald must have thought that our school was doing a bad job of teaching us history. Little did he know that the problem lay elsewhere: the school was doing its job all too well.

12

The Making of
Another Closet Dissident

I LISTENED RELIGIOUSLY to foreign radio broadcasts, the Voice of America and *Die Deutsche Welle* ("The German Wave"), and learned to tune in to these stations myself when Papa wasn't home. They had news about the activities of dissidents, about political prisoners in the Soviet Union; once they read excerpts from Hedrick Smith's *The Russians*. I suspect that generally, the actual information or ideas in these broadcasts took second place for me to the very act of listening to them, of hearing — *doing* — something illicit.

I also grew accustomed to the fact that we had illegal books in the house, our own as well as borrowed ones. Mostly they were not *samizdat*, typewritten carbon copies you often had to strain your eyes to read, but foreign-published *tamizdat* (literally, "published over there"), from France or America. The thrill of the forbidden fruit dissipated quickly and they became just books, albeit very interesting ones, distinguishable from Soviet editions by the whiter, stiffer paper, the glossy covers of the paperbacks. Most of them came from a friend of Father's who married a Frenchwoman, spent a couple of months in France, and returned to Moscow for about a year before settling permanently in his new homeland. Since his wife worked for the French embassy in Moscow and had diplomatic immunity, her luggage was exempted from inspection, and she smuggled in quite a batch of what is known as "literature prejudicial to the Soviet political and social system."

Interesting tidbits could also be picked up from foreign books that were legally available in the Soviet Union. There were two bookstores in Moscow where one could buy American and British paperbacks (Penguins, Vikings, and others), though at about three times the publisher's price, and I discovered two or three libraries with good selections of such books. Reading the American copy of Kurt Vonnegut's *Cat's Cradle*, I found to my amusement several disrespectful references to the Soviets or to Communists that had been cut from the Russian translation. Vonnegut lists "the Communist party" among *granfalloons*, human associations not based on genuine bonds. In the translation, that was altered to "all political parties." And well after de-Stalinization and the Sino-Soviet split, Stalin and Mao were struck from a roster of "enemies of democracy." I delighted in having caught Soviet censors red-handed.

In the summer after I turned fifteen, I don't think I read a single book that could not have gotten my parents (or me, if I had been older) five years for the possession of anti-Soviet literature. There were the reminiscences of émigré artist and essayist Yuri Annenkov about the great figures of Russian culture and politics whose portraits he had painted, including Lenin and Trotsky, the great stage producer Vsevolod Meyerhold, who was shot during the Stalinist terror, and the hounded poets Pasternak and Akhmatova. Annenkov cited a selection of letters to the Soviet press after the publication in the West of *Dr. Zhivago:* "Having read everything they say in the newspapers about Pasternak's novel, I am profoundly convinced that Pasternak hates not only the Soviet people but humanity in general," wrote a distinguished welder from a Moscow factory. There were also the sparkling, wickedly hilarious books of Vladimir Voinovich: *The Life and Extraordinary Adventures of Private Ivan Chonkin*, the story of a bungling soldier who unwittingly becomes a target of official wrath in the first days of the Great Patriotic War, and *The Ivankiad*, a fact-based story of the writer's fight against pow-

erful *apparatchik* Sergei Ivanko, who coveted the new apartment
in the Writer's Union co-op to which Voinovich and his pregnant
wife were legally entitled. For added zing, it was rumored that
Ivanko, who had been a member of the Soviet delegation at the
UN, had been recalled from the United States after the disgrace
of Voinovich's exposé.

Eventually I was inspired, at the age of sixteen, to start writing
my own slanderous fabrications. They came in the form of a
play, of which I wrote the first scene and part of the second. The
action took place in the mid-1980s, and I am happy to say that I
was utterly lacking in prescience. In my version of 1984, Jews
were being deported from Moscow to Birobijan (the only urban
center in the so-called Jewish Autonomous Republic, a dismal
place in the Far East where Stalin actually had been planning to
deport the Jews just before his demise). The heroine of my play
was a sixteen-year-old high school girl (such a coincidence!)
named Olya, who was not Jewish but whose father got arrested
in the opening scene of the play for making some antigovernment
remarks or something like that. Then my heroine, obviously a
high-minded as well as literate type, knelt and quoted from
Othello (in the Boris Pasternak translation):

> Even so my bloody thoughts, with violent pace,
> Shall ne'er look back, ne'er ebb to humble love,
> Till that a capable and wide revenge
> Swallow them up. — Now, by yond marble heaven,
> In the due reverence of a sacred vow
> I here engage my words.

The scene ended with the appearance of a friend of Olya's father,
a man by the name of Volsky (which to a Russian ear has the
Harlequin-romance aristocratic ring of Campbell). Volsky was a
member of a secret dissident society. From what I dimly remember of my plans for the plot, Olya was to join the secret society,
fall in love with Volsky, and in the end participate in the overthrow of the Soviet régime.

I ran into a stumbling block the moment I got to scene two,
which was supposed to depict a meeting of the dissident under-

ground: I didn't know the first thing about dissidents — what they were like, what they talked about, to say nothing of what they did. I think that in the opening lines of the scene I had them arguing about how they should address each other (the words "comrade" and "citizen" being seriously compromised) and eventually settling on nothing less banal than "brother" and "sister." That was as far as my imagination went. If a dissident had been around to read my scribbling, I'm sure he would have been greatly amused. It was much safer, after all, to write about frail aristocrats and vigorous sans-culottes in eighteenth-century Paris. First of all, I actually knew more about them than I did about Moscow dissidents; second, even if I got a few details wrong here and there, no living eyewitnesses to the relevant events would be there to spot the bloopers.

The closest link between myself and a real live dissident was, ironically, my grandmother's friendship with the staunchly Soviet Aunt Katya, the one who was embarrassed to admit that her aunt had been thrown into the labor camps on a ludicrous charge. God, or Mother Nature, had whimsically blessed her with a son, Vyacheslav, who became a rather prominent independent artist and for all intents and purposes a dissident. He took part in protests, got arrested, was mentioned in the broadcasts of what his mother called "those scum radio stations." Aunt Katya threw up her hands in dismay: why couldn't he be a good boy like everyone else? What did he want? She found comfort in attributing his odd behavior to nothing more serious than wayward youthful restlessness. Indeed, Vyacheslav was something of a footloose, happy-go-lucky fellow; he got married and divorced three times and fathered a sprightly boy who was mostly in the care of Aunt Katya.

For all my curiosity about Vyacheslav, I never got to meet him. When Grandma took me with her to Aunt Katya's place one day, I saw a few of his drawings tacked up high on the wall. They were brightly colored cartoons, one depicting an unkempt young male of the beatnik type with rock-and-roll records scattered about his room (the word balloon said "I think, therefore I am"). On another was a very curvaceous blonde with cherry-red lipstick, in a posture that accentuated the orb of her tight-skirted posterior. I stood for a long time staring up at those drawings, straining my neck until it began to hurt, and was left a bit puzzled as to why the Soviet régime would bother to object so much to them. I was disappointed — I had expected something really seditious.

Two or three days before we emigrated, I met a person who I suppose qualified as a dissident: a writer I shall call Mikhail Kaledin. A friend of a bohemian acquaintance of Papa's, he came to pick up our cupboard, which we had sold. Kaledin eked out a living hauling furniture for a moving outfit, although he had once been a journalist on the staff of some magazine. In 1968, when Soviet troops invaded Czechoslovakia, Kaledin was asked (like virtually everyone with a job) to sign a letter to the government expressing full support for the action. He refused, and never worked as a journalist again. He also became an Orthodox Christian and fathered six children. Some of his writings, mostly on religious topics, had appeared in émigré magazines.

With such impressive advance billing, Kaledin could not fail to stir my curiosity. But the stocky, swarthy, bearded man who comported himself with a quiet dignity quickly disappointed me. Our conversation drifted to religion; I asked our guest if he believed in the immortality of the soul, and when he gave me a curt yes, I pressed on about reincarnation, a subject in which I had a burgeoning interest. "Nothing of the kind," Kaledin cut me off imperiously. "I believe that I am going to survive as a person, as myself and not somebody else." He went on to pontificate about humility and the need to subordinate one's prideful reason to the will and love of God. For someone with humility, I noted to myself, he certainly attached a great deal of importance to the survival of his own intact self. I was also wondering why a person who had refused to subordinate his prideful reason to the Soviet state wanted to hand it over to someone or something else. Finally, Kaledin expressed the view that a society couldn't be all that bad if religion had an important place in it. What about the Spanish Inquisition? I asked. Kaledin, whom I was beginning to find more and more ponderous, replied that he didn't see anything terribly wrong with the Spanish Inquisition. I did not dare ask for his views on the proper role of women. I already knew everything I needed to know about the man.

The *real* dissidents, the ones who were my heroes, remained disembodied names: Sakharov, Orlov, Shcharansky, Bukovsky. I tried to find out more. I was desperate enough to sneak a peek into a pocket-sized paperback entitled *A Hundred Questions and Answers for the Political Educator* (or something like that), which lay unattended on the desk of Henrietta Sergeyevna. What the political educator was supposed to say if asked about the dissidents was that they all were antisocial, sick, or vanity-ridden individuals intent on subverting the foundations of Soviet society. As proof of what felonious miscreants they were, the booklet flatly stated that Vladimir Bukovsky had been found in possession of crates of weapons stored in some wooded area out of town — weapons he had planned to use to overthrow the Soviet government.

Crates with weapons! An armed revolt! Shades of *le quartorze Juillet*, the storming of the Bastille, the Revolution — the romantic and comfortably distant French one, of course, not the nasty one. The bald-faced propaganda lie for which I so enthusiastically fell instantly elevated Bukovsky, in my eyes, to a more heroic stature than ever. An entry in my diary read, "The dissidents: the best and noblest people of our age, our modern Girondists." Perhaps this far-fetched comparison had little to do with reality, but it made sense to me. Both the Girondists, martyred moderates of the French Revolution, and the vague dissident silhouettes of my imagination were people who cared passionately about ideas, who stood up for individual freedom against the crushing, impersonal, inhuman machine of oppression.

An eager proponent of revolution, I got into furious arguments with adults — my parents and their friends — who tended to share the opinion that nothing good ever came of revolutions and that as far as Russia was concerned, one revolution had been more than enough. "But if the French Revolution hadn't happened, Europe would never have become democratic!" I would

shout heatedly, making a hasty and possibly quite flawed historical analysis. I remember pursuing a paunchy, bearded colleague
of my father's into our anteroom after dinner, carrying on in a
loud voice that must have been intolerably shrill with emotion:
"But of course a revolution is necessary! Just look at history! No
despotic government has ever been overthrown except by a revolution!" Father's colleague was nodding with an oh-isn't-she-
precocious grin, saying "Yeah, yeah, you're quite right . . . sure
. . . sure."

Once, in the incongruously idyllic environment of the evergreen woods in Engure on a sunny day in August, while my
parents and I were walking around picking blueberries, my romantic perception of the dissidents' struggles as a kind of French
Revolution without powdered wigs was rudely shaken by a shot
of reality far uglier than the clean and theatrical guillotine. Father
had the radio on — probably *Die Deutsche Welle* — and someone
was reading a letter smuggled to the West from a Ukrainian
religious activist ("Brothers and Sisters in Christ," it began) held
in a psychiatric hospital called Sychovka, which means something like "Owl Place." Did the name really have an eerie, sinister ring, or did it seem that way because of what the man was
saying? (My mother later said that the broadcast was one of the
things that made her finally make up her mind that we should
emigrate.)

The low, intense voice of the radio announcer, with a touch of
vibrancy yet devoid of melodrama, described the malnutrition,
the incredible filth, the brutality of the personnel who tied up
the inmates, beat them, abused them sexually. That last detail
was the one I couldn't forget, not because I found it titillating
but because it bewildered me. Was he talking about women inmates in the same place? Of course I had read about homosexuality in the *Medical Encyclopaedia* and the Criminal Code, and I
had read enough Greek and Roman literature no longer to be
scandalized by references to man-boy love, but *this!* Could it
really . . . ? I didn't have the stomach for any more of this; as if
without design — so my parents wouldn't know I was chicken-
ing out — I wandered off further into the trees and the shrubs,

to a spot where the radio voice would be only an unintelligible murmur.

After that, I briefly considered a plot for an anti-Soviet short story, this one about a young woman dissident who is about to be forcibly committed to a psychiatric hospital, escapes, and is rescued by a young man who shelters her in his apartment. However, this tale, complete with love and politics, never took shape beyond a first scene (winter night in Moscow, snow and moonlight, girl with no overcoat on darting wildly out of a white high-rise and across the frozen street, young man hurrying by, panting girl falling into his arms like a fluttering bird), composed in my mind on the way home from doing some errands.

Another short story I actually started to write but never finished was set, more comfortably, in 1794. A member of the Revolutionary Tribunal suddenly finds himself sheltering a suspect aristocrat fleeing from arrest. A bond develops between the two, and the rigid ideological fanatic is gradually transformed into a human being with a heart and an ability to appreciate the value of politically incorrect human life. Message: the divine grace of compassion defeats revolutionary humanism.

My political views, nuggets diligently recorded in my diaries, didn't have much concrete shape and hardly amounted to a coherent belief system. My readings and reflections, mostly on the French Revolution, left me convinced that to cause human suffering in the name of whatever idea, whatever higher goal, was monstrous. No interests of state or society could ever take prevalence over the individual — his life and his right to think and speak as he pleased — or overrule compassion, a virtue I got into the pompous habit of capitalizing. These nebulous humanitarian notions finally solidified into a startlingly Jeffersonian idea, written down some time after I had turned sixteen: "All in all, the best kind of government is one that makes its presence felt the least in the lives of its citizens." (I have to concede that Thomas Jefferson said it much better and more succinctly — "That government is best, that governs least" — but then, he had the benefits of age, erudition, and never having gone through the grinder of Soviet schooling . . . although in a roundabout way, the latter might actually have been a huge boost to the libertarian direction of my opinions.)

Perhaps my perception of where I stood politically can best be summed up in two words: *I understood*. It wasn't so much a question of knowing some particular facts about the Soviet régime or any realities of life in the Soviet Union, but of understanding a basic, essential truth underlying all these realities. To some extent, not even quite consciously, I suppose, I classified people on the basis of this principle: do they *understand* or not? It took some time before I realized with amazement that one could kvetch about lines or about how hard it was to get salami or pantyhose, and tell Brezhnev jokes, and still not *understand* a thing.

After all, who didn't grumble that of course everything was a mess because there were no owners and how could you expect anyone to give a damn? The most revealing story I ever heard about the nature of a socialist economy came from a middle-aged colleague of Mama's. On a vacation in Kazakhstan, she and her husband were taking a stroll by a field bursting with luscious, ripe, scarlet tomatoes — and saw a tractor combing the field, wiping out the tomatoes. As the tractor rumbled past them, the couple regained enough composure to ask the stolid man behind the wheel what was going on. "Had a really huge crop of tomatoes this year," he replied sullenly and matter-of-factly. "If we turn in that kind of a harvest, they'll jack up our plan for next year. Got to get rid of them." And on he went, a cigarette dangling from his mouth, with his slaughter of the innocents.

Audiences roared with laughter, savoring hints of the forbidden, when the Soviet Union's top comedian, the wildly popular Arkady Raikin, voiced this ubiquitous grumbling in one of his routines: "Let's say I have an apple tree. It's *my* tree, right? I take care of it and I eat the apples. Now let's say we have *our* apple tree. I eat from it. You eat from it. We don't like *him*, but he eats from it too. Everyone going munch, munch, munch. . . . So it's *ours*. Is it *mine*? No. Is it *yours*? No. Is it *his*? No. So what have we got here? *Ours* really means *no one's*, right?" Official reviews and profiles of the comedian emphasized that Raikin was de-nouncing and ridiculing such attitudes, but I wonder if the pub-lic saw it quite the same way.

Our country neighbor *cum* handyman Kostya Ivanov would have made a most intriguing though brain-addling subject for a study of the masses' sentiments about the Soviet régime. When Kostya wasn't mumbling drunken nonsense or panhandling for his booze money, he was most often knocking the way the gov-ernment was running things. Just look, he would grumble, just look at this mess. Nobody wants to do a damn thing because no one owns anything, no one profits from doing a good job, so of course no one gives a damn and everyone's goofing off. That's why everything in the country is going to pieces. People in the country used to have cows and suddenly, *boom*, they took the cows away from all private owners and then they didn't know what to do with them so they just slaughtered most of them. Now you can have a cow again but people have gotten burned once, so who's gonna fall for it? And there you have it, no meat in the stores.

Kostya told Grandma (whom he greatly and anachronistically respected as a lady) a story of workers' riots he had seen in some town in the sixties, when they brought out the troops to shoot at the protesters and the commanding officer couldn't bring himself to give the order to fire, so he shot himself instead (the next in command, who replaced him, harbored no such scruples). Kos-tya even badmouthed the sacrosanct personalities of the leader-ship. After watching TV news reports on the Brezhnev-Nixon summit in 1972, he scoffed bitterly, "Just look at our guy! Can't say a single sentence without looking at a piece of paper! I mean, you look at their Nixon, the way he talks and the way he carries himself and all, and then look at our guy. It's a goddamn embar-rassment."

A few days later, the same Kostya Ivanov would rant, shaking his fists, "Those Americans! Those Chinese! They're all out to get us! Well, I'll tell you what — if any of those skunks just *dare* raise a hand against our country, I'll stand firm as a rock! [A task that would have been quite daunting for Kostya even under less extraordinary circumstances.] I'll die defending our country and our own Soviet power!"

So there: if you asked all the people bitching and cursing about the lack of incentives to work whether they would like to see capitalism brought back and whether they thought capitalism was better than socialism, most would have recoiled in horror — and they saw no apparent contradiction.

I had always taken for granted that Rita largely shared my views; she tuned in to the Voice of America in the manner of one who knew her way around. When she casually said something about "some American senator who had a meeting with one of those traitors," meaning the dissidents, she might as well have thrown a bucket of scalding water over me. Without considering my words, I shot back, "What the hell are you saying? They're not traitors! They are good people!" Rita did not fight back and appeared entirely willing to concede, but a little while later she managed to leave me speechless once again. Moaning about pains in her stomach, she said darkly, "It's all because of that stuff our so-called friends are releasing into our air." I gave her a puzzled look: "What friends?" "Oh, you know what I mean," she snapped. "The Americans."

By and by, through shock treatment, I learned not to confuse bitching, political jokes, utter contempt for civics classes, and lust for all things Western with dissent or opposition. The lesson that really brought it home to me came in eighth grade. Four or five of us girls, on a day when we were relieved from gym by a doctor's certificate (customarily done when you were just recuperating from a flu or a cold), were drafted to mop the tiled floor in the lobby. Our job done, we sat down to a well-deserved rest on the cots lined up against the wall.

We fell into the usual laments for pantyhose and whatnot, and the usual jokes were bandied about. *A Party official is passing by the grave of Budyonny* [the legendary Soviet hero of the civil war cavalry] *and hears a faint voice calling, "A horse! Get me a horse!" He gets real scared and runs to fetch Brezhnev. The two of them come up to the grave and the same voice says, "You dope! I said get me a horse, not an ass!*" And so it went, and I was having a great time in the company of like-minded people, until someone mentioned a news item heard on some foreign "voice": the wife of Arkady Shevchenko, the Soviet UN ambassador who had just asked for political asylum in the United States, had killed herself. There were rumors that her death involved foul play on the part of the KGB. The conversation turned from jokes to real politics. A couple of minutes later, it came over me all of a sudden that the girls' sympathies were not with Shevchenko.

It was a good thing I was sitting down. My mouth went dry. My palms went damp. It was as if I were a character in *The Invasion of the Body Snatchers* and had suddenly realized that all the creatures around me, whom I had taken to be human, were actually pod persons — and God, I had to be very careful not to let them know I wasn't one of them. Anya Petrosyan, and the gentle, shy, wide-eyed Katya Vorontzova, and all the others dropped epithets like "that creep," "that traitor," charitably adding that it was too bad the KGB got his wife and not the creep himself. I listened, trying to find my bearings and not to betray my confusion, and made sounds that were supposed to signify agreement.

They went on to chatter about all those turncoats and misfits who were slandering our society, and Anya mentioned some American movie she had heard about — I can't recall the plot she described, and I have no idea what movie it was or even if there actually was such a movie. I gathered it was about political or religious persecution in the Soviet Union, or perhaps about the tribulations of someone trying to escape from the country. She spoke in the tone of someone describing a patently absurd, outrageous lie, so self-evident that it didn't even merit counter-arguments, only contemptuous amusement or anger (the way one might say, "You know, this tobacco company is claiming that smoking has nothing to do with lung cancer"). The other girls disapprovingly shook their heads and snorted scornfully. Isn't it ridiculous! Those Americans!

About a year later, the exact worth of the talk I had always taken to be anti-Soviet was brought home to me most forcefully

when my classmates learned I was emigrating. Anya Sevostya-
nova said to me worriedly, "But because you're leaving doesn't
mean you're against socialism, does it?" What could I say, except
to mumble no? This reassured Anya. "You know," she added in
a tone of alarm and disbelief, "there's a boy in tenth grade [we
were in ninth grade at the time], and he actually says, 'I hate
socialism and I think there ought to be capitalism everywhere
instead of socialism,' just like that, you know?" *Oh really*, I
thought. *How come I never get to meet such boys?*

Even before that final test, I searched around, almost despair-
ing to find someone else who saw the world the way I did. My
Jewish classmates may have been slightly more likely than the
others to be negative toward the system. Among the malcontents
was Mark Kozlovsky, the boy on whom I had once had a crush.
When, in ninth grade, we were assigned that essay on what we
could learn from Lenin based on Marietta Shaginyan's book,
Mark acted far more honorably than I did: he handed in a blank
notebook. Lydia Davydovna, lenient though she may have been,
gave him a stern look and asked, "And what is this supposed to
mean?" Mark replied in a level voice, "I haven't read the book
and I can't write anything," which earned him a 2. I looked at
him with a surge of admiration and envy (*I wish I had the guts to
do that!*), and almost fell in love all over again. Mark and his
mother paid us a visit when we were about to emigrate; the man
of my dreams and I exchanged anti-Soviet jokes while his mother
kvetched to my mother that she too would like to leave, except
she was working in the chemical industry and she wasn't sure
they couldn't hang the tag of "access to state secrets" on her.

Misha Belikov, the blond, round-faced boy (nothing Jewish
about *him*) who refused to have his considerable drawing talents
harnessed into the service of the wall newspaper, was definitely
one of those who *understood*. So I concluded from a few passing
remarks I heard him make, in a voice lowered and clipped —
something about Sakharov and about the invasion of Czechoslovakia. This was all the more amazing, all the more admirable,
since the educational level of Belikov's family was not very high.
Unfortunately, he and I never developed any kind of closeness.

We had an even more unlikely nonconformist in the thuggish, utterly unintellectual Borya Fedoseyev. He was simply an all-round cynic, I suppose, holding no brief for sacred cows of the official or unofficial kind. Once in the Soviet government and law class, our pathetic middle-aged teacher, Lyubov Andreyevna, declared in an elegiac voice that rang with conviction, "I would never leave our country for any other — not if they gave me a million dollars." "You wouldn't for a million?" Fedoseyev piped up lazily from his seat. "Well, I'm sure I would." Lyubov Andreyevna shook her head reproachfully and repeated, "No, I *never* could do that." But Fedoseyev hardly qualified as a soulmate.

My favorite moment-of-truth story has to do with Sergei Yesenin, a lyrical poet of peasant background whose poignant, simple, melodic verse has enjoyed an enduring popularity with Soviet readers. An unruly, impulsive lover of the village and of wilderness, he committed suicide in the 1920s. At the time that we studied his poetry in our ninth-grade literature class, I was reading a contraband *tamizdat* collection of reminiscences about famous literary figures of the era by émigré poet Vladislav Khodasevich. The essay on Yesenin presented him in a rather different light from the biographical notes in our textbook. I thought I'd share the information with Rita, and as we walked down the hallway after the class was over, I said, "You know, I've read that Yesenin really hated the Soviet system." Rita took this with equanimity; not so Katya Vorontzova, who happened to overhear. "Well, so what!" she blurted out, visibly upset. "He still was a wonderful poet and I love his poetry! It makes me so mad when instead of looking at the great poetry someone wrote, people say nasty personal things about him!"

By that time I shouldn't have been surprised, but I still was at a loss for words. After all, I couldn't very well defend myself by saying that I had meant no insult to the memory of poor Yesenin — quite the opposite. And that, I suppose, was what it all boiled down to, that *je ne sais quoi* one was supposed to *understand:* that to hate the Soviet régime was not a fault but a virtue.

*

The middle-of-the-night knock on the door of the Stalin era, the arrests over a remark incautiously made, the knowledge that they could grab you over nothing — all these things, no matter how much I heard and read about them, remained something mythological, something completely unconnected to me on any sort of personal level. The powers that be had gotten lax, as some of the older folks liked to grumble. For all the tightening of the screws under Brezhnev, people had gotten a taste of greater freedom, and it stayed with them. Portable radios tuned in to foreign broadcasts could be heard turned up to a devil-may-care volume in parks and on beaches, and sometimes even in more public places. Grandma remembered waiting at a bus stop one day in August 1968; the person standing next to her had a radio, on which a woman was talking about waking up to see tanks rolling in the street, soldiers charging crowds, people running from the tanks, screaming, sobbing. It dawned on Grandma suddenly that the voice was talking about the Soviet troops entering Prague. She was enough of an innocent to wonder in shock for a moment: *this* is on the radio? Then she realized it was a foreign broadcast.

Yet of course I knew that there were things to be afraid of if I didn't keep my views and my questions to myself. From the days when, as an eleven-year-old third-grader with a ponytail, I memorized my mother's lesson that Papa would go to jail if I told anyone at school what kind of things he talked about at home, I knew that political heresies called for discretion. It didn't take me long to find out that a good many people (starting with my own father) didn't exercise it much. Others overdid it. In truth, it was hard to say just what amount of caution was right. It wasn't — and I suspect still isn't — unusual for people to be cagey and fearful in such matters, far in excess of what the actual danger warranted.

But exaggerated fear is not entirely unreasonable. People have a feeling that the state may tolerate something today but its policy might very well change tomorrow — you never know what *they* may decide to do. Even without a policy shift, *they* might always decide to single you out as an example, to put some fear of the KGB into others, and come down hard on you for a misdeed that most people get away with on a daily basis.

Take anti-Soviet jokes. Virtually everyone went around telling them, including people who weren't opposed to the system at all. Basic good sense suggested that you should at least try to be careful in choosing your audience, and yet in the post-Stalin era, not many people took seriously the danger of getting into trouble because of a joke. But I heard several stories of students being expelled from college for such jokes, after someone had "knocked" on them. Worse, it was rumored that in at least one case, a young woman guilty of this offense was exiled from Moscow to some small town a hundred miles away.

Our most unusual adventure in the don't-take-politics-from-strangers department happened, or rather began, on the last day of our last trip to Latvia, late in the summer of 1978. As usual, our Moscow-bound train was leaving from Riga that night, but we came to the city in the morning, checked our luggage at the train station, and spent the day in Riga. After making the rounds of the stately Gothic cathedrals and the enchanting narrow meandering streets, complete with cobblestones, old-style street lamps, and cast-iron doorknobs, we had particular bad luck in finding a place to eat. There weren't that many in the first place, and all those we could find were either full or booked to capacity. At last, famished and exasperated, we ducked into a humble café and were seated at a table with two other people (no surprise there). Both were men about the same age as my parents, one tall, dark-haired, and balding, the other short, bearded, with flaming red curly hair; both were instantly recognizable as fellow Russian Jews. Indeed, they turned out to be Muscovites, vacationers like us. They introduced themselves as Arkady and Mark.

The small things that can give a conversation between strangers a dangerous turn! The dour waitress came up to take our orders; every item we chose from the menu was out of stock. We had to reconsider hastily, and luckily our choice was made easy for us: of the six or seven entrées listed, beef patties were all they had. My mother, very suspicious of the quality of ground meat she hadn't ground herself, decided to content herself with soup and salad. Mark and Arkady picked strawberry pie for dessert; the café was out of that, too.

When our order was finally given and the waitress went off, Mark, the red-headed one, remarked, "Well, that's life in a totalitarian state for you!" That broke the ice. From beef patties and strawberry pie, it wasn't a long way to political parties, Solzhenitsyn, and emigration. We were already waiting for our papers; Mark was burning to emigrate, but his wife was against it. (Arkady had some other problem that stood in the way.) My father said that Mama had been reluctant too but he had finally managed to bring her around. "We all ought to get together sometime," Mark said to Papa with a heavy sigh. "Maybe you'll be able to straighten my wife out."

Arkady seemed the more level-headed of the two; Mark was a hyperactive, blustery bundle of nerves with an acid tongue. It seemed that we almost instantly developed a mutual sympathy. After we finished our dinner *à la totalitarian*, they wanted to walk us to the train station. On our way there, Mark, getting more excited by the minute (one might have thought the café had been serving alcoholic beverages), flailed his arms wildly and screamed at the top of his lungs, "Hitler was a puppy compared to Stalin!" This looked like the beginning of a beautiful friendship, and we decided before parting to exchange phone numbers. Either right then and there or later, the thought that this dynamic duo might actually be a team of *agents provocateurs* crept into my parents' minds, or at least my mother's. (*The Soviet version of Russian roulette is talking politics at a party even though you know that one of the six guests is an informer.*)

About two months went by and we didn't hear from either Mark or Arkady. My parents didn't call them either, perhaps because of that little worm of suspicion, perhaps just because they never got around to it. And then the phone rang one day in November — the day before we were having a dinner party for my father's birthday. It was Mark. No matter what suspicions Papa may have harbored, he was glad to hear Mark's voice. They talked for a little while; Mark suggested it would be a good idea to get together, and then Papa invited him and Arkady, and the wives, to the dinner party.

The next day the guests began to arrive, many of them, as it happened, either "in application" — waiting for their exit visas — or in some stage of getting ready to apply. (The first stage is thinking it over.) When Papa said that four more guests were coming and explained how we had met, there was an instant outcry: "How do you know they're not KGB?" "I'm *sure* they're KGB, it looks like a classic setup!" Flabbergasted and indignant at our naiveté, the guests began to insist that we find some way of backing out — quite a task, considering that we were expecting Mark and Arkady within the hour. Someone suggested tacking a note on the door saying that there had been an emergency and we were very sorry but we had had to leave, and of course keeping quiet inside lest they should hear voices. The phone was not to be answered, either.

My parents offered some weak resistance. I was dead set against the idea. I shouted that it was awkward, unseemly, low, indecent, anything else I could think of. Finally my parents uneasily caved in to public pressure. Left all alone against a grown-up majority, there was nothing I could do but acquiesce. The note was written and tacked onto the door, and we all sat down at the table, the party getting off to a none too happy start.

Every time we heard the creaky old elevator stop on our floor with a slam of the door, a hush would fall over the room (just like in our classroom when the teacher approached). We would wait, listen to the steps on the flight of stairs from the elevator to our door — no, it was someone going to the apartment across the hall — going up two flights of stairs to the top, fifth floor, going to the apartment next door . . .

In an anticlimactic twist, Mark and Arkady never showed up; we were very alert, and we never heard anyone approach our doorstep. Nor did they call, on that day or ever again, and needless to say, my parents made no effort to get in touch. We did think about them occasionally, even years later, trying to figure out the mystery. Why didn't they come, or at least call to say they wouldn't be able to make it? One possibility is that they actually were KGB informers who got reassigned at the last minute to watch larger fry than ourselves and our dinner guests. The other is that they may have thought *we* were KGB informers inviting them to step into our parlor. So much for beautiful friendships.

Still, the barrier of wariness wasn't insurmountable. Some took longer than others, and some never got there at all, but eventually, after knowing someone for a while, people would let their guard down.

Nadya Kozhevnikova, the girl who rescued me from the plight of age discrimination at the Moscow Foreign Languages Library, was a student of my mother's from the age of six. By the time she was eighteen, Nadya was coming to our place to read *The Gulag Archipelago* and other illicit books. She argued with my more vehemently anti-Soviet father, but only on the question of whether Lenin may have been a good man and worked for a good cause, no matter how rotten a system he and his heirs ended up creating. My father would brook no compromise: "Oh, come off it, Nadya! A butcher and a demagogue like the rest of them, that's all he was." Nadya protested, but rather meekly.

The road to such trust, however, had not been an altogether easy one. Nadya's parents held relatively high-ranking jobs and definitely were upright Soviet citizens, both Party members. One day after class, Nadya, then about sixteen, told my mother with some embarrassment that there was something she had to talk about. "You see, Marina Ilinishna, I read in the papers and they tell us in school that our country is the best in the world and our government is the most caring government and we have more freedom and are better off than people anywhere else, and at the same time, the things I see going on around me — it just doesn't seem to be that way. I've tried to talk to my parents about it, but they say that I'm a silly girl and I have very negativistic attitudes, and that the papers and the teachers at school are right about everything. Marina Ilinishna" — Nadya's voice quivered, and tears welled up in her eyes as she spoke — "you see, you're my last resort. I don't trust any of the other teachers, but I trust you. Please tell me what's going on. Am I really wrong? Is everything the way they tell us? I'll believe whatever you say."

Mama was on the spot. It's not that she could for a moment suspect Nadya of trying to set her up; she knew the girl well and never doubted her sincerity. But suppose she said, "Yes, you're right, everything they tell you in the papers and in school is a lie," and then suppose the impulsive Nadya got into another argument with her highly moral parents and exclaimed, "Well, Marina Ilinishna told me I was right!" Nadya's parents were just the kind of people who would go to see the principal over something like this, and Mama might well be kicked out of school. Apart from these selfish considerations, she worried that Nadya, who was quite prone to letting her mouth run away with her, would herself get into trouble. She was also hesitant to nudge Nadya in a direction that was clearly not what her parents had in mind. However, she couldn't find it in her heart to keep lying to the poor girl. My mother was reduced to muttering something ambiguous like "Well, Nadya, different people have different opinions, you know" — with a not very well-hidden implication that at the very least, she didn't think Nadya was wrong.

One of the most memorable eye-openers of my teenage years was a conversation on our country house veranda between Mama and a colleague of hers, Lisa Kaplan, an attractive, stylish, boyish blonde in her late twenties. Former colleague, I should say, for by that time we had applied for permission to emigrate and Mama had quit her job. Lisa was seriously considering the same option. In view of these circumstances, it was only natural for the conversation to take an unwholesome turn. I was sitting there too, hanging around the adults as always, and occasionally chipping in with a remark of my own.

I think it began with Lisa telling Mama she was lucky not to be at the school anymore. Lisa was getting fed up. She taught tenth grade; the ideological inclinations of the student body at that age were thought to warrant close attention. Lisa knew that there were informers in her classes, recruited to report on what the other kids *and* the teachers were up to. But that wasn't the worst. One day, Lisa told us, the principal had called her in for a talk and said, "Elizaveta Lvovna, we need your help in a rather delicate matter. We know that you get along very well with your students, they like you a lot, and they must confide in you. We are very interested in the students' attitudes, their ways of thinking. So tell me, please, do your students ever talk to you about their ideological views? What kinds of things do they say?" An utterly flabbergasted Lisa had said she didn't know anything, they had never talked to her about such things. "Well, then," the principal had said, "perhaps you should ask them what they think — draw them out, you know. It would be a big help." Lisa had muttered something and gotten out of the office as quickly as possible; luckily, the matter was never brought up again.

Actually, the principal, a timid middle-aged Jew, wasn't really a bad person or a martinet. He wasn't issuing an order, just asking Lisa for a favor. Most likely he hadn't the least intention of going to the KGB to turn in those kids who might reveal inappropriate attitudes. He may simply have felt that he was responsible for the ideological stewardship of the flock and ought to know if any of the sheep had gone astray so he could pay special attention to steering them back. Besides, he was scared to death of the Party activists on the teaching staff.

On another occasion (we heard about it, too, from Lisa Kaplan), a history teacher came to the principal's office with an item confiscated from a fifteen-year-old student: a copy of the Russian émigré newspaper *Novoye Russkoye Slovo*, which had somehow found its way from New York into the classroom of the Gnesin Ten-Year Music School. Reading extraneous materials in class — usually mystery novels or science fiction — was a bad offense, but reading *anti-Soviet materials!* Still, the principal did not report this to higher and more sinister authorities; all he did was give the student a proper tongue-lashing.

The history teacher who took the compromising item to the principal wasn't a bad guy either. Like the principal, he was middle-aged, Jewish, mild-mannered, and prudent in the extreme, as Jews loyal to the Soviet régime tend to be. Not to report such an incident to the principal would have meant taking the risk that someone in the class would report it — certainly not a prudent option.

As for the student, the dressing-down apparently failed to have the desired effect on him. Not much later, the cleaning woman tidying up Lisa Kaplan's classroom brought her a notebook forgotten by the same boy in his desk. The notebook contained hand-copied extracts from *The Gulag Archipelago*. Lisa returned it to the boy without comment.

Among my most vivid memories of listening to the foreign "voices" are some undramatic comments by Solzhenitsyn's wife, Natalya. I lay stretched out on a beach towel on the pale golden sand in Engure as the woman spoke on the radio of her own political awakening, of the realization that the dominant aspect of Soviet life was *lying*. You had to lie about believing in Communist doctrine. You had to lie and pretend that you believed Soviet life was great and getting better when in fact you could plainly see what a mess everything around you was. She spoke of the famous Solzhenitsyn motto, "To live not by the lie."

Perhaps that was when I became aware that this necessity to lie was perhaps the one real way in which I experienced oppression in my own life. It wasn't just that I couldn't say what I believed — *I had to say things I didn't believe*, a distinction of no small consequence. At best, I had to sit still and submit to a stream of high-flown platitudes that turned my stomach; at worst, I had to open my mouth and emit these same platitudes.

There were the meetings at school, and the civics classes. The textbook for Soviet government and law in eighth grade offered this gem of a question at the end of a chapter: "In sessions of parliaments and assemblies in capitalist countries, proposed bills and resolutions are often debated for months. In contrast, the Supreme Soviet always makes its decisions unanimously and quickly. Why is that?" I couldn't believe that this question hadn't been put in by a saboteur in the publishing house, although a saboteur might not have done that kind of thing for fear of being too obvious. The proper answer, I guess, was that legislators in capitalist countries represent all sorts of conflicting muckety-muck interests, while the deputies to the Supreme Soviet represent the interests of the Soviet people, one and indivisible.

Ksenia Stepanovna Obukhova, who succeeded Gena the Crocodile as our ideological guardian, was also our chemistry teacher. She was in her early fifties. Her grave, worried, weary face always wore a hint of a perplexed and slightly annoyed frown. She had two dress suits, a blue one and a brown one, which she tried to enliven by wearing blouses with lacy frills and a brooch of sparkling paste diamonds. Her face was powdered and her hair curled in a pathetic perm. She held class meetings with impeccable regularity once a week and harangued us as lengthily as Gennady Nikolayevich had, except that her joyless monotone was most unlike his fireworks. She preached and nagged and dragged us into various public activities, and an almost pleading look could be detected in her eyes, as if she were saying, "Come on, kids, give me a break, will you?" I think most of us viewed the woebegone lady with a mixture of scorn, irritation, and not unaffectionate pity.

Rita Kuznetzova and I had the good luck of sitting in the very back of her classroom, and during her sermons we could do anything that wasn't noisy or conspicuous. Of course we had to be on the alert when Ksyusha began to pace between the rows and came perilously close to our desk, or perched herself on an unoccupied desk a few steps away. Busy with my math homework or with copying poems into the back of a notebook, I did catch snippets here and there.

"You know, it's amazing how little patriotic pride people have these days." As our ideological guardian droned on and paced back and forth and frowned and cocked her head, she looked more like a nagging housemother than a vigilant watchdog of patriotism. "The other day I was in a store, for example, and there was a raincoat on the rack, a really nice raincoat. And a woman standing next to me said, 'Oh, isn't this a beautiful raincoat! Must be imported.' And then we looked at the label and what do you think? It was ours. People ought to be ashamed of themselves, saying things like that. Instead of taking pride in our country, they talk about salami. Well, I'll tell you, there are some

things in life that matter more than salami." She embarked on a
discourse about the accomplishments of the Soviet system, and
rattled off the figures we had heard a hundred times, showing
how gloriously Soviet industrial and agricultural output had shot
up since 1913 — presumably thanks to the wisdom of the Communist leadership: kilowatts of electricity, tons of steel, tons of
wheat per acre . . .

The most memorable speech Ksenia Stepanovna ever delivered was after our "public studies" teacher, prim, stern, unsmiling Henrietta Sergeyevna, complained that we weren't taking her
subject seriously enough. "I just don't know what it is with you
kids." Ksyusha sounded like a doctor trying to talk sense to a
patient with a bad heart who obstinately smokes four packs of
cigarettes a day. "I see this very irresponsible, very flippant attitude toward such important things. Now, I don't know *what* it
is — maybe you're just politically immature, or maybe there are
unwholesome conversations going on at home in your families."
A nasty, slightly ominous note seemed to be creeping into her
voice. But perhaps I was just imagining things, knowing as I did
that the conversations going on at home in *my* family were probably beyond Ksenia Stepanovna's worst nightmare of unwhole-
someness.

"Public studies," *obshchestvovedeniye*, started in ninth grade.
The word can be literally translated as "sociology" but was much
closer to ideology — or, to use a neutral term, political theory. I
hardly paid any attention to the class or the textbook. I do remember, though, one section that ingeniously made short work
of the whole irritating question of freedom. If you're lost in the
woods, reasoned the authors of the textbook, you may decide
that you have the freedom to go whichever way you want —
except that of course you will come to no good with that kind of
attitude. The only true and meaningful kind of freedom is to
follow the directions of someone who knows the way. The authors could have taken this line of argument further, adding a
few more constructive observations. For instance, it should be
obvious that if you're lost in the woods and you insist on going
the wrong way, someone who forces you to go in the right direc-

tion is actually doing you a favor, even if you have to be walloped into submission. And if a party of hikers is lost in the woods and one or two of the group insist on going their way, could the guide who knows the directions be justified in bumping off the troublemakers, if that is what it takes to get the others home safely?

The last chapter of that textbook painted a broad, uplifting picture of life in a completed Communist society of the future, its features still indistinct but gauzily beautiful. It must have occurred to someone that the targeted teenage audience might find this vision of total harmony too sedate to be inspiring. As a remedy, we were cautioned not to think that nobody would be unhappy under communism, that there would be no conflicts or personal tragedies or that life would be boring. Oh no, conflicts and disappointments and even tragedies would still exist, but they would be personal, not social — a big consolation to hypothetical believers in the advent of communism.

I knew there was more of this down the road. Going to college meant enduring four years of Marxism-Leninism, history of the Communist Party of the Soviet Union, and so on. I was beginning to bristle at the thought. (Imagine for a moment that every college or university a student can go to is a Bible college, with requirements of at least one course in Bible studies or history of Christianity every semester, taught in the strictest accordance with fundamentalist evangelical doctrine.) Besides, Marxism-Leninism professors, trained to be good watchdogs, had a reputation for being especially tough and nasty and out to get you with trick questions. Ideology may have occupied a quarter or even less of the total course time in college, but in my feverish, exaggeration-prone imagination, these three or four hours a week grew to a giant specter of tedium and nausea hovering over my college years. And then a job — and obligatory weekly, or biweekly at best, "political instruction" meetings.

"Comrades! We all know that it is very important for us to train professional musicians at a high level of excellence." That was the principal droning piously at such a meeting at Mama's school. "However, we have an even more important task, an even more important obligation to our country and to our students. That, comrades, is to educate them as good Soviet citizens, in the spirit of Communist morality. And I am sorry to say, dear comrades, that we have a serious problem. Some teachers, year after year, fail to show up at the gala evenings celebrating our state holidays, such as May First or November Seventh." His doleful gaze went straight to my mother and her close friend Nadya Berkovich, who were indeed guilty as charged. "Now, tell me, comrades, what are our students to think if they repeatedly see that their own teachers, the teachers who are supposed to be their *guides* and their *models*" — again his eyes wandered to the same two culprits — "do not care to attend the events celebrating the holidays that are so important, so *sacred* to every Soviet man? What conclusions are the students to draw? And what are we to think? Either that we have some teachers who are just too lazy to attend these events . . . or, comrades, we might draw some really sad conclusions, of the kind I don't even want to mention."

There had been a time when things had been a bit more relaxed at the Gnesin school, and Mama had been able to wriggle out of political instruction duty simply by invoking her status as mother to a small child. Then the screws were tightened. Several activists of the school's Party bureau, all women as it happened, now ran the show. Attendance at the meetings became mandatory, with sick leave the only valid excuse. For Mama, who taught three days a week, this meant an extra trip to school; as luck would have it, the civics meetings were held on one of her free days. And the Party bureau ladies took pains to make sure the meetings were taken seriously. Every teacher who wasn't working on the day of a meeting got a reminder by telephone *please* to attend. But no one bothered to make any calls if a meeting was canceled on short notice. Of course the idea that teachers — many of them not so young, most burdened with household responsibilities — would drag themselves to the school on congested buses, trolleys, and subways for no purpose wasn't nearly as important as the chance that someone would skip her biweekly dose of political instruction.

As a teenager, I chafed at the meetings and the rallies at school, and rubbed salt in the wound by telling myself that I was lying, lying, lying. It may be symbolic that when I finally worked myself up to rebel, the cause was a rather dubious one. It was 1979; Vietnam had just invaded Cambodia, deposing the murderous Khmer Rouge, and Chinese troops made an incursion into Vietnam. There were screams of indignation in the Soviet press, the public was supposed to be in high dudgeon, and in the middle of the imbroglio we were told at school that a rally in support of Vietnam would be held the next day in the gym hall. That night I paced in front of Papa in the kitchen, shivering with excitement, rehearsing a speech that I was going to step forward and give at that rally, arguing that Vietnam was the aggressor in Cambodia. Papa knew full well that I was going to give no such speech (I may have been hyped up, but I wasn't nuts), and he could afford to sit back watching me composedly and making comments such as "Your problem is, you're tense and too nervous. You're never going to make a good speaker if you're going to twitch your face and twist your hands like that." He also remarked that he wasn't so sure I was right, because after all, the Vietnamese invasion had probably saved millions of Cambodians from death and worse at the hands of the Khmer Rouge. If my father took the same side as the official position of the Soviet government, the reasons had to be very good. I fidgeted in the middle of the kitchen, torn by doubt in the face of a moral dilemma. All these vacillations made no difference whatsoever when it came to the actual rally; even if I had been rock-solid in my conviction that truth was on my side, I would not have done more than castigate myself inwardly for my cowardly silence and for living by the lie.

I tried not to lie more than was absolutely necessary — and even, with occasional spurts of ingenuity, to smuggle in a bit of truth when possible. Once our class guide, Ksenia Stepanovna, asked each of us to write down what we believed were the two most important political or social issues in the world today. I wrote "peace and human rights," surely no lie; fortunately, we were not required to elaborate, only to state the issues, and "human rights" could well be a reference to the rights of Chileans under Pinochet or of South African blacks. I felt stupidly proud of myself. But how many times would I get a question couched in such vague terms?

The last day of shame I remember with strong emotion was the gala at school commemorating the sixtieth anniversary of the founding of the Komsomol, the Communist Youth League. There were to be speeches and songs, and I, dogged by my reputation for versifying, had been approached by Ksenia Stepanovna and by Lyuda-the-Pioneer-master to write a poem for the occasion. Back home, I fumed and whined and swore I wouldn't, but what else could I do? Mama, tired of my bellyaching, suggested, "Write something, but don't make it too sycophantic." Writing a not-too-sycophantic poem about the sixtieth anniversary of the Komsomol was rather like writing a not-too-racist defense of the Ku Klux Klan. Come to think of it, it should have been easy to say I had tried my best and I wasn't up to it. But I suppose vanity got the better of me. I wrote the poem, four banal stanzas entitled "The Komsomol Banner."

The gala organizers were very pleased with the result of my efforts. Dressed in a long skirt and fancy blouse I had mooched from Mama, clutching in my damp hand the sheet with the poem on it, I waited in the wings of the performance hall stage. My turn to go on.

> Over our heads you soar high to this day,
> Our banner! Your light to our eyes still appears!
> O Komsomol banner, you've shown us the way
> Over these sixty victorious years!

I got through the last stanza in a surging singsong. The audience applauded with sincere joy, because this was the last item on the program and after a short break we would go on to the good part — the dancing. I slipped away into the ladies' room, my face blazing, and in a melodramatic gesture (but not before glancing around to make sure no one was watching) tore up my poem into small bits and flushed it down the toilet. As I was coming out, I ran into two girls from my class, and Lena Kalinina said, "That was a really good poem," by which I presume she meant that it rhymed and scanned. I looked away and mumbled something, and having had my fill of self-flagellation, went back in for the dance.

My worst sin against truth, however, was committed entirely of my own will, which must be why that was the only time I felt *real* shame. The shame still needles me a bit every time I think about it.

At the age of fourteen, on my annual visit to Leningrad, I suddenly heard English speech while wandering through the halls of the Hermitage Museum. Overcoming my inhibitions, I approached the flock of tourists and asked, in my specialized-school English, whether they came from America. They did, as it turned out, and we struck up a conversation. I got along especially well with two tall, blond, athletic-looking young women, sisters named Belinda and Brenda. Forgetting all about statues and paintings, I tagged along after them like an overeager puppy, wagging my tongue for lack of a tail. The girls must have found my chatter at least mildly interesting (after all, here they were conversing with a native who wasn't a tour guide), and they egged me on with a few questions — about my school, my parents, this and that.

And all the time that I spoke to these two innocents abroad, bursting with health and vitality and pursuit of happiness, I, the would-be revolutionary, was arduously trying to put the best possible face on our life. I wanted them to think that this was a normal society just like any other, and I had a normal life just like they did. One detail is still fresh in my mind, perhaps because it was particularly shameful. One of the sisters asked me whether we had a car. I could have — *should have* — told them the truth, which was that if we borrowed enough money to buy even the homeliest car, we would spend the next God knows how many years repaying our debts and living on bread and potatoes. At the very least, I could have said no and left it at that, with no explanation. But no, I didn't even want them to conclude for themselves that we couldn't afford a car. And so I hastily came up with something about my mother not wanting to buy a car because she was afraid we might get into an accident. In one stroke I put a whitewash on the Soviet way of life and made my mother look like an idiot. (She might in fact have said, after hearing of someone getting hurt in a car crash, something like "Well, perhaps it's for the best that we can't afford a car . . .") Almost immediately after I left the sisters, I wanted to kick myself: why, why had I been so stupid? Of course I knew why. It was not that I was afraid that anything I said to them would somehow come to the attention of the bodies known to worry about such things. No, I was driven not by fear but by a foolish pride: I didn't want these girls with their suntans and their all-American smiles to feel sorry for me.

But I atoned for my sin later. In some other Leningrad museum, I had a lively chat with an elderly Parisian couple, and they took my address and told me that their niece was coming to Moscow in a few months and would love to have someone show her around the city. I was only too glad to volunteer. A few months later, in the summer, the niece wrote to me from her Moscow hotel. I conscientiously tried to be a good tour guide to Josette, a smart-looking redhead in her midforties, but it was not an easy job, considering that my knowledge of Moscow was restricted to my own district (where there wasn't much to see) and a few other scattered spots, mostly libraries. Be that as it may, Josette seemed quite pleased. She even liked the spicy chicken, Georgian style (the only edible meal, my parents had warned me), at the nearest restaurant, a few bus stops away from our home.

When I invited Josette to our summer house, I had no idea that I was doing something illegal. It seems that the Zelenograd area was off-limits to foreigners because there was a military-related research institute in the area. If I had been caught, I might have become an example of the rule (which we had re-

cently learned in our Soviet government and law class) that ignorance of a law is no excuse for breaking it. Everything went
smoothly, though. Josette stayed at our dacha overnight; we
strolled in the woods where no foreign foot was supposed to
tread. Trying to make up for my sorry performance with Belinda
and Brenda, I hurled brickbat after brickbat at the Soviet system,
explaining to Josette that there were books we weren't allowed to
read and things we couldn't say openly ("For instance, if anyone
overheard what I'm saying to you now, I could go to jail for
that"), and that we had to stand in lines, and that people from
other towns had to come to Moscow to buy food. Yet again I
managed to say something that made me squirm a bit inwardly
when I thought about it later on — this time, not because it
wasn't factually true but because it wasn't true to my own prin-
ciples. I told Josette that virtually all Soviet mothers had to work
because a man couldn't earn enough to support a family. My
tone left little doubt that I thought mothers should not work
outside the home. In fact my own views leaned toward the opposite. But I had heard grown-ups talk that way, and couldn't
resist another opportunity to take a jab at the Soviet régime.
Josette was not particularly shocked, and drily remarked that in
this respect, things weren't all that different in France.

When, having escorted my guest back to Moscow, I returned
to Kryukovo with a scarf from Josette and an account of my
educational efforts, my mother was not pleased. What if the
woman was working for some newspaper or magazine? What if
she were to go back to France and write an article quoting my
animadversions?

I pooh-poohed her fears, but to be honest, I too got a little
nervous. However, I have to conclude that Josette was not after
all an undercover journalist on assignment to find out the straight
dope on Soviet life from a freethinking fifteen-year-old schoolgirl. The only consequence of her visit was a small, dainty packet
I received a few months later, a collection of Maupassant stories
and a mass-market paperback about the French Revolution. I
began to leaf through the latter, and was aghast when my eye fell
on familiar phrases about the Girondists and the Dantonists rep-

resenting the class interests of the haute bourgeoisie, about the shining virtues of Robespierre, and about the reactionaries who shut down the guillotine. It turned out the booklet came from the pen of Albert Soboul, a prominent French Marxist scholar. Just the kind of gift I needed from abroad: Marxist history books! What shocked me most of all was the thought that people could write this kind of crap voluntarily, when they didn't *have* to.

My fourteenth birthday, which made me eligible for membership in the Komsomol, came and went with the usual party. Rita, who turned fourteen less than two weeks later, lost no time in shedding her Pioneer tie. One day after school in March or early April, she headed to the District Party Committee headquarters — a mammoth high-rise of yellowish brick with a huge banner of Lenin and a red flag fluttering on the roof — for her Komsomol interview. She had dutifully memorized recent newspaper articles about "the international situation" and something about the history of the Komsomol as well. We came out of the schoolyard together and trudged along Stromynka Avenue with its wet, brown, creaky crust of months-old snow, and I wished Rita luck before we parted ways. At that time I still cared enough to press her afterward as to what questions they had asked her and whether they were really tough. I vaguely recall that the secretary of the Komsomol section had asked something about Chile, among other things, and that Rita had messed up and answered at least one question wrong or not at all, and the Komsomol secretary was rather nice and had accepted her anyway.

It used to be — so my grandmother told me — that membership in the Komsomol was reserved for the true ideological zealots, or at least for those who could put on a very good show of ideological zeal. That was in the 1920s, when Grandma was attending a technical institute, and she herself almost joined the Komsomol then. (Grandma came from what had been, before the Revolution, an upper-middle-class family. Maybe such a background has a universal tendency to predispose young people toward ideas of social justice, equal distribution of wealth, and power to the masses.) Then it turned out that the secretary of

the institute's Komsomol cell had been using the funds collected
in membership dues from the half-starving students to throw
posh parties with champagne and girls. Grandma was utterly
disgusted and gave up the idea of joining the Komsomol, perhaps
for the wrong reason. (I'm sure such party-loving Komsomol
secretaries wrought far less damage to the country than the true
believers did.)

By the time I was ripe for Komsomol membership, joining
that organization certainly wasn't a matter of zeal. It was still,
theoretically, a voluntary matter; you applied for membership on
your own initiative. In fact, though, joining the Komsomol was
not only routine but implicitly mandatory. You went to school,
you joined the Little Octobrists, then you joined the Pioneers,
had a few more birthdays, and joined the Komsomol. (Today,
however, according to a recent *New York Times* article, the pressure has slackened, and about one fourth of all young people
never join.) It's true that not everyone was accepted at first try,
because of bad grades or bad behavior or abysmal ignorance of
"the international situation" (if you said Pinochet was the leader
of Communist Bulgaria, or something like that). But eventually,
everyone either passed the tests or was admitted regardless of
performance and record.

As we entered the ninth grade, the number of necks sporting
red ties in our class dwindled steadily, until it dropped to none.
Those who were not yet Komsomol members were still officially
counted as Pioneers — until what age, I do not know. There
must have been some rules regarding Pioneers who never went
on to the Komsomol, but maybe such anomalies didn't merit any
special provisions. By the middle of the year, everyone except
for myself and Misha Belikov, the boy who refused to do drawings for the wall newspaper, was wearing a Komsomol badge
(almost identical to the Pioneer badge: a head of Lenin in profile
on the background of a red flag). I continued to wear the Pioneer
badge on the brown dress of my uniform and left my worn-out,
crumpled, and rather shabby neckerchief to languish at the bottom of a bureau drawer. Now that my unadorned neck no longer

stood out in the crowd, no one bothered me about it anymore. We were all around fifteen, and the guardians of morality at school were on the lookout for more serious lapses, like makeup or earrings.

Some time before the winter vacation of 1978–79, Ksenia Stepanovna asked me to stay after her chemistry class. As I stood facing her, a little nervous, in the aisle between desks, she folded her arms and with her usual solicitous frown said, "Katya, how come you're not in the Komsomol?"

I muttered something more or less unintelligible in reply.

"I don't understand," Ksenia Stepanovna pressed on. "Just look at this! You're the only person in the whole class who is not a member of the Komsomol. Oh, all right, there's also Belikov, but he's a very poor student, he's really a good-for-nothing, and you — you have good grades, you're a well-behaved girl. What's the matter?"

"Well, I guess I'm just not ready," I mumbled miserably, staring down at my feet. Our perplexed class guide made a few more comments, something about how my failure to join the Komsomol was reflecting badly on the entire class, and then let me go.

I think some girls tried to talk to me as well. Now that we were getting older, "public service" or "being socially active" was no longer child's play but a very serious matter. If you wanted to succeed in life, being active in the Komsomol was the place to start. "How are you going to get into college when you're not a Komsomol member?" said those who tried to talk sense to me — and they included some relatives and acquaintances of my parents'.

I said I wasn't going to join the Komsomol. I even said that I was not going to go to college. I wonder to what extent I meant it. There were so many stories about Jews not getting admitted to good colleges and being deliberately "sunk" at the entrance exams that I was beginning to doubt whether it was worth it even to apply. Why give them the pleasure of failing me when I could keep my dignity?

By the time of that conversation with Ksenia Stepanovna, a different prospect for my future was already taking a discernible shape, and it was looking more and more like I wasn't going to need the Komsomol, or a good public service record, or college in Moscow. We were thinking seriously about emigrating.

13

To Be Young,
Restless, and Jewish

THE DAY AFTER I turned sixteen and had my last birthday party
on Russian soil, I walked to the local police precinct a few blocks
away and filled out the form for a passport, with name, date of
birth, address, and nationality.

Like most Soviet offices, the passport desk of the police precinct had steel-tipped pens that had to be dipped into inkwells;
they made scraping sounds on the thick yellowish paper of the
form. I dimly recalled that only a short time before — a year?
two years? — I had eagerly anticipated this day, a rite of passage
into adulthood and citizenship. Yet now that the time had come,
I felt no stirrings of joy or pride. My family was to apply for our
exit visas, and this was nothing more than another formality to
get over.

The last thing I expected when I showed up a few days later
to pick up my brand-new red passport was entertainment. Looking over my papers, the weary-looking woman at the passport
desk solicitously inquired, "Why did you choose this nationality
for yourself?"

That was a shock. Since my half-Jewish mother was listed as
Russian in her passport, I had the option of listing myself as
either Russian or Jewish. I should add that in Soviet terms,
"Jewish" is not a religion but a nationality, like Russian, Arme-

nian, or Ukrainian. (*How do you unmask a Soviet spy abroad? You ask him if he's Jewish, and he will hastily say, "Oh no, I'm a Russian!"*) But the benefits of being registered as a Russian or the drawbacks of being registered as a Jew were not something to be discussed publicly, certainly not to be brought up by clerks at police precinct passport desks. Ill prepared, I stammered, "Well — my mother is actually half Jewish, so you see, I'm really three quarters Jewish . . ."

The woman looked at me and shook her head. "Did your papa tell you to take this nationality?" she probed gently, lowering her voice a bit as if we were discussing a dirty little secret.

"No!" I shot back abruptly, riled by the preposterous idea that Papa could tell me to do something like that. "I chose it myself." With that, I took my passport and headed home.

About an hour later, after my parents and I had already had a good laugh at the expense of the sympathetic desk clerk, I started looking through my passport (with maybe just the tiniest bit of pride after all) and discovered that they had mixed up my address: instead of "2nd Boyevskaya, 6" it said "2nd Boyevskaya, 2." Technically, this could mean that I had no legal right to reside in the apartment of my parents but had to live in a nonexistent Apt. 35 in Second Boyevskaya, No. 2 — which happened to be a factory. It was better not to leave such things to chance, especially when we were about to apply for exit visas. So it was back to the passport desk of the police precinct.

She remembered me, the good woman. When I explained the problem, she made the necessary change in my passport, and then, giving it back to me, suddenly said, "I suppose it was your papa who made you take this nationality?"

I held back a chuckle. "No, I took it all by myself. My father and I didn't even discuss it."

The clerk shook her head and sighed. "Well, you shouldn't have. It may cause you a lot of problems you know, later in life."

I don't know whether I was more stunned or amused. The poor woman was not too smart (she herself could have had a lot of problems if I had reported her remarks to some higher authority), but kind-hearted in her own way. She only wanted to help, an impulse that under the circumstances deserved to be appreciated.

Actually, about two years earlier there had been some tentative discussions at home of whether I should be listed as Russian or Jewish. A little while later, in my rebellious phase, I was full of determination to list myself as Jewish as a statement of defiance, shove it down the throats of the powers that be. Now that we were going to emigrate, it simply made no difference. A lot of people said that it didn't really make any difference in any case. As the saying went, "They hit you in the face, not in the passport," which in Russian also has the neat double meaning of "When they hit you, they look at your face, not your passport."

But many still tried to be listed as Russian. Mama's music professor told her about being approached at a party by a colleague's husband, who took him aside and said in a tone of utmost gravity, "I'd like to talk to you about a very personal matter, as one Party member to another. How can I get my children registered as Russian?" His children had not a drop of any but Jewish blood in their veins. And who knows how many Jewish fathers swallowed their masculine pride to give their children the last names of their Russian wives, because life would be considerably easier for a Mikhailov than for a Levin? A couple my father knew, he a tarnished Weisberg, she a plain Klimova, fecklessly listed the father's name on their daughter's birth certificate and only then started to think about it. A few months later they decided to have the baby's name changed, but were told at the registration office that this could not be done. Undaunted, the parents got divorced and then remarried after a period of time, during which the child's last name was changed to Klimova.

The question of Jewishness was never of much concern to me until I was a teenager. I don't remember how and at what age I first learned that I was Jewish. I was five or six when I had a fight with Vasya, a ruddy-faced, russet-haired boy in our yard, and he, sulking and pouting at something I had said or done, yelled, "Get out of here, you miserable Jew! And your father's a Jew too! And your mother's a Jew! And your grandmother's a Jew!" I was taken aback but not particularly mortified, and when

I came home and recounted the episode to my parents, all they did was laugh, if only because Vasya's sweeping indictment of my whole family had struck even at Grandma, wholly innocent of anything Jewish.

Later, when I went to school, there was the "nationality" column on the roster. In those years it was up to us, the students, to choose what nationality to claim, and there were Rubins and Bermans who listed themselves as Russian. I always gave my nationality as Jewish, without ever giving the matter much thought. Then one day in eighth grade, I was walking home with Olya Sukhova, one of the diplomats' daughters, and some turn in the conversation led Olya to say breezily, "You know, we all respect you because you write on the roster that you're Jewish and you're not trying to cover it up." This compliment left me mildly befuddled. Oh, it was a compliment all right . . . but how odd that such issues should be discussed among the girls.

I was beginning to pay a little more attention to these things than before, and for a good reason: it was time for me to start thinking about college. I was doing a lot of writing and translating by then, and I had my mind firmly set on becoming a writer. In ninth grade, I placed second in a citywide essay contest, winning no prize but a certificate with a fancy seal. (In the contest, we were magnanimously offered two topics: "Why I like to write" and an analysis of Mayakovsky's "Verses on the Soviet Passport." I dashed off an impassioned essay in which I said that I liked to write because it was a way for me to express my ideas and values and to convey them to other people. Of my twenty or so fellow contestants, one or two chose the same topic I did. The first-prize winner, of course, had chosen the other one.) The Literary College or the Philological Department of Moscow University seemed like natural choices. Then a friend of Mama's, herself Jewish and working as a translator, told her that both were virtually off-limits to Jews.

I couldn't quite bring myself to believe it. Not that I couldn't believe such things would happen under our Soviet laws. But when you're fourteen, it's very hard to come to grips with the fact that you don't have a chance, that you're at the mercy of malevolent or just indifferent forces, faceless men and women who sit on admissions committees and play God with the rest of your life, and there's nothing you can do about it. I knew that there were two or even three strokes against me: being Jewish, being a girl, and having no connections. For a while I just kept telling myself that I'd pull it off, I'd study a lot for the entrance exams and pass them with flying colors. After all, I had a very good memory, just right for cramming, and I didn't have to worry about the essay.

But I also knew that the oral exams — there would be at least three — would include one on the history of the USSR, and if they were out to get you, that one was it. They could ask you about something that was discussed at the plenary session of the Central Committee of the CPSU in year such-and-such. All those countless speeches and resolutions and programs and congresses! From what people said, it looked hopeless: you couldn't possibly memorize everything they could quiz you on. No matter how many sleepless nights you spent, no matter what a phenomenal memory you had, they always had something up their sleeves. (A joke illustrated, in a whimsically exaggerated fashion, the routine method of taking care of Jewish applicants. *Three young men are taking a college entrance exam in history. "Ivanov, what is the date of the bombing of Hiroshima?" "August 6, 1945." "Good! Petrov, how many people were killed or injured?" "About seventy-five thousand." "Good! Now, Rabinowitz, list all the victims by name."*)

Besides, it was becoming abundantly clear that no matter how perfectly you knew the material, no matter how perfectly you answered every tricky question, you were still at their mercy. In the late fifties, when my mother applied to the Moscow Conservatory, she got all 5's on the oral exams and the music exams; they gave her a 2 on the essay, and she wasn't admitted. (The next year she made it into the less prestigious Gnesin College.) She had never gotten anything less than a 4 for an essay in all of her school years. No applicants ever got to see their essays or their test results after they were graded, and it was usually pointless to argue.

Legally, you could demand to see your graded essay or test

results. Sometimes you could even win. A Jewish girl who graduated from the school where Mama taught was slapped with a 2 on her college entrance essay. Her mother decided to fight. She went from office to office, sat in waiting room after waiting room, and finally got as high as some Ministry of Education official. She was a dynamo, and besides, she probably had good connections: her husband was a doctor at a prestigious hospital or clinic. Finally she was able to see her daughter's essay, on which not a single spelling, grammatical, or stylistic error was marked. What was wrong? Nothing, the admissions committee official sheepishly conceded. Then why the failing grade? "Er — well — it was a mistake. The next person on the list got a two on the essay and we mixed them up and accidentally gave your daughter a two. But we can't admit her now, it's past the deadline. We'll admit her next year, though." The indignant mother began to protest, but was told that she'd better make the best of what she had. The next year the girl had to take the exams all over again; this time she was admitted.

A boy registered as Russian but in fact three quarters Jewish who got a 3 on his essay and was not admitted to Moscow University had the good fortune of having a prominent scientist for a father and a prominent journalist for a stepfather. The father and the stepfather joined forces and went to see the dean of admissions, demanding to see the essay. Again, not a single correction had been made. Why the 3? The dull-faced dean looked at the essay and said, "It's written in a sloppy handwriting, that's why." Under heavy fire, he consented to change the grade to a 4, which was a passing grade. Knowing that the competition was very tough, the two men kept pressing for a 5. The dean dug in his heels and produced some rule book that in fact said that a top-grade essay not only had to be well written and have no spelling or grammatical errors but also had to be neatly written. Finally he told them in plain Russian that he couldn't just up and change a 3 to a 5 — it would be awkward, really quite unseemly. The highest grade he could give the young man was a 4. But he reassured them that "everything would be all right." The boy's grade was changed from a 3 to a 4 and he was admitted.

The most hilarious thing happened to one of my father's co-workers. Her son — this time, a bona fide non-Jew — was a math whiz who won nationwide contests competing against kids older than he was, and graduated from some top specialized math school with a gold medal (that is, with straight 5's). However, when he applied to Moscow University, he got a 3 — a failing grade — on his math test. The boy, deeply puzzled, was sure he had gotten all the answers right. Luckily for him, his father, who had some high-level job in scientific research and was a Party member to boot, knew scores of people in all the right places. What he discovered from the hems and haws of these people was that the admissions committee had apparently taken the boy to be a Jew. The family had not the slightest trace of Jewish blood; it just so happened, by some whimsical chromosomal joke, that their son and daughter both *looked* Jewish. Of course the boy's passport said he was an ethnic Russian, but this was a perfect illustration of the folk wisdom "They hit you in the face, not in the passport."

The father did a lot of talking, presumably stressing the fact that his son had been failed not just unfairly but for the wrong reason as well. The mess was straightened out and the boy, Jewish looks and all, went to the university. This tale evidently got some notoriety; somewhat later, my mother heard about it from a friend's husband, who taught at Moscow University. His story was that after some VIPs made phone calls on behalf of the boy, the dean of admissions grudgingly agreed to change his grade, saying, "Well, since so-and-so is asking me for a favor, we'll take this fellow. Just don't tell me he isn't a Jew — you can't fool me."

I could easily see that in my case, this approach wasn't going to work. My parents might have had some uncultivated connections lying dormant, Mama in particular; quite a few students attending the prestigious Gnesin Ten-Year School of Music had well-placed or well-connected parents. For these parents, the music teacher was a near godlike being, holding in her delicate hands the future of their children's careers. Other teachers, even at nonprofessional district or community music schools, where the parents were generally of lower status and didn't consider music that important, got all sorts of things through their students' parents — salami, blue jeans, a sheepskin coat, an oak bedroom set, medical supplies, a room in an exclusive spa or a bed in a high-class hospital. But my mother hated asking people for favors, and hardly any ever came her way. (A couple of times the father of one of her little girls arranged for my parents to book hotel rooms, and rather nice ones at that, on trips to Leningrad and to Yaroslavl.)

And so I began to say, "I'm not going to go to college. They won't admit me anyway, so why should I waste any effort?"

"Don't be a fool," my mother would snap back at me. "What do you mean, they won't admit you anyway?"

"Because I'm Jewish."

"Don't talk nonsense. As if Jews never got into college! Well, of course they say that some colleges don't admit Jews, but not *every* college, for heaven's sake."

We argued ourselves hoarse, as we did on many a subject, without arriving at any conclusion.

My mother wasn't having that pleasant a time at school, either. A student of hers who was supposed to play at a televised recital was incomprehensibly passed over in favor of a good but far less interesting performer; Mama was baffled until someone quietly explained to her that the boy was Jewish and the girl chosen instead of him was Russian. Then there was the parent-teacher meeting at which a Party activist teacher, snide and honey-tongued, addressed the father of a boy named Volodya Ostrovsky as "Comrade Ostrovsky," though she knew full well that his name was Lifschitz. When he uncomfortably corrected her, she made him repeat it twice with an "Excuse me — what was that again?", then archly raised her eyebrows and said, "Oh, Comrade *Lifschitz?* And you're the father of Volodya *Ostrovsky?* Would that be his mother's name? Oh, I see . . ."

A student from the school, Dima Rakhmanov, emigrated with his parents. The school's Party organizer, stately and dignified Anna Borisovna Simonova, who had opposed admitting Dima when he transferred from another school in fifth grade, went around saying gleefully, "You see? You see? I was right! I think we ought to be more careful as to whom we admit, to make sure that this doesn't happen again."

Dima's piano teacher, a soft-spoken and genteel but straightforward woman in her fifties (also Jewish), innocuously inquired, "You mean to say that we shouldn't admit any more Jews?"

Imperious though she was, Simonova backed off: "Oh, come on, come on, don't put words in my mouth."

"Well, what else could you mean when you say that we should be careful as to whom we admit so that we won't have any more émigrés among our students?"

The dauntless little woman may have won the battle (Simonova, thus cornered, had to wriggle awkwardly out of her predicament), but the war was being lost. It got to the point where the fact that all but two of Mama's ten students were Jewish became something to worry about.

"Those Jews who emigrate — I'd kill them with my own hands if I could!" So declared an elderly Jewish piano teacher at the Gnesin school, talking in the hallway to a small group of other teachers, all of them Jewish, Mama among them. "It's because of them that there's all this anti-Semitism! They make things worse for all of us!"

In those days Mama was not even thinking of emigration yet; nevertheless, she furiously rallied to the defense of the maligned émigrés. "How can you say that?" she lashed out. "First of all, don't you know anti-Semitism was around long before there was any emigration? There was anti-Semitism when I was applying to college! Besides, what's wrong with people leaving if they don't want to live here? And even if they are doing something wrong, what right does anyone have to punish you and me for it?" Her counterattack was so vehement that the older woman had nothing to say. She was, however, by no means alone among Jews to take the view that emigration fostered anti-Semitism.

Value judgments aside, there was some truth to it. Jewish emigration and anti-Semitism (whether in the form of institutional discrimination or spontaneous popular sentiment) became locked in a vicious circle: the indignities and the practical difficulties of being Jewish were the main thing that pushed many people to emigrate, while emigration whipped up the bias. Émigrés, after all, were traitors, turncoats selling out the Motherland.

Pragmatic considerations played a part as well. Any dean of admissions at a college could now rationalize his reluctance to accept a Jewish student, no matter how bright: what good would it do to waste money and resources on educating someone who was going to make a run for it instead of repaying his debt to the Motherland? And a personnel manager at any workplace knew that if an employee applied for permission to leave the country, the management would be compromised. Why take the risk of hiring someone who could pull that kind of trick on you? This is not to say that discrimination against Jews was anything new; it just seemed to have gotten much worse in the 1970s. (A Gorbachev-era joke updates the situation. *A Jewish applicant is told by a personnel director, "I'm sorry, but we don't hire Jews." "What!" the man exclaims, flabbergasted. "But don't we have* glasnost *now? What about the new openness?" "Well, don't you see?" the director calmly explains. "I'm not trying to cover anything up. I'm* openly *telling you that we don't hire Jews.")*

People with no say in hiring employees or admitting students would express the same attitudes in less subtle ways, ranging from snide remarks to outright assaults. An elderly Jewish friend of Grandma's was knocked to the ground while standing in line by a fellow customer who yelled, "Why don't you croak on your way to Israel!"

Such ugly scenes were so far removed from my own experience that I truly could not imagine them happening to me. But I heard about all these things — the increasingly clouded atmosphere at Mama's school, the tart remarks, the slurs, the attacks, the injustices — and they could not but shape my view of the world I lived in. In the high noon of my dissident aspirations, being Jewish — and up-front about it — became another way of tweaking the nose of the system. It was just around this time that I started my heretical play with stick-figure dissident heroes and references to Jews being exiled *en masse* to distant and dismal

Birobijan, capital of the Jewish Autonomous Province that Stalin set up in Siberia. (I didn't just pull this out of thin air; there was some talk about it, but it was mentioned only as a very remote possibility, something not even at the stage of a rumor yet.)

If Jewish issues were of any interest to me, it was only insofar as Jews were victims of injustice — random, capricious, senseless injustice. That there could be any *positive* Jewish identity (apart from the gratifying aspects of being a pebble in the shoe of authority) never occurred to me. That being Jewish could entail a religion or a lifestyle, and not just an ethnic tag, was something I did not fully grasp until I came to America. What did I think it meant to be Jewish? A word in item five of the passport, a peculiar last name, and a "Jewish look," whatever that was. I don't think I ever bothered to ask myself why some people didn't like Jews and how Jews were different from other people. It was just a fact of life, as illogical as a hurricane — one more of the many absurdities of daily existence.

When I was eleven years old, I suddenly wanted to convert to Christianity — a curious side effect of reading very dumb antireligious propaganda books I picked up at the local children's library. I told my parents, in a most categorical tone, that I wanted to be baptized. (They did not get too alarmed, because they knew I would soon forget all about it.) I even had images of Christ and of the Holy Virgin with the child pinned up over my bed, icons I had copied from my parents' art albums. I had no idea that there was any contradiction between being baptized and being Jewish, and I certainly did not think that converting to Christianity would make me any less of a Jew.

By now, it is perhaps redundant to say that I knew next to nothing of Jewish culture. Granny Polina, my grandmother on the Jewish side, once told me about the holiday of Purim and another time about Hanukkah and the custom of giving children money — *geld* — as a gift on that occasion. She and most of my father's relatives took a simple-minded pride in their Jewishness. Papa could never forget two of his aunts discussing someone's unseemly behavior: "But darling, is it possible that a Jew could have done such a terrible thing?" "Well, dear, we have to admit that there are bad people among Jews too." Yet even they weren't all that mindful of their Judaic heritage.

I found it merely amusing when some Jewish visitors from Great Britain (acquaintances of Granny Polina's cousin who lived abroad) came to see us, after we had already applied for our exit visas, and seemed shocked by the albums of Russian icons in our bookcase and the miniatures of wooden churches decorating our shelves. And when Mama mentioned that a daughter of some friends, a would-be émigré, had suddenly turned into quite a Jewish zealot and was saying things like "I went to the synagogue the other day and it felt so good, you know — all those Jews, being among my own people," my natural reaction (which, judging from Mama's tone, seemed natural to her too) was to shake my head and chortle.

Now, years later, I tend to react with a certain coolness to impassioned pleas from Jewish activists on behalf of Soviet Jews denied the right to "live as Jews." I have good reasons to be leery of the idea that a majority or even a substantial portion of Soviet Jews — if those I have known are any indication — are all that worried about being unable to eat kosher food or light candles or wear yarmulkes. Even my father's proudly Jewish aunts were no exception. One of the dear ladies got a notice from the post office that there was a parcel for her from abroad (Jewish organizations used to send, and probably still send, parcels to aid Soviet Jews — always with return addresses of individuals, since Soviet citizens are forbidden by law to receive parcels from foreign organizations). Thinking it was a package full of clothes, she rushed to the post office, hailing a cab in her elation. The parcel contained several boxes of matzos. Aunt Tosya's disappointment turned into the fury of a woman cheated — these so-called benefactors had made her, an old lady of poor health and modest means, rush over by cab to the post office! She refused to accept the parcel and went home in a huff. I'm sure that if the senders were ever notified that the addressee had turned down the parcel, they must have taken this as an ominous sign of how Jews were terrorized by the Soviet system.

My own conjecture is that most Soviet Jews would much

rather live as Russians than as Jews, if only the powers that be would let them, if only it wasn't for that accursed item five. I am in no way trying to write out of existence all the stout-hearted men and women, famous and unknown, who have affirmed their Jewish identity and sought to reclaim their cultural roots in the face of all odds, of ostracism, brutal harassment, all the way to imprisonment. But I cannot help wondering how many of them embraced Jewish cultural and religious traditions, consciously or unconsciously, out of protest. (Perhaps they are the very people who, if raised in an oppressively traditional environment, would have turned rebellious and secular.) Who knows, maybe if I had stayed in the Soviet Union long enough to have my Jewishness shoved in my face countless times, and long enough to grow even more impatient with official dogma, I would have been drawn toward some form of Jewish self-awareness as well. Maybe — but I doubt it.

One summer when we were vacationing in Engure, we had for co-lodgers a refusenik family. The husband and wife were both strongly Zionist, and the wife, having lost her regular job (as people in her situation usually did), earned her living dangerously by typing Jewish *samizdat*. I read some of those typescripts. I also picked up, for reading on rainy days, the couple's smuggled-in but luxurious edition of the Torah: leather-bound and with gold lettering on the spine and the cover, the text running parallel in Hebrew and Russian, with commentaries and with backward pagination. The fierce insularity of the Chosen People, the insistence on the submission of the individual to the rules of the group, the harsh line drawn between the Jews and the outsiders — all of this turned me off. So did the Biblical references to women; and even more offensive were the cloying commentaries to these passages, pointing out how enlightened and progressive they actually were ("Look! They even acknowledge that a woman is a human being!"). This was not for me.

But there still was that matter of tweaking the nose of the system. In ninth grade, a chance suddenly turned up for me to make a public — and safe — protest against anti-Semitism. In our literature class, we were studying Yevgeny Yevtushenko's

The Bratsk Hydroelectric Station, a lengthy epic poem consisting of many episodes, some of them monologues of people whose fates are somehow intertwined with the station. Each of us had to pick a segment and memorize it, to recite later in class. I scanned the poem, and the opening line of one segment jumped out at me: "I'm a light dispatcher, Izzy Kramer." Characters named Izzy Kramer were not exactly a staple of Soviet literature as I knew it.

I read on. I have never had much admiration for Yevtushenko, the virtuoso walker of the tightrope of the permissible, but that poem, written in a simple, direct language, made my eyes tingle (I still get goose bumps every time I recall it). Izzy Kramer is thinking of the contrast between his present self as a respected member of the community and his other identity, still indelibly inside him, as a seventeen-year-old boy in a ghetto in Nazi-occupied Latvia, with a yellow star on his sleeve: "To the one they shout, 'Hello there, buddy!'/To the other, 'Hey, you lousy kike!' " He remembers his clumsy adolescent yearning for Reva, whose hair is "long and misty like a rabbi's prayers." Taken to Oswenzim, he one day suddenly sees a wan, thin, ghostlike Reva on the other side of a wire fence. Before his eyes, a Nazi guard strutting about in shiny new boots that are too tight for her forces Reva to put on the boots and run in circles to stretch them. Reva runs and runs, as a sobbing Izzy begs God to put an end to her torment . . . and at last the girl collapses in exhaustion: "God has heard me, Reva: you are dead."

> Izzy Kramer does amount to something:
> At his feet a world of splendor lies.
> . . . Somewhere yet, Reva still runs in circles,
> Somewhere yet, Izzy still cries and cries . . .

That was it. I was going to memorize this poem and recite it in front of the whole class, and not only because it had moved me so much — no, this poem did not just have characters named Izzy and Reva but included numerous references to Jews, and even the word "kike" (the Russian pejorative *zhid*). The word "Jew" cropped up only a few times in our curriculum or our class discussions, in connection with World War II, and even then in passing. (In seventh grade, when we read Gogol's *Taras Bulba*, I noted with amusement that the abridged version in our textbook left out the numerous anti-Semitic passages, such as the grotesque Jewish characters and the not unsympathetic description of a pogrom by the Cossacks. This was done, I am sure, not out of sensitivity to the feelings of Jews but simply to avoid any controversial references to an issue that was not supposed to exist. It is noteworthy that the even stronger anti-Polish motifs in the story were left intact.)

I would put an end to this silence. I was going to stand up defiant, a Joan of Arc in brown dress and black pinafore, and throw it in their faces:

That the word "kike" should forever vanish,
And no longer stain the name of Man!

I don't know what consequences I expected, for myself or for the world at large, from my act of so-called defiance: some kind of martyrdom? Catcalls from my classmates? A bad grade (from Lydia Davydovna, of all people)? What happened was that I got up there, pumped up as could be, and recited the poem, and Lydia Davydovna gave me a 5 and asked me to prepare this in a week or so for a schoolwide poetry recitation contest, the winner of which would be sent to a districtwide contest, and then on to a citywide one. As I went back to my seat, the boy who sat behind me, strawberry-blond Litvinov, a sourpuss and a pain in the neck, leaned over and whispered, "That was pretty good" — the only time he ever said anything nice to me.

The following week I went to the contest, which had no audience, just a panel of judges at a long table in the performance hall. The panel included our dreaded headmistress, Nadezhda Pavlovna, and the long-nosed assistant principal, Vera Nikolayevna, who had donned the mantle of poetry conoisseurs for the occasion. I stood before them, and did myself in. I was so overwhelmed by emotion, both by the poignancy of Yevtushenko's lines and by the proud, nervous consciousness of my public statement, that I stumbled in midpoem, couldn't remember the next stanza, and had to be prompted by Lydia Davydovna. Somewhat shaken, I managed to recoup and continue without a hitch, and gave it to them in a strong, vibrant, triumphant voice:

> That the word "kike" should forever vanish,
> And no longer stain the name of Man!

And they, the powers that be, looked at me sympathetically and kindly; I even thought I detected a haze of warmth in the eyes of Nadezhda Pavlovna herself. Maybe they were thinking, *The poor kid — she must have suffered a lot from anti-Semitism, see how strongly she feels about it.* They told me that my recitation had been good, very good, and if only I hadn't stumbled. . . . If only I hadn't stumbled — who knows? — I might have appeared at a citywide poetry-reading contest with a poem that openly spoke about Jews and about the word "kike." A regular Joan of Arc at the stake.

14

Parting Is
Such Sweet Sorrow

ONCE, ON A SUMMER DAY in the country with nothing better to read, I somehow became absorbed in a Polish detective novel in a paperback fiction anthology borrowed from a neighbor. It started out as a straightforward mystery: an undistinguished white-collar resident of Warsaw kills himself for no apparent reason by jumping from the window of his tenth-floor apartment. The police are suspicious. At once a foreigner appears on the scene, a cousin from France who was visiting the poor devil at the time of the suicide. Is he the villain? It was not quite as simple as that. After many twists and turns of the serpentine plot, it was revealed that the undistinguished Polish citizen actually wasn't dead. He had knocked his French cousin unconscious, changed clothes with him, and hurled him out of the window, so he could pose as the foreign visitor and use the victim's passport to leave Poland.

It occurred to me after I put the book down that the story might (surely unbeknown to the author) contain seeds of subversion. What did it say about the quality of life in Poland, that a person would connive so intricate a murder scheme to get out? Moreover, would it not be easy to make such bizarre crimes unnecessary by making it possible for people to leave the country without masquerading as their murdered cousins?

Although I never heard of anyone pushing people out of windows or swapping identities to get out of the Soviet Union, devious arrangements of a less daring kind were common. The only Soviet wedding at which I ever was a guest, at the age of fourteen — a wedding with a lavish feast, champagne and vodka and singing, a dark-haired groom who cut a dashing figure, a bride in a flowing, lacy blue gown — was just such an arrangement.

The wedding bash was thrown by the bride's ex-husband, Sergei, a former schoolmate of Papa's who had grown into an arrogant bearded bohemian artist. He was known to be a pathological liar, and Papa was barely able to suppress a chuckle when Sergei first broke the news of his impending marriage to a lovely Frenchwoman who worked for the French embassy in Moscow. Michelle confounded us all by turning out to be quite real and quite lovely. Sergei then set about arranging for his ex-wife to marry a Frenchman, not for a *ménage à quatre* but in order to get their two small children out of the Soviet Union. Although this union was intended solely as a means of transportation, the newlyweds called each other "darling" every time they spoke on the phone, just in case there was anyone else on the line who had to be fooled.

Sergei, who must have really taken to his role as matchmaker *cum* travel agent, also started looking for a Gallic bride for his brother. He would have found one all right, but the groom wasn't willing. He said he had heard that in the West you have to work for a living. In Moscow he was getting along beautifully by loafing nine to five at some office and dabbling in the black market in his spare time — a lifestyle that suited him perfectly.

The magnetic fascination that all things Western, and especially American — from blue jeans, chewing gum, and rock music to Jane Fonda and Kurt Vonnegut — hold for Soviet people from all walks of life is well known by now. The high expectations generated by this fascination sometimes make the real thing quite a letdown. I must have been fourteen or so when Grandma's relatives in Leningrad, with whom we were visiting, brought home a surprise bottle of Pepsi-Cola. (It had just been introduced in the Soviet Union, but — it goes without saying — it was very difficult to get.) The sight of the bottle with the red-white-and-blue logo was quite a thrill: *Pepsi-Cola!* I don't quite know what sort of nectar I anticipated, but when I took a few sips, my immediate reaction was *This is it? A carbonated drink — that's all there is to it?*

The clunky anti-Western propaganda dished out daily by the Soviet press tended to have a reverse effect on many people. I found it especially delightful when *Pravda* or *Izvestia* earnestly reported the declaration of some American that the United States was turning into a police state where people were no longer free to speak their minds, or something along these lines. As far as one could tell, the courageous American who had made that statement (if he held a teaching post at a college or had published a book, that was enough to promote him to the rank of "one of the most distinguished scholars in the U.S." or "a well-known writer") was not yet languishing in a jail cell. As a result, when the press spoke of runaway inflation or of crime in the New York subway, many of us brushed it off as just another canard. And when yet another newspaper quoted yet another American politician or activist as saying that the cost of medical care in the United States was obscene, I paid more attention to the thrilling freedom of being able to say something like that about your country than I did to the message itself.

I was too consumed by the French Revolution to take a passionate interest in more contemporary Western ways (my general feeling at that time was that interesting things had abruptly stopped happening at some point after the 1830s), but of course I was curious. I picked up some entertaining details from American mystery novels and science fiction, which depicted a world of private detectives and reporters hot on the trail, of suburban houses and swerving cars and motels and dimly lit bars where bartenders served cocktails topped with red cherries. The thing that startled me the most was not the widespread availability of cars, guns, and eateries, but the apparent ease with which a man and a woman would rip off their clothes and tumble into a bed, or if one wasn't conveniently nearby, onto the living room rug — sometimes just minutes after learning each other's names! In disbelief, I was inclined to attribute such behavior to the authors' flights of fancy (which is not to say that such things didn't go on in the Soviet Union, only that I didn't know about them).

More humdrum but nevertheless intriguing aspects of life in the West emerged from the stories of the lucky few who had been there. My father's brother, Uncle Willy (named by Granny Polina after William Shakespeare), had toured the United States with the Moscow Symphony Orchestra, where he was a cello player. Two of his especially memorable anthropological observations were that Americans never wore any headgear, not even in the coldest weather, and that they always smiled, even at total strangers.

Others — upstanding citizens, usually Party members — sometimes got a chance to go abroad as tourists in groups. Their impressions of foreign life usually boiled down to variations on "home good, West bad." It seemed to me that more often than not, the focus wasn't on the bad politics of the Americans, the French, or the Austrians, nor on their bad morals, but on their bad *manners* — not on social inequities but on lack of cultural sophistication. The Party organizer at Mama's school, self-satisfied, imperious Anna Borisovna Simonova, back from a trip to France, did not talk about beggars in the streets or any such capitalist horrors but about an altogether different, previously overlooked Western vice: "Just imagine, when they go to a concert or to the theater, they don't leave their coats at the coat check in the lobby like we do, they just go in and sit in the audience with their coats on, or drape them over the back of the seat. For us, going to a performance is something special, a festive occasion. And they don't even bother to take their coats off. They don't care about culture. They have all those great museums and no one goes there. At the Louvre, you hardly see a soul except for the staff." (The first observation was by and large true, though I'm not sure it merited such harsh condemnation. As for the latter . . . well, maybe museum attendance in France skyrocketed between the midseventies and the mideighties, when my parents and I stood in lines to get into the Louvre.)

I recall reading in the literary magazine *Novy Mir* a woman's snide account of her trip to England. Back in the USSR, the lady invites her friends to a party and announces she is going to entertain them Western-style. She serves tiny sandwiches and crackers with bits of cheese and cream, and drinks in little glasses. Her friends' reaction is to say, "Look here, if you've got nothing to eat at home, we'll run down to the store and buy something. [Of course, nothing could be easier in Moscow.] You don't invite people over and feed them *this!*" The none-too-subtle implication was that the Brits, and Westerners in general, are just tightfisted, which is why they serve ridiculous snacks instead of a bountiful tableful of hard-won delicacies as the Russians do.

Even trustworthy, more or less freethinking people often did no better than the official journalists who got paid to churn out these damning impressions of the West. How many times, for instance, did we hear the story that in the West, it's quite common to invite people for dinner and then send them a bill for the food they've eaten? (My mother's former music professor swore that this actually happened to him in Germany — but that was *East* Germany, hardly a reflection on capitalistic mores.) Moreover, the story went, the host will pour you a drink in an itsy-bitsy glass and then lock the bottle away in the liquor cabinet.

When and how did I hear for the first time that people emigrated to become part of that unknown world? In the beginning, in addition to those who married into it, there were people who "ran off" — who went on a trip abroad and never came back. If they were famous, like the figure skaters Belousova and Proto-popov, they were excoriated in the newspapers as venal traitors who sold their souls and their country for dollars and luxuries (and parties with tiny hors d'oeuvres to nibble on, and stingily dispensed drinks).

In 1970, all of a sudden it became possible to emigrate legally, with an invitation from relatives in Israel. By the time the seventies were half over, jokes on the subject had mushroomed. *A group of scientists decides to come up with the quintessential joke. They collect thousands of jokes and put them into a computer for a synthesis. After a lot of blinking and whirring, the machine gives them this:* "*Brezhnev meets Lenin in Red Square, and one asks the other* [with a Jewish accent], *"So, Avram, when are we going to Israel?"*

Even the beloved singer Vysotsky wrote a song about emigration, here transmogrified into a good-natured farce where the goofy hero and his equally goofy friend Mishka Shifman have a discussion, over a few bottles of vodka, about going off to Israel:

> Well, at first I wasn't drunk,
> And in fact protested:
> "Moshe Dayan," so I said,
> "Is a one-eyed bastard.
> "He's a real pharaoh,
> "An aggressor, too!
> "And where there is aggression,
> "What's there for me to do?"

Eventually, however, Mishka Shifman persuades the hero to join him in emigrating to Israel, except that there's one little hitch: the hero is pure Russian, with not a drop of the required Jewish blood in his veins. Then comes the punchline: when the two go to the exit-visa office, Mishka is turned down while his non-Jewish pal gets a green light.

> "Wait a minute! I'm the Jew!"
> Mishka starts to shout.
> "Hey," they said, "don't raise a fuss!
> "And anyway, get out!"

The conclusion: Mishka drinks himself to death, complaining that they always give preference to Russians rather than Jews.

Vysotsky also pulled off a terrific emigration joke in his capacity as an actor, on the stage of the Taganka theater while appearing in Chekhov's *The Cherry Orchard* (my parents were in the audience). In the last scene, the character he played raises a glass of champagne "to those who are leaving — and good luck to those staying behind." Vysotsky spoke that line *to the audience*.

I overheard talk about this or that family leaving, and jokes like *Why are Jewish children so smart and good-looking? Because they're produced for export*, and perhaps I knew somewhere deep down that it was only a matter of time before they exported me too. My father would have pounced at the first opportunity that presented itself. Mama was reluctant. (I didn't learn about all these arguments until much later.)

"You say you don't want to live under the Soviet system," my mother would say. "Well, I don't really feel that I'm living under the Soviet system. I have my job, my friends, my family. I have nothing to do with the Soviet system. I really love my school and my students. I know I'm never going to have another job like this abroad."

To which my father would reply, "Well, you'll see — the Soviet system will catch up with you someday. Then you'll change your mind."

For better or worse, he was right: the Soviet system came to Mama's school. It didn't happen overnight, of course; things started to change slowly but perceptibly, with the mandatory political instruction meetings, and the high-handed attitudes of the Party activists on the staff, and the subtle warnings to the teachers who did not show sufficient zeal. Bit by bit, it got to a point where the job Mama loved so much was a source more of aggravation than of satisfaction. That was one of the things that swayed her to cross the Rubicon. Many little things played a part, including that chilling *Deutsche Welle* broadcast of the letter from the Christian prisoner of conscience held and tortured in a mental ward. There was something else as well.

I remember a conversation on our way to Latvia for our summer vacation with Vika Veksler, the mother of Mama's little student Yulya and our co-lodger in Engure, who with her family was about to take the plunge and file an application for permission to leave. In our small, cozy train compartment, late at night before turning in, we talked about emigration and why it was the right thing to do, about freedom and anti-Semitism and our Jewish identity. Mama said, "I don't want to pretend to be more highminded than I really am. I'm scared by all this talk about rationing here and rationing there. There seem to be food shortages everywhere, and it's closing in on Moscow, too. The idea of lining up for food at six o'clock in the morning and spending hours out in the cold in front of the store — that frightens me. I just don't think I'm up to it." (Papa's only, laconic comment, in a flat voice that was somehow more striking than any dramatics, was, "I don't know about anybody else, but I'm leaving because I want to get out of here, to get away from this system. I think that's the only valid reason to leave.")

Valery Geller, my father's go-getter colleague, was also on the move. After applying to emigrate, he was promptly fired from his job at the State Radio Broadcasting and Sound Recording House — a job considered sensitive, since it involved the media. Indefatigable as he was, he just couldn't leave it at that, and with hardly any hope of success, he sued his employer. The case went to court. Geller lost. To avoid going through the humiliating charade of getting fired, my father quit his job two weeks before we filed our papers on March 1, 1979.

Mama quit even earlier, in the fall of 1978, without telling her superiors or most of her colleagues why. Formally, she explained that the job was just too demanding, too stressful, and she couldn't handle it any longer. She later realized that this wasn't entirely untrue: since the students were aspiring professionals, and future careers and competition prizes were at stake almost from grade school, the strain *was* great. An extra grade point in the finals or participation in a school recital assumed a vastly overblown importance, leading to rivalries between teachers, angry outbursts, accusations of conspiracy. In our last year and a half in Moscow, when Mama was no longer teaching at the Gnesin school, she felt almost relieved to be outside the fray as she listened to former co-workers spill out their woes. When she was quitting, though, it was with regret. She simply didn't want the administration to know that she was emigrating, because she was afraid it might cause trouble for her students, who were hastily redistributed to other teachers.

The principal was shrewd enough not to buy Mama's explanation, perhaps because he knew how much the work and the students meant to her. Confidentially, he said to another teacher, who later relayed it to Mama, "Either she has some really bad illness, or she's leaving the country." Perhaps by then it wasn't such a hard thing to guess.

But I am jumping ahead of the story.

One afternoon in the spring of 1978, when I was fifteen and in eighth grade, I came back from school and sat down for dinner at the kitchen table, and Grandma, the only one home, said suddenly and abruptly, "You know, the folks have decided to leave."

Perturbed, I looked up and blurted, "They have? But I don't want to leave."

"Well, if you want to do something about it, you'd better talk to them now," Grandma said gruffly, as if implying that my parents had really gone gaga and her only hope was that I'd be able to bring them back to their senses.

Why was she — so avidly curious, so hungry for new things to see and experience — at first so hostile to the idea? And why was I so upset? I think that my reaction, and perhaps hers too, was an instinctive resistance to anything that threatened to disrupt the familiar course of life. Whatever the reason, I did not acquit myself very honorably that night when my parents came home. I marched up to Papa and said, "You've decided to leave, haven't you." Yes, he replied. "I don't want to leave," I declared belligerently. "Over there, women do not have equal rights." My father stared at me incredulously as I went on (conscious, not even very far in the back of my mind, that I was about to say something dumb), "For example, in Brazil, a woman cannot get a job without her husband's consent." I had picked up that bit of information from our eighth-grade Soviet government and law textbook, from the chapter on marriage and family, which somewhat tendentiously contrasted Soviet family laws and practices with Western ones. This must have been one of the very few times I appealed to the moral authority of a textbook. In addition to the tainted credibility of the source, there was such an easy, obvious answer, which my father of course threw back at me without missing a beat: "But we're not going to Brazil!" Surely I could have come up with a more intelligent objection. But this was probably an argument I had no desire to win. I needed only the satisfaction of being persuaded, of knowing that whatever reasons I could find for not wanting to leave were weak and easily overcome.

With quiet assurance, Papa said, "Come on, Katya, I'm sure that in America no one is going to prevent you from doing the work you want to do." And that was enough. My doubts dispelled, I was soon, if not instantaneously, transformed into a gung-ho enthusiast of emigration. It didn't take a long time for Grandma to be won over, either.

In the fall of 1978, we received an "invitation" from Israel, from an obscure great-aunt of my father's. We could have filed the application in November or December. The problem was that I was turning sixteen in February, which changed my status from a child, included as an appendage in my parents' application, on a joint passport with Mama, to an adult individual in my own right and with my own application. If we filed our documents before my birthday, additional documents, photos, and such would have to be submitted afterward. To avoid going through the hassle twice, my parents figured it would be better to wait until February.

After I got my passport, we nearly had another delay in filing the documents, this time because Uncle Yura, Mama's brother, was up for a promotion at the research institute where he worked and was afraid that his chances would be hurt if his family were compromised. Papa was actually willing to wait a few more months, but this time it was the formerly reluctant Mama who rebelled. Now that we had made up our minds, she insisted, it should be done as quickly as possible. To wait was to play with fire. Who knows, she said, what's going to happen in the next few months? The door could slam shut at any moment. Papa shrugged and rolled his eyes and grumbled about panicking, but complied. Eventually, of course, it turned out this was one of those occasions when my mother's seemingly exaggerated fears proved quite justified, not to say prophetic. The door did all but slam shut, and we were among the last lucky ones to slip out while it was still open. If we had applied three months later, we might still be there, or we might have left after six or seven highly unpleasant years of struggle, harassment, and efforts to make ends meet.

By the way, Uncle Yura did get his promotion, the stain on his family's reputation notwithstanding. He did have to sit through a talk with a Party representative who made inquiries about his sister's intentions. My uncle's straightforward answer ("Am I my sister's keeper?") apparently satisfied the questioner. What a liberal time we were living in.

Because I was sixteen and an adult with my own individual application, I had to get a letter confirming my attendance at School No. 1 of the Sokolniki district, just as my parents needed papers confirming their past employment. That meant there was no way to keep the whole thing a secret at school, as my parents and I might have wished to do. There were good reasons: a boy beaten up by his classmates, a girl driven to a nervous breakdown after her best friends stood up at a class meeting to denounce her as a traitor — we had heard enough cautionary tales, and even some funny ones. There was the boy whose name remained on the roster until the end of the semester after he emigrated, and the burly math teacher who went through the following routine every time he took attendance at the beginning of a class: "Timashov, present . . . Petrova, present . . . Sidorov, ill . . . Rosen, betrayed the Motherland . . ."

When I realized that exposure was now inevitable, I was glad. I was, after all, at the peak of my defiant mood and actively seeking a safe but spectacular taste of martyrdom. One day at the end of February I appeared in school with a written request from the OVIR, the Visas and Registrations Department, for a letter from the principal. I deposited the letter with the principal's secretary first thing in the morning and trotted off to class, tingling with anticipation.

At the beginning of the third period (algebra), the teacher told me the principal wanted to see me after class. I fidgeted in my seat until the bell rang, then scampered downstairs and, a little breathless, knocked on the door of the principal's office. Nadezhda Pavlovna, her face heavy and stern as always, was looming over her desk. With her was Vera Nikolayevna, superintendent of the teaching staff. I suddenly felt intimidated and awkward, and a confrontation was the last thing I wanted. Mercifully, it seemed that they were not looking for one either. "Sit down," Nadezhda Pavlovna commanded in a level voice. I took a seat, probably feeling for all the world like any ordinary, non-dissident student called on the carpet.

She probably wasn't completely at ease, either. How did I feel about all this? she asked.

"Well, it's really my parents' decision." I spoke in a small, strained voice, staring down at my hands.

"It's too bad," Nadezhda Pavlovna pronounced in a tone that was authoritative but devoid of hostility. She then added, as if in an aside, her eyes fixed on some object on her desk, "Perhaps someday you will really regret this. There was one family — they emigrated to Israel and then the father was killed in the war and the girl was left an orphan. Such a sad story." The tone of her voice implied that, sad as it was, the family was of course to blame for its own tragedy: if people insist on doing silly things, they'll have to pay.

She asked me, I think, whether I had tried to influence my parents and talk them out of making such a mistake; I evasively answered that nothing could be changed. Finally, after a perfunctory question-and-answer session that lasted only a few minutes, our dreaded headmistress heaved a sigh and said, "All right, you can pick up your letter from the secretary. You may go now."

Our next class was chemistry, with our class guide, Ksenia Stepanovna. As I might have expected, she had already gotten the news. After the bell rang at the end of the lesson and my classmates noisily got up and stuffed their books and notebooks back into their schoolbags, she came up and muttered, "Katya, will you please stay for a few minutes."

When everyone had filed out of the classroom, I walked the gauntlet of the empty seats toward Ksenia Stepanovna's desk. It's not that I was afraid. Although she might represent the powers that be, she wasn't that bad a person, just a pathetic one. I didn't want to cause her any distress. Besides, I knew that she was going to start asking me questions that I would not be able to answer truthfully (after all, I couldn't tell her *why* my parents, and I too, wanted to leave the Soviet Union), and I was going to have to squirm and put on an act.

"Well . . . Nadezhda Pavlovna has told me about what's happening . . . in your family," said Ksenia Stepanovna, surely as uncomfortable as I was, if not more. She was like a Catholic nun trying to talk to a student who has gotten pregnant. She looked at me with rueful, somewhat disconcerted solicitude. It was as if there had been a sudden death or grave illness or messy divorce in my family.

"So that's why you did not join the Komsomol," she added reflectively. I nodded yes. We went through an already familiar question-and-answer routine. Wasn't there anything I could do to influence my parents? Had I tried? My role was to stand there and shrug helplessly. Then Ksenia Stepanovna delivered her *pièce de résistance.* Shaking her head with the same look of forlorn sympathy, she said, "And then, you know, you'll have to listen to all that slander against our country. Can you imagine how painful that's going to be for you?"

At the time, it wasn't even funny — that's how awkward I felt. With eyes downcast, I murmured something intended to indicate that yes, it would be awfully hard, but I'd find the strength to bear it.

Ksenia Stepanovna let out a sigh and said, "Well, you'll tell them the truth about our country, won't you?"

This time, I realized, I could give her an honest answer. I was even beginning to appreciate the irony as I answered, "I will."

I was dismissed — and still not a soul in class knew a thing, with the exception of Rita. She had known for a few months. One day as we were walking home together from a movie, I braced myself and said, "Rita, I've got something to tell you."

As I paused, searching for words, Rita beat me to the punch. "You're leaving," she said, not asking a question but making a flat statement. It wasn't such a wild guess on her part. We had swapped émigré jokes, and I had recited to her Vysotsky's Mishka Shifman song; I had also mentioned our acquaintances who were leaving or had left, and she had remarked a little wistfully more than once, "Someday you're going to leave too."

My appetite for persecution aside, I was simply curious to see what would happen when my schoolmates found out. Perhaps I also wanted to be the center of attention, wanted them all to know that I had such an unusual destiny. Having gotten my letter with the school seal and Nadezhda Pavlovna's signature, I stood in the girls' restroom chatting with Rita and waving the letter around in a rather conspicuous manner. Not surprisingly, my efforts paid off: Katya Vorontzova asked, "What's that paper you've got?"

I showed her the letter confirming that I was indeed a student in the ninth grade of School No. 1 of the Sokolniki district, a letter addressed to the OVIR and "pertaining to an application for exit for permanent residence in Israel." Of course it was a big surprise to Katya, and of course a little flock of girls clustered around us right away, and of course by the next day, when we had gym and all the girls were gathered for our social circle in the changing room, everybody knew all about it. I was shelled with questions, including the inevitable "Are you going to America?"

"No, we're going to Israel," I feebly protested, mindful of my parents' admonition to be careful. Officially, that was our destination; the rationale for the Jews to be singled out as virtually the only members of Soviet society allowed to emigrate was that they had a "historic homeland," and relatives, in the state of Israel. In fact, by that time nearly 90 percent of all émigrés were going to the United States or to Canada.

"Oh, come off it. Israel, my foot," sharp-nosed Lena Karpukhina retorted scornfully. "They all go to America. We know this elderly couple, their kids went away and landed in California. And now they're trying to get the parents to join them too. Well, they're gonna get what's coming to them," she snorted.

I was no good at obfuscating. Once cornered and confronted with what I knew to be true, I meekly surrendered and did not exactly admit that yes, we were headed for America, but I didn't deny it, either.

"Will you be able to come back for a visit?" someone asked.

"They say that you can come back once you get your citizenship, in five years," I said. (That was what we had heard. Oh, the twists and turns of fate. Soon after we came to the United States, we found out that it was all but impossible for a recent émigré, even a citizen, to get an entry visa from the Soviets — so impossible that the few people whose visa applications were approved immediately were suspect, in émigré circles, as KGB agents. And then suddenly along came Gorbachev with his reforms, and lo and behold, the coming-back fairy tale we had all believed in came true and émigrés started traveling to the Soviet Union in droves.)

"I can just imagine Jung coming back a few years from now," one of the girls taunted. "Pale, worn out from hunger, unemployed . . ."

"Drug addicted," someone else chipped in. They were smiling and joking around, but it occurred to me that behind the jokes, they really believed that was the way people lived in America.

"And she's going to have black babies," tittered Natasha Timina, sparking a roar of laughter.

"And yours are going to be slant-eyed," I sniped back, referring to the widespread fears of the Chinese, hovering on the Soviet borders and poised to invade. (One joke projected a 1990 news broadcast: *In today's news, skirmishes on the Golan Heights, and everything quiet on the Finnish-Chinese border.* And the lyrics of a popular song, "Yellow leaves are circling all around,/With a rustle landing on the ground," were modified to "Yellow men are circling all around,/With their rifles landing on the ground.") Models of racial sensitivity we were not.

Ella Shimanskaya, with her utter inability to take things

lightly, had a look of helpless dismay on her little face. "I just don't understand how you can leave the best country in the world," she said with quiet desperation. "I mean, it would be different if you were moving to Czechoslovakia or Hungary. But to a capitalist country . . ." This was the daughter of stylish, trendy intellectuals who breezily ran down the Soviet way of life and could discuss Solzhenitsyn.

Granted, by that time I did not expect much from the girls by way of dissent, or any sort of opposition to orthodoxy, or what was to me an almost inexpressible *understanding* of the system. Their references to the Voice of America, their griping, their contempt for civics classes, their cynicism about public service, didn't fool me anymore. Still, they managed to astonish me. Katya Vorontzova (it was she who had leaped to Yesenin's defense when I said he hated the Soviet régime) unwittingly echoed almost word for word Ksenia Stepanovna, of whom she made fun as wholeheartedly as anyone else. "Well, don't you let them slander our Soviet society, all right?" she said earnestly, then added, "And by all means vote against Jimmy Carter. He's such an anti-Soviet." (Carter's human rights initiatives did not sit well with the Soviets.)

And Rita, my dear Rita, whom I thought I had at last succeeded in educating? Oh, she was supportive all right, though she too teased me about black babies. She even mentioned that when she told my parents about me, her father said that he would leave too if he had an opportunity, while her Party member mother said she wouldn't think of it. And then I happened to mention that a friend of my mother's, Zina Petrova, had been really upset when Mama told her about our plans and had lashed out at people like us, who jumped ship when things were bad, leaving everybody else to tough it out. "What the hell did she mean by that?" Rita retorted sharply. "What's so bad about living in this country? I, for one, am very glad I live here." *She still didn't understand!* "Well," I stammered, recovering from the shock in time to look for a quick way off the dangerous ground, "I guess she meant that there may be a war with China or something."

Gradually, the curiosity died down and I again became just another member of the class. If some part of me secretly craved to be martyred, ostracized, given a chance to proudly hold up my head in the face of ridicule, that part must have suffered a crushing disappointment. There wasn't even a hint of hostility. Things would have been different if I had been a member of the Komsomol. Then they would have had to expel me at a meeting, and who knows how many of the same kids who came to my birthday parties and whom I occasionally hung out with in Sokolniki Park would have risen to voice their horror at my infamy? (After all, what meeting would be complete without patriotic speeches and angry denunciations?) I might have gotten far more martyrdom than I bargained for.

There is a moment in Vladimir Nabokov's *Lolita* when Humbert Humbert, briefly back in the town where the long and fateful chain of events began, and having already made up his mind to kill his archenemy, Quilty, enjoys "a delicious dream feeling" as he calmly breaks all decorum, uttering the most unspeakable incivilities to the faces of shocked suburbanites. (In his own Russian translation of the novel, Nabokov speaks of "the marvelous freedom characteristic of dreams.") About to commit murder, the ultimate affront to society and its rules, he can afford the luxury of disregarding lesser proprieties — and of not worrying about the consequences. After March 1, 1979, when we submitted our applications and all the documents for exit visas, my life at school was often marked by something I think was akin to Humbert Humbert's "delicious dream feeling" of freedom. I would soon begin a new life (still that unshakeable faith that things could not go seriously wrong), and these last months were only the drawn-out conclusion of the old one. Whatever I did now would be of no consequence to my future. Was it that different from living in a dream?

No more worrying about grades, or about being on good terms with the teachers. Of course I wasn't about to go around being rude to teachers, not even in my dreams. But magically gone, all of a sudden, was the universally familiar feeling of acute embarrassment and discomfort that comes when a teacher calls on you to answer a lesson and you flounder and mumble without the slightest idea of what you're supposed to say.

The subjects I was interested in, literature and English, still mattered as much as ever. But when it came to physics, for example, the dream freedom truly was delicious. I all but stopped doing my homework and hardly ever bothered to open the textbooks. My grades slipped from an average of 4 to 3's and even 2's. I remember one time when our wisecracking teacher, Valery Vasilyevich, called on me to do a problem on the blackboard. I approached the blackboard, picked up the piece of chalk, stood silently for about a minute, then turned around to stare serenely at Valery Vasilyevich and said simply, "I can't do it." I felt lightheaded and powerful. Valery Vasilyevich shrugged, smirked, and said, "All right, you get a two. Bring me your journal." I went to my seat, picked up the journal, and, clowning a bit, sauntered back to Valery Vasilyevich's desk, bearing the journal on my open palms like a sacrificial offering. There was giggling in the class. Valery Vasilyevich penned the 2 in my journal and then said, not unkindly, "I'm not going to put it down in the teacher's journal for a while, in case you start doing better." A grade not marked in the teacher's journal did not count toward the final grade for the semester.

"Oh no, Valery Vasilyevich," I protested jauntily. "Please put it down in the teacher's journal now."

Valery Vasilyevich measured me with an ironic gaze and granted my request. The titters in the class grew louder, and I thought I could detect a certain amount of admiration, even awe: I was defying authority, perhaps doing what everyone else in the class wished they could do. Did they realize that I was living in a dream, and therefore did not deserve to be commended for my courage?

"Someday you'll regret it." Valery Vasilyevich squinted at me with a mixture of pity and gloating. "In tenth grade, when it dawns on you that you'll have to pass your final exams if you want a diploma, you'll panic and sit up all night studying physics and making up for the two years you spent goofing off." Secretly

I smiled to myself: *He doesn't know that for this student, there aren't going to be any final exams at the end of tenth grade.*

Now that we had placed ourselves into the almost outlaw category of people wishing to leave the best country in the world, some of our acquaintances were wary of associating with us. No one broke it off with us altogether, but one woman came pretty close. She happened to be one of Mama's closest friends, Zina Petrova, a former schoolmate and pal from the age of eleven or twelve. When Mama first told her of our decision, Zina was annoyed and resentful. "So when things get tough, the rest of us will have to grin and bear it, but you people just pack up and leave and you're sitting pretty," she said sharply. "You people" had a certain undertone that became much more explicit when Zina added that the Jews were always walking all over the poor oppressed Russians, running the whole cultural establishment, getting all those cushy jobs. Mama often scoffed at the hypersensitivity of those Jews who had a tendency to imagine anti-Semitism everywhere, but Zina's remarks left little to the imagination. The friendship cooled off almost to freezing point.

In addition to feeling personal resentment and piqued ethnic pride, I suspect, Zina was fearful for the future of her only child, Natasha, a student at the Bolshoi Theatre Ballet School whose precious career had to be protected. (After we had arrived in New York, a mutual friend mailed to Mama a playbill for a ballet program with Natasha's name in it. Later she wrote that when she casually mentioned this to Zina, Comrade Stage Mother pounced on her like a fury, shouting, "How could you do this? Don't you understand that this could damage Natasha's chances?" even though the playbill bore no indication that Natasha Petrova's name was the object of special interest to the recipient.)

Other people, too, worried about possible consequences to their jobs or promotions, though few went to such extremes. Some absolutely would not call us from their home phones, but used pay phones instead, so they couldn't be traced if our telephone was bugged. Among those who took such conspiratorial moves was a genteel old lady of Grandma's acquaintance, long retired and with no prospects of promotion. None of my classmates or their parents shunned me, not even Rita's mother, with her managerial job and Party membership, or Alla Makarova's diplomat parents. All in all, the only pattern seemed to be no pattern at all.

How a particular individual would react to the news that we were leaving was totally and often hilariously unpredictable. One day Papa met a neighbor of ours, a quiet, shy, retired Jewish barber. They said hello, and Papa inquired about the man's daughters, noting that he hadn't seen them around in a while.

"Oh, they don't live with me anymore," the barber explained. "They're married, you know, one's in Leningrad, the other's in Kishinev, and they're doing very well, thank you. And how are things in your family?"

"Well, actually, we have decided to emigrate," Papa said. "We applied for permission in March."

"Really, you have?" Our neighbor's face suddenly dissolved in a warm glow. "Well, then, let me tell you — my daughters have really emigrated, they've been gone for a while! They're in Boston! And I'm thinking of joining them!"

When we filed our papers, the standard waiting period for either a yes or a no was three to five months. So when I walked out of the sun-drenched, lusciously green schoolyard on the last day of classes in late May, I had good reason to think I would never again enter that building. By September, though, we were still waiting. Back from our dacha, I called up Tanya Tumasian a couple of days before the start of classes, and she exclaimed, "Katya! Where are you calling from, America?"

At home things went on almost as usual, except that my parents weren't working. Papa had some free-lance recording jobs once in a while (there were a few studio people with enough guts to hire someone who was, as the expression went, "in application"); Mama taught a few students privately. Otherwise, our income mostly came from parcels of clothing sent by Jewish organizations abroad. My parents eschewed the far more lucrative black market in favor of unglamorous used-clothing stores, with about one third of the profits and none of the risk. Even such tame trading was, strictly speaking, illegal: Soviet citizens aren't supposed to receive any gifts in parcels from abroad that are "not intended for personal use." But of course you could always say the jeans were really meant for you, it's just that they didn't fit, and with grief in your heart you had to sell them.

Time went on. My parents were diligently studying English. A conventional wisdom among would-be émigrés and their friends held that learning English was really a cinch, you just arrived in America and plunged headlong into an English-speaking environment and *boom*, before you knew it, fluent and near-flawless English speech began to roll off the tip of your tongue — "Don't you worry — a couple of years and you'll speak like a native." On the basis of their first encounters with the English language, my parents had serious doubts about this, and therefore sat hunched over textbooks on the metro, moving their lips as they laboriously read the unfamiliar phrases and occasionally wondering if they looked like morons to their fellow passengers. Once on the metro I saw a man in his twenties absorbed in an elementary school English textbook. I wanted to ask him if he too was on the go, but I chickened out.

The emigration subculture in which we now moved much of the time had its own self-published textbooks, which gave advice, gleaned from letters and other communications from those who had gone before, on what to do in various situations arising in transit, on dealing with Jewish refugee assistance organizations, and so on. Some friends and acquaintances were getting ready to take the plunge. Still others were agonizing over it. (*There are three kinds of Jews in the Soviet Union today: those who are leaving, those who are going to leave, and those who think they are not going to leave.*) Some people hesitated because they were working in a technical field — chemical engineering and such — and they had no idea whether their jobs would all of a sudden be classified as giving them access to technological secrets.

In the last days of 1979, we anxiously listened to the Voice of America's reports about the Soviet troops' invasion of Afghanistan. At school, Misha Belikov, who sat behind Rita and me in literature class, breathed into our ears in an agitated half-whisper, "Know something? We're giving the Afghans a helping hand . . . like we gave a brotherly helping hand to Czechoslovakia in 1968 — like this." He held out his hand and clenched his fist, the claws of a vulture sinking into its prey. "Yeah, yeah, that's it," Rita snickered, enjoying the secrecy. "A helping hand."

Then came the winter vacation, and my parents and I went to Pushchino, a charming town not far from Moscow that even had nice restaurants, including a seafood restaurant with fishing nets and anchors and steering wheels and mounted fish trophies adorning the walls. The days were sunny and crisp, and we went skiing in the snow-spangled woods. Mother's cousin Vega and her close friend Lena (now respectively in New Jersey and Boston) were staying there too, all of us in hotel rooms obtained *po blatu*, by way of pull.

What a idyllic week it was. I have two vivid Pushchino memories — the last memories of the Moscow teenager who was still a part of the relatively quiet flow of everyday Soviet middle-class life, despite the limbo of being "in application"; my last memories before the haze of the frenzied weeks of preparing for departure. The first memory is of our visit to a riding stable, the first one I had ever seen, where I begged my parents to let me take a ride. All the vacationers lucky to be in the vicinity were in stitches as I unsuccessfully tried to mount the horse, assisted by a grim-faced stableboy of twelve or so. Finally I gave up and settled for a pony, which the same taciturn stableboy led in circles around the track for about five minutes. The second memory is of a dinner at a restaurant where they served us broth with an egg floating in it; I tried to cut the egg in half with my spoon, and it catapulted from the bowl. I tried to catch it, in the process knocking my glass of tomato juice all over my father's light-colored pants. Papa rose and exclaimed, "You pig! You ought to be held in a pigsty — on a leash!" The waitress (who, strangely enough, was nice about the whole thing) arrived to clean up the mess, and I had the nerve to ask, "May I have another glass of tomato juice?"

And then, a day or two after we came back from Pushchino, on January 13, 1980, we found the postcard in our mailbox.

Now we had only thirty days left for the packing and the final goodbyes and whatever else there was to do. I went to classes one last time — the first day of the new semester. My memories of that day are no more than disjointed patches. In the morning, before the start of classes, I ran into Ella Shimanskaya and Lena Karpukhina walking arm in arm through the hallway, and said in a worried voice, "You know, Sakharov has been exiled to Gorky." (The Voice of America report had been followed by an *Izvestia* article saying that the traitor Sakharov had finally exhausted the enduring patience of the Soviet government, and at the request of the people was getting his just deserts.) Curtly and almost gleefully, Ella threw back at me, "Well, very good! It serves him right!" Without a word, I turned around and walked in the other direction, not even bothering to hide my disgust or my obvious sympathy with the wrong side. The thought ran through my mind: *I can't blow it now, of course, but if we weren't leaving, I would pick up a piece of chalk and write on the blackboard,* FREE SAKHAROV!

Later that day, at the end of physics class, Valery Vasilyevich, the usual sly grin on his ferretlike face, made some wisecracks about the success awaiting me in the future, and remarked, "You know, Golda Meir was from this country too — from Odessa. Perhaps someday you'll be prime minister of Israel."

Another teacher who had an interesting reaction to my impending departure was our English instructor, Cheburashkin. He asked me to stay after class, calmly directed me to take a seat facing him, and said, "So you're leaving." Again I muttered something hardly intelligible, wondering what he was going to say next. Was he going to explode, as he had on some occasions (though never on political grounds but only over someone's inveterate thickheadedness or laziness)? Was he going to make some stinging comments on the depths to which I had sunk? Not that I had anything to fear from him now — but I liked him, and he had always liked me, and it would have been sad to part in that way. But I looked at him and his face was benign. "Very, very interesting," he drawled reflectively. "I hope you don't mind my asking you to stay after class — I just wanted to talk to you, because I have often heard about people leaving but I have never actually met anyone in the flesh who was, er, doing this, so it's really interesting to me. Well," he added cheerfully, "you have my support. I've always thought everyone should live in his own country. So good luck to you."

As I walked out of that classroom for the last time, I reflected uncomfortably on the ambiguity of his well-wishing. *Everyone should live in his own country?* Did that mean he thought that because I was a Jew, my country was Israel and I didn't belong in Russia? Or did he think that *I* thought so? Cheburashkin was still a good guy in my book, so I opted for the version that made him look nice.

Perhaps it was also on that day that Tanya Tumasyan asked me if I wasn't worried about unemployment, and I told her that in America, people who are out of work get five hundred dollars a month in unemployment benefits. I don't remember where I had picked up that figure, but at the time it seemed like a whopping sum of money. "Really? Then I'd just stay unemployed and collect benefits," said practical Tanya. I thought about it for a moment — really, why wouldn't everyone just hop on such a wonderful gravy train? — and then I said, "I guess it doesn't work that way; maybe you have to prove you're looking for a job or something like that." Tanya looked disappointed, then perked up and added, "Well, I'm not going to work anyway. I'll find myself a husband who'll support me!" I glanced at her with a bit of shock (such backwardness!), but I think she was being facetious. The Cinderella scenario may not be very plausible in 1980s America, but it is even less — *far* less — realistic in the Soviet Union.

I came back to school one more time, just a few days before our departure. To think that I was in the school building but I didn't *have* to be there! I could just come in, in the middle of the schoolday, lounge about in the hallway outside the room where I knew my classmates were shackled to their seats in the current class period, chat with them during the break, and stroll out! They were in the history class. The bell rang shrilly, and the indistinct hum of voices, growing in volume, began to fill the building. About a minute later, the doors of the classroom swung open and my ex-classmates streamed out into the hallway. Henrietta Sergeyevna, the teacher, walked past me, her face a frozen mask of displeasure. No goodbyes to be wasted there.

My friends seemed glad to see me. I have no idea what we talked about, except that a couple of people asked me to write. I have no memory of the farewells. I had brought little gifts, something to remember me by, for several of the teachers, including Cheburashkin and Ksenia Stepanovna (things like a painted cutting board, a ceramic tea or coffee mug, a fountain pen), and something — at my parents' suggestion — for the cloakroom attendant and school custodian, Nadezhda Konstantinovna. She was the last person I spoke to in the school building where, for better or worse, I had spent much of the past ten years. I gave her a dark blue ceramic mug with a gilded flower on it and said, "This is for you, as a memory, Nadezhda Konstantinovna." She seemed touched, in her own taciturn way, and thanked me and wished me the best.

My school-free life was anything but carefree. Even the library was out. I worried that I wouldn't find another such library in the West; my parents dismissed my fear as ridiculous. (My first visit to the New York Public Library's reading room proved them right. A few years later, I made the breathtaking discovery that many of those nineteenth-century volumes, leather-bound, with gilt letters on the spines and the brisk fragrance of yellowing pages, were available in the student library at Rutgers University — in the *borrowing* section.)

The chore assigned to me was mailing parcels. Most of the luggage of émigrés, after a customs inspection, traveled to its destination by boat (also known as "low speed"), which could take over a year. Most people therefore preferred to transport at least some of their things, as much as they could, by mailing them to acquaintances who had gone before. For us, it was mainly books that had to be lugged to the International Post

Office on Komsomolskaya Square, five or six trolley stops away. (Only three post offices in all of Moscow accepted parcels with foreign destinations; this number was later reduced to one.) There I had to stand in line and present the contents of my parcel to an unfriendly clerk, who made sure I wasn't sending out any anti-Soviet literature, state secrets, or valuable antique books (defined as anything published prior to 1940). She weighed the books, issued the stamps, and wrapped and sealed the package — this unexpectedly high quality of service motivated by the concern that she should know exactly what was inside. Then I took my packages to the crowded table in the middle of the always jam-packed room, pasted on the stamps, and painstakingly penned the addresses: strange, mysteriously alluring words like "Brookline, Mass.," "Jackson Heights, N.Y.," "Brooklyn, N.Y.," "Forest Hills, N.Y." Names of real places somewhere on this planet.

The post office on Komsomolskaya Square had become a den of people of Jewish nationality at some stage in the emigration process. (I had quite a shock when I realized from the conversation of a couple in front of me one day that they were ordinary Soviet citizens sending souvenirs to a foreign professor they had met in the course of an exchange program.) My parents had waited until our application was approved to start sending things abroad; others were more optimistic or more devil-may-care. So the lines were long, and it took a while for the clerk to dispense with each customer, and I ended up spending hours at the post office (alone or with one of my parents), nearly suffocating in my winter coat and hat, which I often couldn't take off because my hands were full.

Once the scowling clerk accepting parcels from Mama and me remarked tersely, as if talking to herself, "Look at this! You can't find any good books in the bookstores and here you have people sending them abroad! It's because of people like you that there aren't enough books to go around." (She didn't look like the book-hungry type.) "You'll see," she added ominously, "soon they'll put an end to such outrageous carryings-on." The warning might have been something more than idle chatter. Shortly after we left, the regulations for sending parcels from the Soviet Union abroad were suddenly made much more stringent: each citizen was restricted to just *one parcel a year*, and you had to present your passport at the post office to prove you weren't using someone else's name to get around the quota. In addition, no books published prior to 1976 could be mailed abroad or taken along in the luggage. That would have meant leaving behind nearly the entire library my parents had been collecting with such dedication for over twenty years.

Even with all the parcels we sent by mail, there were at least twenty huge cardboard boxes of books left to be sent by boat. The day before Papa was to take them in for the customs inspection, we had a close call. Among the books were three volumes of collected works by Marina Tsvetayeva, one of the four or five greatest poets of twentieth-century Russia. (Her appeal was heightened by her tragic fate, startlingly unorthodox voice, and long exile from the lists of state publishing houses.) These three volumes were really a replica of the one-volume Poet's Library edition, the first to appear in the Soviet Union and nearly impossible to get. Papa had managed to buy a photocopy and then had it bound in attractive red imitation leather (by an illegally moonlighting private contractor, of course), in three volumes instead of one because the photocopy only had text on one side of the page. As Grandma and I stuffed the books into the cardboard boxes, we packed these volumes along with everything else and didn't even stop to think that a photocopied edition was not, strictly speaking, legal. Not that you could get into serious trouble for possession, but when you were emigrating and therefore already on the spot, it was better not to let an official see that sort of thing. The cardinal rule of Soviet life — *you never know what THEY might do* — applied here with a vengeance. For all we knew, our entire luggage, books and clothes and bookshelves and everything, could fail to clear customs because of this one snag.

So, with less than a day to go, there was only one thing to do: unpack and look for the hapless Tsvetayeva volumes. Slavik, the adopted son of an old friend of Grandma's, came up to help, and was promised the Tsvetayeva books for his labors. In the very first box we opened we found the first volume, and naturally everyone thought, *Great, the other two are going to show up in no time.* In the second box, nothing . . . third box, ditto . . . and so we had to open and empty all those twenty-some boxes, until we found the remaining two volumes, in the very last one.

Though Papa had to exercise restraint for just a few more days, and then he would be able to speak his mind as freely as he wanted, he remained true to himself. Just a week before our departure, he learned that he would not be able to take his violin with him; the rule was that you could not take a violin worth more than a thousand rubles, and the commission at the Ministry of Culture had assessed the value of his instrument at 1100 rubles. When Misha, an acquaintance who worked at the commission, called with the bad news, Papa asked, in the grim tone of someone who had known better than to expect anything but the worst, "Well, can you at least tell me who made the decision? The names of these people?" No, Misha said, he couldn't disclose their names. "Well, of course," Papa said. "When people engage in disreputable business, they don't want anyone to know what their names are." Mama, who happened to be within earshot, let out an appalled gasp, and when Papa hung up he braced himself for a bawling-out.

There were last visits from relatives and friends who were not leaving: Mama's former students and friends from school, Papa's ex-colleagues, Grandma's in-laws and friends. Uncle Yura, of whom we hadn't been seeing very much, became a dutiful son in the last months that his mother was on the same continent as he, although he didn't want us to write to him or call him, for fear of jeopardizing his career, and he never communicated with us after our departure. Grandma's younger sister, Anya, came from Leningrad, and wept as she hugged Grandma and Mama.

Grandma's friend Aunt Katya (she of the stalwartly pro-Soviet views and the dissident son) came over a lot, scarcely disguising her annoyance at our folly. "Listen, Lida," she instructed Grandma as they were saying their last goodbyes, "when you're going to write to me, if you find that life over there is really good, just put at the end of the letter 'Say hello to Nina,' and if it's really bad, write 'Say hello to Masha,' and I'll understand." I don't recall if Grandma asked her why she should resort to such conspiratorial methods to convey the message. It seems that the request wasn't so unusual: a middle-aged émigré later told me that a friend of hers, an opera lover like herself, had asked her to write that she attended a performance of *Eugene Onegin* to signal that things were going badly, and of *The Barber of Seville* if all was well. (A reverse situation appears in a Soviet joke: *A White Russian émigré who decides to return to Russia makes an agreement with his brother to write a letter in blue ink if he likes his new life and in green ink if he doesn't. A few months later, the brother gets a letter that opens with the words, "Dear brother, Things are going very well, except for a few trifling difficulties. For instance, I haven't been able to buy any green ink . . ."*)

A pathetic fiftyish fellow named Volodya Blumenfeld, who had met Papa at some recording studio, became something of a fixture in our apartment in those last few days. He had fallen into the grinder of the labor camps under Stalin for telling a political joke, and had had his kidneys wrecked by beatings during interrogations. For years he had longed to emigrate, but his wife wouldn't budge. He had to settle for the vicarious satisfaction of hanging around people who were about to emigrate, talking to them, offering to help with packing and other chores. He had meek eyes, completely gray hair, and a doleful smile — and after all his trials and tribulations, he was a bit deranged. No matter how intensely one might pity him, he simply wasn't tolerable in large doses; he rambled on endlessly, repeating the same stories over and over again in the course of a single day. Things were hectic enough as it was, and finally one day, when he showed up without warning, my father — who was in the bedroom when Volodya appeared, and had a dreadful headache — asked us to say he wasn't home. "Oh, all right," Volodya declared cheerfully, "I'll wait for him." The situation, with Papa holed up in the bedroom and Volodya sipping tea in the kitchen and talking Mama and Grandma to death, was getting desperate. Finally Mama and I told him we had to make a trip to the Central

Market. Since he had a car, would he give us a ride? He agreed; Papa was rescued.

Mama and I actually did have to go to the market, but we had no idea that Volodya Blumenfeld was going to make it such a memorable trip. Conventional émigré wisdom held that it was a very good idea to take along silver one-ruble coins, which supposedly were convertible abroad. (Those leaving could exchange Soviet money for hard currency only in the piddling amount of ninety dollars per person, although a higher ceiling wouldn't have helped much in our case; there wasn't much left to exchange.) Silver one-ruble coins were relatively rare; we had gathered about fifteen. Volodya suddenly decided that he was going to help us with this, and was all afire with the idea. "Citizens! Citizens!" he began to shout amid the racket and bustle of the Central Market. "Does anyone have silver rubles to trade in to these ladies for one-ruble bills? They really need silver rubles. They're going away to Israel!" Mama and I stood terrified, expecting to be at least verbally lynched by the crowd. However, there was no spontaneous surge of popular ire. In fact, no one paid much attention at all to us or to Volodya. I don't think we got any silver rubles, but we escaped unscathed.

We had another mildly unpleasant but ultimately comical adventure less than two weeks before our departure. One morning between seven and eight, strange voices roused us from our sleep. For a few seconds the voices conversed about something in our anteroom. Then one of them said, sounding rather embarrassed, "Wait a minute — it looks like they're still living here." "Why, no," retorted a loud, boorish female voice. "They've all gone off to Israel." Papa pulled on a robe and went out to investigate. The early-morning visitors were the future tenants of our apartment, accompanied by the owner of the boorish voice, an official from the local housing authority to whom we had had to turn in one set of keys before our papers could be cleared.

Almost everyone who emigrated from Moscow took the Moscow–Vienna flight (for those from other locations, train travel was the only option). And now an embarrassing confession:

Mama and I were both so afraid of flying that we talked Papa into getting train tickets, to the consternation of most of our acquaintances. Our train was leaving on the night of February 8 for the border town of Brest, where we would change for a train for Vienna.

That last day came and there were still some last-minute parcels to be mailed, and it was I who rushed off to the post office, where the line was extra-long. A suave gentleman behind me asked me when we were leaving. "Today," I said, and all the people around me, like the good Jewish fathers and mothers they were, sighed and groaned and clucked in dismay at such recklessness — messing around with packages at the post office hours before departure! They would have been even more shocked if they had known what I did after getting out of the post office. With a few hours left and a few rubles in my wallet, I decided to treat myself to one last trip to my favorite foreign-language bookstore, and picked up a Penguin Library portable Coleridge — just the thing to buy in Moscow before going away to America!

And so I came home perhaps an hour and a half before we were to set out for the train station, and our apartment was full of people seeing us off — Papa's mother and brother and aunt, Mama's brother. Everyone was going crazy because I had been missing. My mother was on the verge of a breakdown, trying desperately to keep herself under control, and she must have been successful because my father's Aunt Busya remarked with an unctuous smile, "You are such a calm mother!" Rita came over to say goodbye, bringing me an address book and a wall calendar with the then-ubiquitous cutesy bear that was the mascot of the 1980 Moscow Olympics. She didn't stay long, just hung about the anteroom for a few minutes without even taking off her winter coat. Granny Polina was crying softly and some of the other people present began to sniffle, and Rita smiled awkwardly — "Gosh, I seem to be getting teary-eyed too" — and in fact her eyes were a little moist as we hugged goodbye.

There was no time to stop for sentimental reflections about the rooms where I had taken my first steps and scribbled my first clumsy letters. With everybody else, I was racing around frantically in a last-minute search for anything we might have forgotten. Then there was the taxicab ride. We were getting panicky, because time was running out. Luckily, we found when we got to the station that the train was delayed. A crowd of people, some of whom I didn't know, shivered in the cold, waiting to see us off. Snow was falling, swirling wildly in the milky light of the station lamps. Mama had packed away her winter coat — it would be much warmer in Vienna, wouldn't it? — and had borrowed a friend's fur coat for the evening, and as she clambered up the steps of the train I shouted, "Mama! The coat!" and she nervously wriggled out of it and tossed it to her friend. That was our last moment on Moscow soil.

From the moment the train took off with a jolt until our arrival in Brest the next morning, I don't remember a thing. Did we sleep? I know only that my mother was still nervous, still not absolutely sure that we were really going to leave. We all shared her anxiety to some extent. We hadn't crossed the border yet and were still within the jurisdiction of the supreme law of the land: *you never know what they might do.* We had heard of cases in which people had boarded a plane and then an official had approached them and said, "Sorry, there's been a mistake, your visas have been revoked," and they had gone back to their stripped-down apartments to wait either for new visas or for a refusal.

In Brest, the morning was gray and heavy. At the station we had to go through a border checkpoint. One by one we faced a uniformed guard behind a glass window in a booth, just like a ticket window. He took our visas, one by one, and looked back and forth from the passport-size black-and-white photograph to the person in front of him, not just looking but intently and suspiciously studying the face on the photo and in the flesh, as if there were a good chance that we were criminals stealing someone else's identity. He was a very young man, with short blondish hair and icy, piercing gray eyes, almost hypnotically unblinking. I saw my mother cringe and freeze, and I myself felt a little like a bunny nailed by the python's gaze. Finally the guard ascertained to his satisfaction that we actually were the holders of the exit visas he had examined, and it was on to the next tribulation. We were herded into the large customs inspection hall, where the bags and suitcases with our modest belongings were thrown open on a wooden counter. The customs agent, poker-faced but human — he didn't look vicious, just indifferently diligent — rummaged through our things, said not a word about the address books and some personal letters we were taking with us (the kind of things that we had heard people were sometimes not allowed to take), but axed the plastic bag with pills and other medicines and said we could not take the measly fifteen silver rubles we had managed to amass. Everyone had quaked at horror stories about strip searches; in our case, however, Papa was asked to step behind a screen, where he had to take off his overcoat and was patted down, and we women were even spared that.

The silver rubles we had to get rid of came in handy to tip the porters, because the train for Vienna was leaving any second now and there was yet another frantic dash. In the aisle of the car, a noisy family of emigrating Georgian Jews — portly daddy, buxom mama, two shapely daughters — began to wail loudly and claw at the rain-spattered windowpane when the train started moving and gaining speed and the Russian land beyond the window became a blur of denuded trees and fields and stocky gray buildings. Moments later they were happy as birds, laughing and chirping about something in their melodic Georgian language. They never bothered to close the door of their compartment, which was right next to ours, and every time we came out into the corridor we could see them sorting out their luggage, heaps of clothes spilled all over the floor.

Then Polish border guards with a German shepherd came looking for narcotics; their chief was a jovial fellow whose idea of banter was to look at my visa and declare, grinning broadly, "Why, that's not you!" then add amiably, "The young lady must be the chief drug smuggler."

Fast asleep through the night, I missed the dramatic moment when we entered Austria and two policemen armed with submachine guns checked our visas and then — since we were theoretically headed for Israel and therefore a choice morsel for terrorists — took their posts on both sides of the door of our compartment. On the next morning (as damp and gray as the one in Brest had been; evidently Mother Nature was not going to provide a metaphorically radiant backdrop for this moment in our lives), as our train was peacefully puffing its way toward Vienna, I woke up a future citizen of the United States.

Epilogue

OUR ARRIVAL in Vienna was only slightly marred by the reception we were accorded by the representative of the Israeli immigration agency, Sokhnut. The moment we told him we were not going to Israel, the gaunt, balding man scowled and remarked stiffly, "It's too bad an invitation was wasted on you." He then added that we would come to regret this. (Whenever we remembered that affable individual later, my father always referred to him as "the Israeli KGB man.") In the boardinghouse where we were taken afterward, two Sokhnut recruiters, both young and brash Soviet émigrés, made subtler attempts to win us over ("You think your daughter is going to go to college in America? Ha! I've been to America, I know how hard it is to get into college over there. She'll end up washing dishes in a restaurant").

On a more pleasant note, we were met in Vienna by Papa's friend Alyosha, who had married into Switzerland and came expressly to see us and help us out in whatever way was possible. And the next day I got a birthday present: walking past a nearby movie theater, my father spotted a poster for *Jesus Christ Superstar*, and shelled out from our modest allowance what then seemed like an impressive sum of money for me to buy a ticket.

Even more memorable was the first time my parents came back from a trip to a supermarket and laid out their catch on the bed of our drab boardinghouse room. Salami, ham, bananas, coconut cookies . . . it took my breath away. I was not ashamed to jump and yelp and almost dance with delight. I was duly stunned by the array of hams and sausages in Vienna's delis and especially by the fanciful window displays of pastry and candy stores.

We spent two weeks in Vienna, not just stuffing ourselves, I should add, but visiting the Vienna Art Museum and the exquisite St. Stephen's Cathedral; we even took an out-of-town trip to Schönbrunn, the dazzling summer residence of the Austrian emperors. Our next journey was to Rome — another night train, except this time I stayed up to look out the window. We went through the Alps, and I saw tunnels and mountains looming in the clear night with their white caps of snow, and a magical white castle lit up in the night, high on a mountaintop. We woke up early in the morning as the train came to a stop; my mother asked me to see where we were. A sign on the platform said Firenze — Florence — and in the next moment a conductor's ringing, operatic voice sang out, "Firenze!"

We continued on to Rome and another unattractive boarding-house, Pensione Mimi, and later a room in an apartment a half-hour train ride away in the beach town of Ostia, which had turned into a colony of Russian émigrés waiting for their U.S. visas to come through. There was a trip to the U.S. consulate, where we found the Stars and Stripes, a picture of grinning Jimmy Carter, and a clean-cut official who asked us to raise our right hands and tell the truth and nothing but the truth about ourselves (were there by any chance Communists or felons among us, or prostitutes, bigamists, alcoholics?). There was pizza, and sandwiches, and pastry, and ice cream. We managed side trips to Florence and Venice, and Grandma and I went on a bus tour, offered at special rates to Russian émigrés by some enterprising bunch, to the south of Italy — Naples, Pompeii, Sorrento, and the island of Capri, a paradise with its mystical Blue Grotto.

The Zion Club, established for émigrés in Ostia by Jewish organizations, had a library stocked with Russian expatriate magazines of every stripe — the conservative, somewhat Slavophile,

Christian-leaning *Kontinent*, the liberal democratic *Syntaxis*, the hard-line Zionist *Zion*, the liberal Zionist *22*, the eclectic *Time and Us* — as well as books in Russian published outside the Soviet Union, what we in Moscow used to know as *tamizdat*. I brought these books and magazines home by the armful and gulped them down avidly and indiscriminately. One of the first things I got was the autobiography of my hero Vladimir Bukovsky, from which I concluded that he was every bit as admirable as I had imagined in my daydreams.

I read the memoirs of Trotsky's personal secretary and of labor camp inmates; I read Orwell's *1984* and *Animal Farm* and Aldous Huxley's *Brave New World*. I followed magazine debates on the moral issues involved in the decision of people who left the Soviet Union on an Israeli visa to go to the United States instead, grudgingly admitting once in a while that I couldn't approach the question in a totally objective manner. Perhaps it was my personal bias that made me notice something uncannily familiar in the rhetoric of hard-line Zionists castigating émigrés headed for America, charging that they had set material well-being and personal convenience above the higher ideals of service to one's people and chosen the Almighty Dollar over devotion to the Cause. The public above the private? No, you don't — this time, *I* am going to decide what my cause is and who my people are.

Two or three times a week, I would get on a train and go to Rome all by myself, savoring the feeling of walking alone in the streets of a strange city, going wherever I wanted: to the ancient Roman temples, to the cathedrals and churches, through the greenery and the marble ruins of the Forum. I climbed up the steps of the Capitol and surveyed the Colosseum, abundantly populated, like all such sites in Rome, by cats of all colors, noiselessly slinking by. I found out firsthand about the notorious habits of Italian males, having become sufficiently fluent in Italian to understand and field questions such as "Have you got a boyfriend?" I got to know Rome much better than I had ever known Moscow, and developed a much stronger attachment to it as well. When the date for the final leg of our journey was set and we made our last trip to Rome, I looked around, intent on taking in as much of the city's sights as I could and keeping the images in my mind's eye. I had not done that when I was about to leave Moscow. Of course, this departure was much less frenetic.

And then there was the Leonardo da Vinci airport and the Pan Am jetliner (no choice this time but to overcome our fear of flying). The movie was *Superman* — who could think of a better introduction to life in America? — though we decided to forgo the earphones, available at an additional charge.

By the time we landed, I must have been very tired and perhaps rather dazed, for I have no memory of our arrival, or of going through customs and immigration, or of any thoughts in my mind in those moments. From JFK airport, a van drove us to a dingy rooming house in a Hasidic neighborhood in Coney Island — a rather dismal place to get our first glimpse of the United States. It was July 1, 1980. Three days later, we were a little shaken up by the firecrackers popping off at close range as we ventured to take a stroll through the normally quiet streets. What was this, revolution breaking out just as we got here?

In another four days, after a brief search, we rented a two-bedroom apartment in Jackson Heights, Queens (the site of a burgeoning émigré community, including a few of my parents' acquaintances), for the whopping sum of $450 a month. "Oh, please, please let's take it," I begged, impatient to have a normal place to live. "We'll pay for it somehow, I'll get a job" — and I did, by the end of September. The typewriting skills I had learned in the vocational courses at school came in handy, though I had to rent a rickety manual typewriter to get used to the Latin alphabet keyboard. When I first appeared at an employment agency, dressed nicely and wearing makeup, I did rather miserably on the typing test, but they graciously let me come in and practice on their IBM electric. My first job was as an office worker for the Greater New York Chapter of the Boy Scouts of America. I got to go to my first cocktail party and my first American movie (*Gloria*). We were sold a home-delivery subscription to the New York *Post* and immersed ourselves in American mass culture via the day-by-day accounts of the trial of Jean Harris for shooting the Scarsdale Diet doctor.

At the end of *Crime and Punishment*, after Raskolnikov undergoes his moral rebirth, Dostoyevsky concludes by saying that here a new tale begins — the tale of the hero's gradual transformation and entrance into a new life: "This could be the subject for another story — but our present story is finished."

Without comparing myself to Dostoyevsky, or the change in my life to Raskolnikov's regeneration, I think I too have reached that point in my story. To use a contemporary metaphor, I will now fast-forward through the next eight years to a where-are-they-now update.

My grandmother, who remained her active, energetic, intellectually curious self to the last, died five years ago, at the age of seventy-eight. Her greatest happiness was that she had gotten to see something of the world in her final years.

My father works as an assistant editor for a publisher of music books in New Jersey, where we moved in February 1981 — a year to the day after our departure from Moscow — and moonlights as a violinist for local orchestras. My mother teaches piano at the Hebrew Arts School in New York, and at Rutgers University and the Monmouth Conservatory in New Jersey. I graduated from Rutgers with a B.A. in English in 1988. We became naturalized American citizens on October 9, 1987. Quite a few people have told me I speak English without an accent. (A couple of years ago, when I saw *Gloria* again on cable TV and did not miss a single line of the dialogue, I realized how much my comprehension of the language has improved over the years.)

I have often wondered, as I have learned to find my way around the maze of American political and cultural issues, about what differences growing up in Moscow has made in shaping my opinions. With indisputable arrogance, I would much prefer to think of myself as a free mind making perfectly objective judgments, not in the least affected by such lowly things as personal experience and environment. Still, something tells me this is not the case.

I certainly was not objective in the beginning, in the early surge of euphoria. Today, a sense of outrage, even helpless outrage, over a domestic news item is no longer an unfamiliar emotion. Sometimes, as when I get angry because an order of ham steak with a pineapple ring is brought to me sans pineapple ring, I have to take a step back and ask myself if I have lost perspective. But then again, becoming an American in a way means losing perspective. One can't go on forever overlooking the negative sides of American life with the excuse that it's worse in the Soviet Union. And even if I try my best to refrain from claims of complete objectivity, I do bristle when someone argues that I hold a particular opinion because of my Soviet background. If I criticize the bloated bureaucracy of the welfare state, I have been told, it is because my bad experiences in the USSR have turned me into a knee-jerk opponent of government programs. If I criticize the excessive leniency of the justice system, the argument is exactly the reverse: my Soviet habits make it hard for me to digest the American dedication to civil liberties even at the cost of sometimes letting the guilty go free.

Needless to say, I can never be considered objective about the Soviet Union. That cuts both ways, too. Once in a campus political argument, a blonde with an icy manner declared in response to something I said that she was really tired of people who had never been to the USSR knocking that country. A brief explanation of my origins did not help much. Before long I was listening to the familiar line that I, a victim of Soviet oppression, could not be truly objective about the Soviet system. Apparently the right to judge the Soviet system is reserved for those who have been there, but for no more than, say, a month.

During my first six American years, Russia drifted further and further into a dreary fog. I wrote extensively for Russian émigré papers in New York, but all my topics were from American life. My correspondence with Rita dwindled to nothing by the end of the first year; I know only that she entered a teachers' college in Moscow after finishing high school. My parents maintained closer ties with relatives and friends — with those who were not afraid to maintain such ties. Some (including Mama's brother) never wrote, never called, and emphatically did not want to be contacted. Others enclosed their missives, often bearing just an initial for a signature, with the letters of those brave souls who used their own names and return addresses on envelopes. Everyone took it for granted that mail was being opened and read before it reached its destination (a few of our letters arrived in Moscow with one of the two or three pages missing from the envelope). This has been a recurring scene in our American life: Mama, the household censor, reads a letter Papa is writing to Granny Polina and starts berating him over some outspoken remark ("This is very unfair! You're not risking anything, but you're putting them on the spot. You have no right to do that!"). Papa bristles but finally caves in and rewrites the entire letter.

You never know (what a sense of *déjà vu* that "you never know" evokes!) just what you might write that will cause anxiety to circumspect correspondents. When my mother was hospitalized for about a week, her cousin Vega, also a New Jersey resident now, wrote about it to an elderly acquaintance in Moscow. She mentioned how nice it was in the hospital: a bed in a room for only two (Soviet hospital wards contain ten or twelve people in closely spaced beds, with two nurses per floor), a TV set, a phone on the nightstand, a daily menu to choose from. Some time later she was shocked to receive a harsh, not to say rude, letter from the seventy-year-old retiree: "I only want news about your personal life, your work, and so on," she wrote. "I am not in the least interested in hearing about how Marina was in the hospital or how wonderful the hospital was, so please don't ever write to me about such things. By the way, Maria Petrovna was in a hospital recently and it was every bit as good." (She forgot to mention that it was a privileged hospital for high-ranking Party officials, their family members, and unaffiliated but well-connected individuals.) The same lady was just as upset by a casual mention of goods available in a supermarket, and repeated her plea to be kept up-to-date *only* on personal things.

And the elaborate precautions people have taken when writing

letters from the Soviet Union! For a long time, Granny Polina
kept us posted on the struggles of a relative to join her English
husband in Great Britain, referring to the whole affair as "Minna's medical problem." "Minna went to see a doctor and he said
that there wasn't anything he could do for her right now" meant
that Minna had been to the visa office and had been turned
down. Granny's real literary *tour de force* came when Gorbachev
took power, bringing new (and, as it turned out, well-founded)
hopes. Her comment: "Minna's health might get much better.
We'll see what the new doctor will say." This ingenious code
had one drawback: what would Granny Polina do if she really
wanted to write about Minna's *health?* Remarkably, Minna was
in no way doing anything illegal, only trying very hard to leave
the Soviet Union through perfectly licit channels.

A few years ago, a friend of Mama's was coming to the United
States with a touring musical ensemble, and a mutual friend (one
of the few who have steadily kept in touch with us) wrote, "Nina
is looking forward to her trip — she's so eager to see you." The
next letter was on a more downbeat note: "Marinochka dear, if
you see Nina after a concert, don't be surprised and for heaven's
sake don't be offended if she treats you in a rather cold manner.
I hope you will understand *what* the reason is."

These obscure fears, these tangled webs of references to any
potentially touchy matters (like the difficulties of shopping, to
take another example), have been a running reminder of what we
escaped from. For a long time, the only way I ever thought of
the Soviet Union was in the there-but-for-the-grace-of-God-go-I
mode, reliving the feeling of utter helplessness, of being in the
hands of an absolute and malevolent power, of revulsion at having to prevaricate. Every once in a while, realizing how soon
after our departure the door had slammed shut, I was gripped by
a spasm of fear and simultaneous relief (*Whew, that was a close
shave!*).

My reacquaintance with the country of my birth began just
about two years ago, when I sat down to work on this book and
started to go through the closets of memory, turning up faces,
feelings, thoughts, and episodes that I didn't know were there.

And what a coincidence that at just around the same time, the Soviet Union should suddenly become interesting and — of all things — unpredictable! Less than a hundred pages into this book, I realized that I had to change many of my observations about Soviet life from the present to the past tense. It seemed that things were changing, and who could tell what they'd be like by the time the book was finished?

My initial instinct, based, as most instincts are, on experience, was to dismiss Mikhail Gorbachev's "democratization" campaign (also known by the buzz words *glasnost*, which can mean anything from free speech to public disclosure, and *perestroika*, or reconstruction) out of hand as a propaganda ploy, clever window-dressing for the consumption of gullible Westerners. But time and time again I would say, "Well, I'll believe it when they do such-and-such," and only a little while later they would up and do exactly that. Perhaps the solid barrier of my disbelief received its first crack when Andrei Sakharov was not only released from exile in Gorky but became something of a public figure, gingerly accorded favorable mentions in the official press. Other things followed. Soon it was obvious that whatever my opinion of *glasnost*, my old assumptions about the possible, the unlikely, and the unthinkable in the Soviet Union did not hold any longer.

Formerly banned books are now openly available or about to be printed. Novels by George Orwell and the memoirs of Nadezhda Mandelshtam are among the most famous examples. The Soviet press (which I have recently started to read — something I hardly ever did in Moscow) now talks about the need to reform education, to encourage more independent thinking among students. The following, for example, comes from a letter that recently appeared in the Soviet magazine *Yunost* ("Youth") in response to a questionnaire. It is signed by "Galya, 19 years old, a medical college student in Moscow."

School brought me the first very strong disappointment in my life — because of the duplicity, the lies that pervaded everything, absolutely everything. And the students who tried to fight this, or at least to say what they thought and not what they were supposed to say, were considered "recalcitrant." Half of our classes were such "recalcitrant" students, and so they kept explaining to us that we had "degenerate attitudes" (their exact words). When I finished school, I was very happy. I believe that an honest person intolerant toward falsehood simply could not, in our school, engage in that much-touted social activism. Our teachers, in every way they could, consistently exterminated in us the very civic spirit they were always shouting about. . . . I hope that I can think for myself, the ten years of that hated school notwithstanding. Just to spite it, that school.

And that letter is just one of many in a similar or even harsher tone, including one from "E. S.," an eighteen-year-old Moscow boy who gave this answer to the question "What do you love? What do you hate?":

> I'm not going to talk about what I love, but I really hate inform-ers. [The word E. S. uses here is *stukach*, "stoolie," a word with decidedly countercultural overtones that I always assumed was far beyond the pale of officially approved vocabulary.] I detest that scum so much I can't even think clearly. What use does our society have for these bastards? If it didn't have any use for them, they wouldn't exist.

More bluntly yet, a writer in the letters column of *Izvestia* wondered if socialism was invented just so people would lead miserable lives. This rabid heretic was mildly rebuked in a note from the editors for taking too extreme a position.

I would be at a loss to list the most startling examples in recent Soviet newspapers and magazines of how different things are. There have been so many. How about this gem from the letters column of a leading newspaper, in response to some articles that had appeared previously: "Dear editor! What are you doing? They're going to jail these people! But the stuff was great, simply astounding! I pray to God they won't jail them!"

Or the debate in *Literaturnaya Gazeta* about the sensational play *Forward . . . Forward . . . Forward*, by Mikhail Shatrov. (The play is a meditation on the evils of Stalinism, in the form of a conversation among some dead Communists, including Lenin and Stalin.) In his comments, historian Lev Ovrutsky argued that Stalinism was the result of flaws inherent in the system, not just of Stalin's personality, and he went so far as to say that Lenin's words should not be taken as absolute dogma.

Or the story of Vladimir Soloukhin in *Novy Mir* (written in 1967, published in 1987), recounting the author's real-life efforts to get a Christian burial for his mother. Describing his labors to obtain a coffin, he pauses to reflect on the "peculiar rationing system that extends to all spheres of life" in the Soviet Union: you can't buy what you want, only what is available, "and the choice, as a rule, is very limited if at all possible." Further on, when the author is told by the village priest that he needs written permission from the local authorities to conduct the funeral mass, Soloukhin declares, "If this were happening in some conquered country where the occupation powers hold the local population so tightly harnessed, under such a yoke that they forbid them even to bury their dead according to their native customs without permission from these same occupation powers, that would at least be comprehensible. But I don't know if there are anywhere in the world such occupation powers, if there is anywhere in the world a people that would put up with such a yoke."

Another change: it has suddenly become possible for recent émigrés to travel to the Soviet Union, and more amazing still, a small but steadily growing trickle of Soviet citizens are visiting the United States at the invitation of relatives and even friends. That, my father confidently said only a month or so before we heard about the first such visits, was never going to happen. After all, when the Soviet government allows émigrés in as tourists or visitors, at least it gains something, and something it wants badly: an influx of hard currency. In contrast, when a Soviet citizen goes on a trip abroad, the state suffers a slight loss: some money is exchanged for dollars — a small amount, but hard currency nonetheless. Well, they do allow these visits now, and in the past few months we have been able to hear eyewitness accounts of *glasnost* and *perestroika* from friends who had been dead and buried to us for eight years, surviving only as disembodied words on little sheets of paper in airmail envelopes — friends who have come over from Moscow to visit their relatives here.

From these stories, a picture emerges that is intriguing but less than happy — a picture of a society sharply split along too many lines to keep track of. Some people are nervously optimistic, some wearily cynical, some in a hurry to catch whatever breaths of fresh air they'll be able to get before democratization collapses and things go back to the way they used to be. The division, at least among those people whose views have reached us, is mostly between those who think *perestroika* is a sham — just a lot of talk, and talk is the one thing the Soviet state has always been good at — and those who bask in the new freedom but tell you that it may all come to a grinding halt at any moment. Perhaps the explosion of unorthodox and sometimes startlingly heretical revelations, opinions, and barbs in the Soviet press is more exciting to us than it is to Soviet citizens; they have been following it day in and day out for nearly two years now, and the thrill has somewhat worn off. Yet one of our visitors has pointed out that the excitement remains because the boundaries of the acceptable keep getting stretched, and one never knows what taboo will be smashed next week. So at least for the time being, it looks as if my father was wrong when he categorically declared, in those endless to-go-or-not-to-go arguments ten years ago, "Things can't get any better! Under this system, things can only get worse."

Of course, I suppose that in some ways they have. From what I have heard, shopping is at least as traumatic as it was when I experienced my first brushes with it, and quite possibly more so. Recently an old friend of my parents' on a three-week visit to the United States came over for dinner; he was visibly delighted when chocolate-coated *zephir* (a delicacy made of marshmallow and soufflé that in our time occasionally made an appearance at the local confectionery) was served for dessert. Mama inquired, "Do they still have this in Moscow?" "Marina, darling," said our guest, "there is a joke where a guy is on trial for killing his wife, and in court he is asked, 'What was it about her that made you hate her so much?' and he says, 'Well, first of all, everything.'

When you ask me if they still have chocolate-coated *zephir* in Moscow, I can begin by saying that first of all, they don't have anything."

Of course they do have *something* — except that it's less for more: less quality and less variety; more effort, sometimes more money. That was just the kind of thing Mama used to worry about, and perhaps she did know best after all. Today there are also semiprivate co-op stores where you can buy things like ham and salami and smoked fish, but at prices nearly as mind-boggling as the liberties taken by the press nowadays.

Probably the most unanticipated aspect of *glasnost* for me was to find out from *Soviet newspapers* things about Soviet life that were much worse than I had thought. (Western newspapers never did anything of the kind for me.) It's not that I didn't know about the miseries and the squalor that most people, all over the country, endured from day to day, but these miseries have now been revealed, with the blessing of official Soviet mastheads, on a scale that shocks me. Hundreds of thousands of people live in the streets and train stations; large numbers of elderly people go hungry; thousands of children are injured and hundreds killed every year in accidents on collective farms because they are forced to perform heavy tasks for which they are not physically fit; families of four live for years in eight-by-eight rooms (the size of a prison cell for one in upstate New York). Likewise, I didn't think anyone could tell me anything new — at least not anything shockingly new — about corruption and abuses of authority among Party big shots. But the head of the Communist Party of Uzbekistan having private prison facilities built to order, to jail individuals he didn't like, without even the Soviet version of due process? Torturing people with his own hands? Administering public beatings to subordinates? If I had heard it over the Voice of America in 1979, I might have wondered whether the Americans were letting their imaginations run too wild.

To see, from letters to editors, how many true believers in the goodness and the great achievements of the Soviet state there are in all walks of Russian life is sad but not surprising. Today these true believers take up the pen in baffled rage at newspaper stories that denigrate the Soviet way of life and give ammunition to the enemy (to me, for one). The impassioned pleas, the vehement diatribes, the raging debates all over the Soviet media can be rather touchingly amusing, as if one were watching people argue in earnest about whether the Earth is round or flat, or seeing the wheel proudly presented as a great invention. Look, someone says, it's wrong to kill people because their opinion differs from yours (yours being the same as the Party's). Moreover, it's wrong even to *put people in jail* because their opinion differs from yours! In fact, they should be able to express those opinions openly in the press! And you know something? When the opinion of the Party is set up as infallible dogma not to be questioned, thought is stifled and society is paralyzed!

Amusing as it may be, I suppose that reinventing the wheel is an honorable enterprise if things are so bad that it needs to be reinvented. I find myself vacillating between optimism and cynicism, often depending on the latest thing I have read or heard or see on TV. I hear that peaceful demonstrators calling for a multiparty system have been brutally dispersed, and new laws that crack down on demonstrators and give police even broader powers to enter and search private dwellings have been passed. Yet thirteen Supreme Soviet deputies voted against these laws, breaking the traditional unanimity. I see articles that call for the restoration of Soviet citizenship to Alexander Solzhenitsyn and for the publication of his books. Yet when *Novy Mir* published a back-page announcement that Solzhenitsyn's *Cancer Ward* would appear in an upcoming issue, the authorities stopped the distribution of the magazine and ordered that the back page be reset without the offending announcement.

A daily parade of articles, essays, or letters to the editor that provoke gasps and exclamations of "Well, this is really something!" does not a reconstruction make. Besides, too many taboos still remain; too many of the revelations about the no longer quite heroic past are of the "Lenin good, Stalin bad" variety. Most important, it is still the state that sets the limits of the new freedom (although there seems to be no shortage of people willing to test them), and no one is ruling out the possibility that the state could roll back.

The dark spots are many. In the official press, the cloying unanimity persists, only now, instead of heartily joining our efforts to build communism, we are cheerfully joining our efforts to rebuild Soviet society, which, though the most democratic in the world, is suddenly in need of across-the-board democratization, and though the best in the world, is suddenly in need of a total overhaul. Lenin is still the dominant icon and the "Leninist course" a golden age in the past. Ironically, those who are now hailing democratization are holding up a fantastic portrait of a tolerant Lenin, a Lenin who had great respect for differences of opinion, a Lenin who tried to secure legal safeguards against unjust repression of suspected counterrevolutionaries even in a national emergency. This is the same Lenin whose articles and pamphlets display a rich vocabulary of colorful invective against his opponents — "lackeys," "scum," "political prostitutes," who never say anything but "pule," "whine," or "talk as if chewing on a sponge in their sleep." This is also the same Lenin whose letters are filled with orders and exhortations to arrest, jail, deport, and shoot people "without asking questions" and "without too much foot-dragging."

The moving testimonials of victims of Stalinism omit the fact that many of these victims, such as Marshal Tukhachevsky, had themselves been executioners only a short time before, in the previous, Leninist wave of terror. Nikolai Bukharin is now touted as a quasisaintly humanist, and no mention is made of his efforts to justify "proletarian coercion, in all its forms, from executions to forced labor," as "the method of molding communist humanity out of the human material of the capitalist period." A recent article in *Pravda* on Leon Trotsky was widely seen as a positive sign simply because it admitted Trotsky's important role in the Revolution and portrayed him as a three-dimensional human being rather than a cartoon villain. Yet the article was prefaced with an editorial note that contained typically coy phrases ("Trotsky made a certain contribution to the October armed insurgency") and staples of Soviet jargon such as "After his emigration, Trotsky sunk so low as to take anti-Soviet, anti-Marxist positions." So much for the truth-telling every Soviet historian worth his salt is now urging.

The perfunctory nods to the mystique of socialism (which in the Soviet press means only and exclusively Soviet-style socialism) persist as well, sometimes made utterly ludicrous by their seemingly unselfconscious proximity to scathing attacks on Soviet realities. Thus a recent report on drug abuse, issued by two high-ranking Ministry of Internal Affairs officials as a guideline for educators, journalists, and other professionals, piously recalls the orthodoxy that "we all learned in our schooldays" (and how!): drug abuse in capitalist countries is an escape from a reality that is too painful to face. Of course, the authors continue on the same pious note, nothing of the kind happens or could happen under socialism . . . although "there was something in the realities of 1970s socialism" that caused just such things to happen. And then comes a litany of evils of the "stagnation period," as the years that coincided with my childhood and adolescence are now officially known: self-seeking, careerism, hypocrisy, materialism, the gap between words and deeds. Could there be a deliberate irony hidden here, or is that too much to expect of Ministry of Internal Affairs officials?

Sometimes I think there is something faintly repulsive about the spectacle of Soviet intellectuals falling all over one another to come up with bold ideas for reform, to bash the dead Brezhnev, denounce Stalinism, and thunder against such evils as dogmatism, forced unanimity, and suppression of information. Where were all those brave souls ten years ago? Silent at best, and in too many cases clamorously applauding Brezhnev and heaping scorn on "antisocialist distortions" remarkably similar to what they now proclaim with such abandon, such fiery conviction.

In the category of the not-so-faintly repulsive, I would place the convenient habit of blaming all the evils of the past not on the system but on some bad people who somehow managed to abuse the system for their advantage. Take a short piece in *Literaturnaya Gazeta* in August 1988, which had the ostensibly noble purpose of clearing the name of the late Alexander Galich. Galich, a poet and balladeer akin to Vladimir Vysotsky but with a more wryly intellectual and detached voice — more pointedly sarcastic, more scathingly and explicitly political — was pilloried as an anti-Soviet slanderer in the 1970s and forced to emigrate. The *Literaturnaya Gazeta* article, even as it lauded Galich and decried his persecution, made it look as if the poor man simply had had the bad luck to run into some unnamed heartless bureaucrats who hounded him and made his life unbearable, and all because he had written anti-Stalinist songs and ballads. In reality, although anti-Stalinism was a strong theme in Galich's work, some of his most cutting barbs were reserved for contemporary Soviet life.

It is especially sickening to see on American television those weathered, smooth-talking Soviet spokesmen who were loyal servants of the "stagnation period" leadership and assiduously peddled the "everything is perfect" line of the times, now vested in the garments of *glasnost* and just as proudly proclaiming, "We have finally stopped pretending everything is perfect! We are courageously facing up to our problems!" Courteous American interviewers never ask them point-blank the question it all seems to beg: Just over two years ago, on this very same program, you were serenely denying the existence of the various social blights (homelessness, drug addiction, and so on) that have become the subjects of a spate of exposés in your press. You were asserting, too, that Soviet citizens had all the freedom of thought and expression anyone could possibly wish for, and today Soviet newspapers are filled with bitter laments about the squelching of all critical or independent opinion at the very time you said those things. Does all this mean, esteemed colleague, that you were lying? (Which begs yet another question: If you are in fact a certified liar, why should we believe you now?)

And the most discouraging dark spot of all is that the dissidents, who made mostly the same criticisms of Soviet society (only without the pious disclaimers) that have come to be daily fare in the official press, are still counted among the bad guys. Some of them remain in prisons, labor camps, mental hospitals.

Others are targets of constant police and KGB harassment. They are still the slanderers, the traitors, the turncoats, and the language reserved for them in the newspapers that trumpet *glasnost* and expose social ills revives the traditions of the "stagnation period" at its best. The occasional appearance of these articles, with telltale titles like "Once More on the Games of the Turncoats" and telltale stock phrases like "so-and-so spews forth filthy and vicious slanders against the Soviet state," are like a sudden whiff of a distasteful and all-too-familiar smell.

What is certainly an indicator of changing times, though, is that these days, such titles and phrases come as a shock to me — at least as much of a shock as the forays to the outer limits of *glasnost*. Along with the disappointment, and the strong temptation to doubt whether there is any substance to all the changes, one has an oddly, perversely comforting feeling of finding oneself in familiar territory.

I wonder if these "holdovers from the accursed past" (a phrase familiar to every Soviet schoolchild as the standard description of any phenomena that shouldn't but maddeningly do exist under socialism) are just relapses, perhaps reflecting a kind of peevishness: the Soviets are reluctant to eat humble pie and admit that the people who challenged the régime, and whom it ejected from its midst, were actually right all along. To apologize is tough. It is interesting that Sakharov, probably alone of all the dissidents, has been more or less brought back into the orbit of official recognition and respect, but at the cost of pretending that his brutal, often savage persecution — the exile and forced isolation, the constant surveillance, the libels in the press, the medical tortures — never happened. Sakharov's demands for public retraction of the many stories in Soviet newspapers that dragged him and his wife through the mud, and for charges to be brought against the individuals responsible for the particularly vicious aspects of his persecution, have never, to my knowledge, been publicized in the Soviet media.

Or could it be more than pique, more than fear of embarrassment? Perhaps the state is affirming a deliberate, carefully considered policy: it's all right to criticize the system, but only when and only to the extent that the state sanctions it. Those who practice *glasnost* without a license remain outlaws as much as ever. If this is the case, *glasnost* means only a somewhat longer leash, a somewhat looser straitjacket, a prison with liberalized rules — and a better camouflaged prison.

I have seen some of our Soviet guests anxiously watch TV news reports on shakeups and apparent power struggles in the Kremlin, agonizing over what it might bode for the future. Then I suddenly realize what it is like to feel helpless, to know that a change in leadership or a change of heart at the top can turn your whole life upside down, and *there's not a thing you can do about it.* The more things change . . .

So perhaps *glasnost* is not the genuine article but only a short-term relaxation, a temporary, aberrant diversion. It is quite possible, perhaps likely, that the current democratization will shrivel before it can bear fruit, killed off by an early frost. I doubt that it will go far enough to create the kind of society in which I would want to live — a society in which I could maintain my integrity. But if ever true democratization is to come to the Soviet Union, I think this is the only way it can start. Dreams of revolution are absurd; a violent overthrow of the Soviet régime, of which I fantasized at the age of fifteen through the heroine of my aborted play, would almost certainly result in a bloodbath, perhaps on a scale yet unseen. I do not see much chance that it would result in peaceful, democratic rule; revolutions hardly ever do, even in societies not bedeviled by problems and contradictions of such daunting complexity.

Whatever happens, there are grounds to be optimistic on at least one count, despite all the hypocrisy, the silences, the half-truths woven into official *glasnost*. Even if an early frost comes, the awakening now before us is likely to leave some lasting effects. People are being told, on the authority of the printed word, that they were fed lies for many years; that problems they were told did not exist were covered up, to fester beneath the surface; that it's a good thing for individuals to have their own opinions. The genie has been let out of the bottle and will be awfully hard to jam back in. Even assuming that books and articles published today may be banned in the future, no state (unless it develops some horrendous brainwashing techniques) will be able to erase them from the memories of its subjects, and even to make sure that no copies remain in the hands of the populace would be quite a task. (I hear that provident Russians are now collecting current newspapers and magazines with materials that might well turn into dangerous controlled substances in the event of a backlash. Wouldn't it be funny if today's *Pravda* and *Izvestia*, to say nothing of *Ogonyok* and *Moscow News*, were to become the *samizdat* of tomorrow?)

Meanwhile, I'll be watching, and pursuing a life in America, whose problems are of more immediate, more visceral concern to me now than the faraway rumblings of *glasnost*. Of course the political quarrels shaking up Soviet society today are riveting, because the stakes are so much higher, the lines drawn so much more sharply, and the issues under debate so much more fundamental. Whether or not Gorbachev will stay in power and stay the course makes infinitely more of a difference in the lives of Russians than the victory of one or another presidential candidate makes in the lives of Americans. With the higher stakes, there is naturally a much higher degree of emotional intensity, further exacerbated by having had all these emotions, thoughts, resentments bottled up for so long.

I am reminded of the legendary Chinese curse, "May you live in interesting times!" It is not a sentiment I admire or really share. But, at the risk of appearing battle-shy, lacking in adventurousness, and overly concerned with my own petty well-being, I prefer to watch the interesting times unfold from across the Atlantic — with no regrets.